DOWNSIZING

DOWNSIZING

Reshaping the Corporation for the Future

Robert M. Tomasko

amacom

American Management Association

This book is available at a special
discount when ordered in bulk quantities.
For information, contact Special Sales Department,
AMACOM, a division of American Management Association,
135 West 50th Street, New York, NY 10020.

Library of Congress Cataloging-in-Publication Data

Tomasko, Robert M.
   Downsizing: reshaping the corporation for the future.

   Bibliography: p.
   Includes index.
   1. Industries, Size of—United States. 2. Middle
managers—United States. 3. Industrial organization—
United States. 4. Corporations—United States.
I. Title.
HD69.S5T59 1987   338.6'4   87-47709
ISBN 0-8144-5907-2

Printing number

10 9 8 7 6 5 4 3 2 1

In
Memory
of
M. O. T.
and
W. W. T.

Acknowledgments

This book has a number of sources. It is based partly on a review of the growing business literature on companies that are downsizing, as well as the writings of management scholars such as Chris Argyris, Elliot Jaques, Harry Levinson, Henry Mintzberg, and Thomas Peters. As a management consultant, I've noticed that some of these experts' best contributions have been overlooked by busy executives, while some of their most popular ideas are discussed far more than practiced. This book is also based on conversations held over the last several years with several dozen chief executives, line managers, strategy planners, human resource experts, and other consultants as we all tried to make some sense of the dramatic and often painful changes many companies have made as they shed surplus staff. I have also talked with a number of middle managers who were out of work, with disrupted careers, and seeking jobs. They have all helped me better understand the down side of downsizing.

Several individuals have been very helpful in researching some of the companies and practices discussed in this book. I'm especially grateful for the help of Ann Figura, Eric Hochstein, and Christopher Krebs.

Carl Sloane, one of the founders and now President and CEO of the consulting firm Temple, Barker & Sloane, Inc., for many years has exhorted corporations to develop a strong sense of mission and purpose. His view that a business cannot be managed through numbers alone is one that I wholeheartedly share and is reflected in this book's treatment of downsizing. Other colleagues of mine at Temple, Barker & Sloane whom I would especially like to thank for their ideas and helpful suggestions are Frank Menser, Patrick Pollino, and Michael Tennican.

Much of this book was written while I was on leave from Arthur D. Little, Inc. While ADL is over 100 years old, it has retained some of the flexibility of a start-up enterprise. For this flexibility, and the support and encouragement of people like Douglas Anderson, Robert Mueller, David Shanks, and Richard Stephan, I am very grateful.

Special thanks also go to a close colleague from Brussels, Jean-Philippe Deschamps. Several years ago he prompted me to think about many of the ideas presented here, when he recoiled in horror at the notion that I would consider writing a book about downsizing. He reminded me that our job as management consultants is to be builders, not cutters, and that a company can go just so far in reducing costs and eliminating employees. He maintained that these actions may be necessary, but without developing new products and winning new customers, they are dead ends. He is right.

Several people have provided strong encouragement to turn some of my ideas into a book. Herman Stein, whom I first met when he was Provost of Case Western Reserve University, opened my eyes to the way political realities frequently shape an organization's behavior, and helped me see that companies were more than just collections of lines and boxes on a chart. Harry Levinson got me to revisit the lessons of Freud and to apply psychological intelligence, not just competitive microeconomics, to understand the implications of the current wave of mass layoffs. Harry also made sure I didn't forget the impact that losing, or having to fire, many of one's colleagues can have on the survivors of downsizing. Both of these seasoned organization observers gently prodded me for several years to take time from consulting to write about what I was doing. Adrienne Hickey, my editor at AMACOM Books, picked up from there and helped convert my good intentions into a publishable manuscript. She also knows how to keep a project on track by providing what a novice writer needs: a careful blend of firmness and support.

There is something to be said at times for the view that the greatest value management consultants can provide is not their own ideas, but their ability to pick up lessons from one client and transfer them to another. Several of the practices cited here were first observed while working with my clients. The confidential nature of our business necessitates anonymity for these people and their companies, but their willingness to be open about their problems, work hard to solve them, and remain concerned for their people as well as their balance sheets certainly deserves a strong acknowledgment.

Finally, a great deal of appreciation is owed to Brenda Turnbull, my wife. She's the only real writer in our family, and has more than once helped me turn a tortured phrase into printable prose. And somehow she managed to nurture a struggling writer-husband while watching over one young daughter, giving birth to a second, and, with a business partner, running her own policy analysis firm.

It goes almost without saying that any fuzzy logic, misapplication of what are otherwise good borrowed ideas, and just out-and-out mistakes are all my own doing.

Contents

Introduction

It finally happened. After decades of corporate executives berating the U.S. government for being slow, unresponsive, and expensive, the other shoe dropped. At a meeting of the Japan Society of New York, then Deputy Secretary of the Treasury Richard Darman said that bloated, risk-averse, inefficient, and unimaginative large corporations make up an American business "corpocracy." He said this corporate bureaucracy was a key reason behind the decline of the United States' global competitiveness, and that it was paving the way for a populist reaction to the nation's economic plight, which might cripple world trade with high protectionist tariffs.

Fortunately, many corporate executives had started to downsize their overgrown structures even before Darman's dire warnings. While responding to the short-term pressures of the stock market for cost reduction, asset restructuring, and business refocusing, some companies had also taken the first steps toward strengthening for the longer haul. For many of them, their actions came none too soon. Just after World War II more than three-fourths of corporate employees were in production jobs. The remainder did staff work like accounting, personnel, and public relations. But by the 1980s, this proportion had almost reversed. A line executive noted that, "It was almost as though engineering, manufacturing, and selling had been replaced as key functions in our company by accounting, financing, and the solving of legal problems."

This bulge in the middle of the corporate pyramid was an especially American problem. In 1980, managers made up about 10 percent of the U.S. industrial work force. In Japan, they constituted 4.4 percent; in West Germany, 3 percent; and in Sweden, 2.4 percent. When John Welch became General Electric's chief executive, he found GE—one of the nation's largest exporters—in a position "where we were hiring people [just] to read reports of people who had been hired to write reports."

And this problem was far from GE's alone. From 1978 to 1985, a great deal of effort was made in all U.S. industries to improve blue-collar productivity, using everything from Japanese quality circles to Silicon Valley factory robots. But almost all the blue-collar productivity gains were wiped out by decreases in white-collar productivity. Something eventually had to give.

And what "gave" were several hundred thousand jobs of staff professionals and managers, as American industry entered a major period of restructuring its assets and organizations. Most of these downsizing efforts have had three targets: headquarters staff, middle managers, and everybody else. This book focuses only on the first two, partially in the hope that if companies do a better job in managing the size and shape of their management work force, they will be able to maintain more employment stability for everyone else. This is not a book about how to fire employees. Massive layoffs have been overused as a tool to downsize; attention here is given to pruning bureaucracy without necessarily firing good performers.

This book has both heroes and villains. Chapters 1 and 2 highlight twin villains: overgrown corporate bureaucracy and the overreaction to it—demassing—in some companies. The consequences of top-heavy organizational structures are already well known. To the extent that they are reflected in high overhead costs, they are also quantifiable. But the equally destructive consequences of deep, across-the-board cutbacks, sometimes happening wave after wave, are only beginning to become apparent. These consequences include diminished employee commitment to their companies; bitter personal trauma inflicted when the reductions were implemented with concern only for their economic impact, ignoring their psychological aspect; and creation of corporate environments that are risk-averse and innovation-fearing. These harder-to-quantify problems may return to haunt many businesses.

Charting a course between these two dangers are the book's heroes: planned downsizers. They are characterized in the third chapter, and the approaches they have taken to pinpoint excess mid-level staffing are outlined in Chapters 4, 5, and 6. Implementing downsizing in a planned manner requires taking the long view, and this, in turn, opens many alternatives to mass layoffs. Some of these alternatives are reviewed in Chapter 7.

Getting lean, however, is not even half the battle. Many U.S. companies are starting to discover what even Mikhail Gorbachev will find in a few years as he works to streamline the Soviet economy: that it is very difficult to change one aspect of an organization's structure without causing ripple effects in all the others. A streamlined company must be managed differently from one with more layers and more staff. New management practices will have to be learned; entire cultures of some companies will need to be redirected. Developing new products will be more like a good rugby scrum than a drawnout 9-inning game of baseball (where every department has its chance at bat). Some businesses will also need to develop a new breed of general manager, who can safely and effectively get results from those downsized organizations.

Chapter 8 considers some of the prerequisites for running lean. But a bigger challenge for many firms will be sustaining their hard-won gains from downsizing. If business history is any guide, when economic pressures let up excess staffing often returns. Companies that want to prevent their size moving like a roller coaster will need to consider "vertically disintegrating" their corporate structures. They will have to limit their activities to those in which the value added is greatest, and buy what else they need in the marketplace. They will have to develop strong human-resource planning functions and will have to weed out aspects of their compensation systems and career paths that lead to inflated numbers of management positions. They must keep up with developments in information technology and must explore using expert systems as a way to strengthen their managers' capabilities. These and related issues are reviewed in the last chapter.

This is a book of examples. It draws on the experiences, good and bad, of companies in the United States and overseas. These examples help illustrate points, showing ways certain management practices have been used. They are not intended to glorify or vilify a particular company. Many companies do very good jobs managing some aspects of their operations and weak jobs managing others. Some that have made serious mistakes downsizing have made them honestly, usually because of crisis pressures or from feeling they lacked other alternatives. Many executives know that today's excellent company may be tomorrow's problem business.

The examples cited here should be used with care. It is very difficult to take one idea or practice that has been successful for one company and transplant it intact to another—unless that company is also willing to bring along any number of supporting practices and a good bit of the exemplary company's culture and history. Instead, executives should use these examples and stories to stimulate their thinking differently about their own companies. They should look for the general principles behind the examples, and ask how they may be applied to their businesses. Redesigning a company requires more of the mentality of an architect than that of a surgeon.

Let's start by examining the causes and consequences of an overgrown corporate bureaucracy. But while reading the first chapter, also keep in mind that sometimes the cure can be worse than the disease. This is especially true when instead of pruning the bureaucracy, efforts are made just to work around it. The Reagan presidency has been weakened by a small headquarters staff unit (the National Security Council) that ran in lean and mean mode, taking action in an area in which the line organizations nominally in charge (the State Department and C.I.A.) were viewed as too slow, unresponsive, and ineffective. As a result, the National Security Council did what it was supposed to prevent: it facilitated improper transfers of arms to Iran and funds to Nicaraguan contras. The criticism of corpocracy made by the deputy treasury secretary cited earlier is worth heeding, but neither his organization nor any of the United States' overseas business competitors have a monopoly on effective management practices. This conclusion did not escape Richard Darman. Several months after his well-noted corpocracy speech, he left the Treasury Department to take a more active role in reshaping corporations as a Wall Street investment banker.

Chapter 1

The Bulge in the Corporate Pyramid

"The Tale of the Tardy Product Innovation." It is a story most of us smile at, but too many of us have also lived through it. Robert Reich, a Harvard professor and seasoned industry observer, tells one of the better versions:

> A salesman hears from a customer that the firm's latest bench drill cannot accommodate bits for drilling a recently developed hard plastic. The customer suggests a modified coupling adapter and an additional speed setting. The salesman thinks the suggestion makes sense but has no authority to pursue it directly. Following procedures, the salesman passes the idea on to the sales manager, who finds it promising and drafts a memo to the marketing vice president. The marketing vice president also likes the idea, so he raises it in an executive meeting of all the vice presidents. The executive committee agrees to modify the drill. The senior product manager then asks the head of the research department to form a task force to evaluate the product opportunity and to design a new coupling and variable-speed mechanism.
>
> The task force consists of representatives from sales,

marketing, accounting, and engineering. The engineers are interested in the elegance of the design. The manufacturing department insists on modifications requiring only minor retooling. The salespeople want a drill that will do what customers need it to do. The finance people worry about the costs of producing it. The marketing people want a design that can be advertised and distributed efficiently and sold at a competitive price. The meetings are difficult since each task force member wants to claim credit for future success but avoid blame for any possible failure. After months of meetings the research manager presents the group's findings to the executive committee. It approves the new design. Each department then works out a detailed plan for its role in bringing out the new product, and the modified drill goes into production.

If there are no production problems, the customer receives word that he can order a drill for working hard plastics two years after he first discussed it with the salesman. In the meantime, a Japanese, West German, or South Korean firm has already designed, produced, and delivered a hard-plastics drill.

Ironically, this unfortunate drill maker has even less bureaucracy than do most American corporations. Six, seven, or even eight layers of management between salespeople and chief executive are much more common than the three described here. So are three- and four-year waits for product improvements.

Losing sales to overseas competitors because of slow product development is only one consequence of the middle bulge in many corporate pyramids. Another consequence, which also diminishes competitiveness, is high prices owing to excess middle-management overhead.

Too Much Management, Too Much Staff

General Motors Corporation has become a favorite target for critics of corporate bureaucracy. David Cole, head of the Office for the Study of Automotive Transportation at the University of Michigan, feels that GM's costs would be reduced by 30 percent if the company adopted Japanese-like leaner management practices. He feels GM's problems are caused by inadequate management, not technology. Apparently, GM's chief executive agrees. Chairman Roger Smith has blamed much of the problem on what he calls the company's "frozen middle management." In North America, GM operates with well over 100,000 white-collar workers. Many are managers spanning the organizational levels between the assembly-line worker and Smith. Others are staff people providing advice, analysis, and services to these managers. An observer of GM who is working with the management to streamline the organization does not think that so many people are necessary. Generally, he finds them all busy, but not necessarily doing things that help make better cars. He also finds that the decisions that could result in more competitive vehicles often require dozens of these individuals' approvals. What will it take for GM to match the Toyota Motor Corporation's management efficiency? Operating the company with at least 25 percent fewer of these salaried positions.

Figure 1.1 shows that this situation is not limited to GM. These Bureau of Labor Statistics numbers show that as the overall employment in American factories increased from 1950 to 1980, the number of jobs held by nonproduction workers increased almost five times as much as those occupied by the people actually doing the producing. And even though nationwide manufacturing employment decreased from 1980 to 1985, the number of nonproduction workers kept rising.

In some industries the situation is even worse. In electrical machinery making, an industry subject to strong Asian and European competition, the work-force mix changed from 46 staff jobs for every 100 production jobs to 56 per 100 in only ten years. And the biggest companies seem to be the most staff-prone. By 1976, the American Telephone and Telegraph Company had 99 staff workers for every 100 involved in production. Some estimates indicate that, currently, one in three AT&T employees is a supervisor or manager.

Systems as well as staff have a way of proliferating, possibly to keep some managers busy. One large and wealthy tobacco

Figure 1.1. Production versus nonproduction workers in U.S. manufacturing industries.

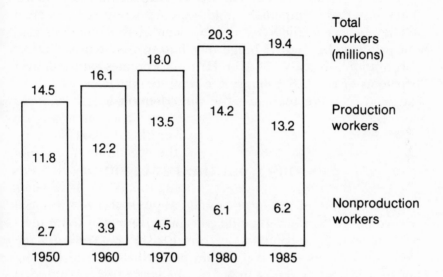

Source: Bureau of Labor Statistics

company was unable to decide which budgeting system it liked best. The systems were not compatible; the company decided to make its managers prepare budgets both ways.

To make matters worse, some smaller companies in high-technology industries have started to show signs of premature bureaucratization. Many thought the way to become the "next IBM" was to organize and staff the same way IBM does today. For example, one brand-new advanced-technology business, which was at the time the most capital-intensive start-up since the Federal Express Company, created an organizational structure that included managers, directors, vice presidents, and an executive vice president, along with a chief strategy planner and the founder-president. The total size of the company needing all this management? Twenty-two employees. Another firm, the pioneer microprocessor builder Intel, had half its work force doing some form of administration by 1979. Processing an order to get an engineer a new mechanical pencil took nearly a hundred steps and a dozen pieces of documentation.

Some executives are fascinated with the military metaphor. They wish their companies would be as quick to execute orders as they believe soldiers are. Unfortunately, the Pentagon has not escaped the midriff bulge that has appeared in so many corporations since World War II; some recent organizational problems of the U.S. military are reminders that bureaucracy can lead to more than just the slow delivery of mechanical pencils.

Lessons from the Pentagon

An examination of the most capital-intensive part of the U.S. government illustrates some deadly consequences of too much management. The commission convened by the Secretary of Defense to investigate the circumstances behind the bombing of a Marine barracks in Beirut, Lebanon, found that the chain of command did not initiate actions that might have prevented the deaths of 241 servicemen. This "chain of command" included dozens of generals and admirals in an organizational structure in which orders, after moving through the Pentagon labyrinth, criss-crossed Europe from Germany to England to Italy before reaching anyone in even the vicinity of Lebanon. This management structure included five layers between the head of the U.S. forces in Europe and the unfortunate commander of the Marine battalion landing team. Military analyst Edward Luttwak felt that this was a recipe for disaster, given the volatile situation in Beirut in October 1983. He noted that because so many senior officers were involved in managing this critical Marine mission, responsibility became hopelessly diluted. People in each of these five headquarters levels would pass on individual orders as required, but none of them took the responsibility of examining the entire situation to make certain the proper security precautions had been taken. The end result was Marine guards with unloaded weapons, left to face a fast-moving suicide bomber.

This is a common problem in too many armies. During World War I, 300,000 British troops left their trenches and became casualties at Passchendaele. The battle lasted four months, during which it was claimed that no senior officer ever visited the battlefield. Daily reports on the condition of the battlefield slowly made their way up a long chain of command to General Headquarters, where they were usually ignored or considered unimportant by the desk-bound military bureaucrats. It was not until the battle had ended that the headquarters realized it had been ordering troops to advance from their trenches into an ocean of mud.

Edward Luttwak is a Georgetown University–based hawk on national defense who wants to see more logic in military management. He attributes much of the excess layering in the Pentagon and in the field to a bloated number of middle- and upper mid-level officers. At the close of World War II, 12 million active-duty troops were commanded by 17,000 officers ranking colonel, navy captain, or higher. Of these 17,000, 101 were three-star generals or admirals. In 1983, a time of international tensions but not global warfare, only a little more than two million troops were on active duty. But to manage this smaller force required over 15,000 officers ranked at the equivalent of colonel or higher. This number included 17 *more* three-star generals and admirals than the 101 at the end of the Second World War.

What do all these officers do? Because only a fraction of them can be accommodated in bona fide command slots, Luttwak has observed that they become managers instead. Since there are not enough senior-management tasks to keep them all busy, many tend to overmanage or micromanage; others become high-level coordinators, relaying orders from one overstaffed headquarters to another. The resulting organizational structure that accommodates them has become over-elaborated and overlapping. Work that belongs in one place is scattered among many departments. Key defense problems that need to be considered as a whole by people relatively close to the action are fragmented among competing services and overlapping civilian and military jurisdictions. And the entire operation is put together in a global matrix organization with a combination of functions and divisions that rivals the complexity of even the most belabored corporate structure.

Since at times there is not enough real action for all the players, when critical missions come up everyone wants to be involved. For example, roles for all the services were found, and sometimes forced to fit, in the Vietnam War. The ill-fated Iran-hostage rescue attempt ten years later repeated in miniature the Vietnam practice. Roles were found for the Army, Navy, Air Force, and Marine Corps. The mission was managed from the West Wing of the White House, through the National Military Command Center in the Pentagon, to a middle-management headquarters set up in Egypt. This closest command was headed by an Army major general assisted by an Air Force major general. The rescue completely unraveled when the Marine pilot of a Navy helicopter collided with an Air Force refueling tanker at the Desert One landing zone in Iran. Eight servicemen died in the collision. At the landing spot itself, to sort things out, were an Army commander of the ground assault force, a Navy commander watching over his service's helicopters, an Air Force commander managing the refueling, and another individual in overall charge of the landing zone facility.

Israeli commando experts have been astonished that, to carry out such a critical mission, the United States mixed people with such different types of training, differing philosophies of warfare, and different career interests linked to their home services. For their successful hostage rescue at Entebbe, Uganda, the Israelis built a single, unified, and elite team, completely separate from normal bureaucracy, with the shortest possible chain of command to carry out an extraordinarily difficult task. (Interestingly, entrepreneur Steven Jobs followed the same practice when he set up a skunkworks to design Apple's Macintosh computer.)

Why pay so much attention to the problems of Pentagon organization? The military, sometimes more tragically than other parts of the government, illustrates the logical outcome of overgrown bureaucracy. It provides corporate executives with lessons, at times outlined in bold relief, of how *not* to organize. The situations facing the military are comparable, sometimes in slow motion, with those facing the private sector.

To be effective, both military and corporate executives need direct visual evidence of their current situation. Layers upon layers of management only separate them from such evidence. During the early 1970s, Detroit executives looked out their office windows at the surrounding expressways and saw nothing but large U.S.-built cars. Had they been based closer to the Pacific port cities, they would have observed an increasing number of small Datsuns and Toyotas filling the freeways. Perhaps then they would have planned a more timely counterattack.

The contrasting approaches to hostage rescues by Americans and Israelis parallel the ways some corporations develop new products. Some companies circulate countless memos up and down multiple layers of staff, while others assemble small teams of committed champions and let the marketplace cast the vetos. The tiny 315-employee Minnetonka Corporation managed to out-innovate the much larger Procter & Gamble. Honda—far from Japan's largest automaker—outflanked General Motors, and Compaq shifted from being a builder of IBM-compatible personal computers to becoming an innovator of new technologies.

Where Did They All Come From?

Very few companies, or government agencies, set out to create organizational structures with an overabundance of staff people or layers of management. But, as these examples have illustrated, bureaucratic bloat seems more common than not. Before considering ways to combat this situation, it is helpful to review its causes. These are some of the most common reasons for excessive management.

□ *Age and prosperity.* In business, unfortunately, time bears a direct relationship to excess staffing. Ironically, the more successful a company has been in the past, the more it is prone to adding unneeded managerial jobs. It is almost a law of nature that, except for a calamitous past, as a business grows in sales it also grows in employment. And a company with past success in taking its market share from competitors in a growing industry—rather than in surviving in a low-cost niche—is often the most prone to problems as its market matures. This situation is further complicated by a social objective that many companies have, at least implicitly, to provide an increasing number of jobs as the company gets older. Whether held by the company or expected of it by society, this objective can result in inattention to managing a firm's size when times are good. It can also slow a company's reaction to early warnings of economic troubles—all of which can leave few alternatives to massive cutbacks as troubles deepen.

□ *Size.* Big seems to breed bigger. As total employment increases, so does the number of management layers required to keep things under control. And so does the number of staff support units. Functions that smaller companies must buy from others (payroll processing, printing, travel and meeting planning, food and security services, medical and counseling help) have a habit of being assumed in-house as the size of the work force grows. The more analytically oriented departments also tend to grow, as the motivation to provide excellent staff work in their functions replaces a more general desire to serve the highest priority business needs. This is often a legitimate narrowing of objectives. With all these new managers and staff professionals around, it just seems harder to keep the "highest priority business needs" constantly in mind. As most companies grow, their goals become increasingly abstract. And staff professionals often feel closer to their counterparts in other companies than to people working in a different department of their own company.

□ *Growth by diversification.* Through much of the 1960s and 1970s, the favored route to corporate growth was through diversification. *Synergy* was the word commonly used in annual reports to justify these decisions, but much of the growth came through acquisition or start-up of enterprises related only marginally, if at all, to the base business in which corporate senior executives spent most of their careers. Managing these expansions required new layers of executives able to cope with the diversity and new headquarters staff to help senior executives manage the new executives.

□ *Management by decentralization.* This was the new management philosophy to support the diversification era. It stressed trust, delegation, and management by objectives—all important parts of the manager's toolbox. Unfortunately, in some companies it resulted in the destruction of economies of scale and the duplication of staff efforts. Decentralized management was espoused by many executives, but practiced by few. Executives uncomfortable with its tenets found themselves looking for indirect ways to regain control over their businesses. Some bureaucratized their senior management structures with group executives and offices-of-the-president. Others embraced the technologies of strategic planning.

□ *Strategic planning.* Rapidly adopted in the late 1970s, strategic planning promised executives a way to get their arms around business diversity. It also created jobs for strategic planners and other staff analysts at several levels in the corporate hierarchy. Planners also bred planners. Some division-level general managers felt the need to hire their own planners to respond to the requests for information from the new headquarters planners. In a number of companies the planning staffs overlapped with line management, resulting in slow and overanalyzed decision making, as well as increased overhead.

□ *Increasing government regulation.* The 1970s was also a period of multiplying government regulation. OSHA, ERISA, EEO, SEC, and EPA, among many others, generated increasing work loads for many corporate staffs. Responding to these agencies' information requests and managing their companies' compliance with government regulations became full-time occupations for new staff specialists.

□ *New management concerns.* Energy conservation, productivity improvement, product safety, product quality, work-life quality, innovation—these are all important concerns that have occupied top management. In many companies the response to these issues has been to set up high-level staff departments.

As one executive commented, "It seems that every time I ask my staff a serious new question, they go and add someone else to the payroll."

□ *New technologies and markets.* Finding opportunities in technologies such as computer-assisted manufacturing and genetic engineering has also led to creation of new staff units. Overseas expansion has added to the complexity of many management organizations, because special divisions or global matrix structures have been used to stimulate international growth. These are important issues; they seem to require net additions to the corporate bureaucracy.

□ *Scarcity of expertise.* Knowledge and experience in dealing with new technologies and markets are often difficult to find and, at least in the early stages, usually expensive. This has often led companies to set up additional elite, centralized staff departments. At times these elite departments acquire decision-making authority over line management, adding the equivalent of an extra layer of management.

These forces all drive the expansion of corporate bureaucracy. Most originate in situations outside the company. They are pervasive and difficult to control because coping with them involves adopting new responses to new situations. In later chapters we will consider some alternatives to the almost knee-jerk tendency to cope with change by inflating the organization with additional staff people.

Unfortunately, these factors are not the only villains. As troublesome as these forces can be to a company trying to control its size, they are not the most significant driving forces. Much greater difficulty comes from internal management practices.

Probably the most persistent causes of management layering and excess headquarters staff are the human resource policies employed by many American corporations. Their consequences are unintended, but unmistakable. The three most problematical areas of human resource policy are compensation, career development, and corporate culture. Let's look first at compensation.

Compensation: Bias Toward Management

Most major American companies, and many government agencies, use some form of job evaluation to help them pay their employees fairly. This process is such a critical cause and sustainer of management layering that it is worth examining in detail.

Compensation-setting usually works something like this: Someone prepares a written description of the responsibilities, performance standards, and qualifications for each job. Suggestions and changes are obtained from a number of sources until the job description is approved. Then either a compensation professional in the human resources department or a committee of workers and managers evaluates the job description, assigning it a certain number of points. After point scores are obtained for all positions in the company, jobs with similar point values are grouped into common salary ranges. Salary surveys are then used to help set dollar values for the salary ranges.

The entire process is comprehensive. It does provide a much needed way to pay people in an internally consistent manner. It does help companies keep their salary levels in line with the job market. And it solves some of the difficulties in comparing the contributions of, say, a sales manager with those of a design engineer. But it is also a major builder of top-heavy management structures. To appreciate how this happens, let's examine the techniques of job evaluation.

Many systems of job evaluation are in use. A number of them have been developed and are supported through periodic salary surveys. Among the most common systems are those that identify a series of factors common to many jobs, which can then be used to help distinguish among them. Typical factors are:

The amount of knowledge, obtained through schooling or specialized training, that is necessary to do the job.
How much judgment, initiative, and closeness of supervision are required.

What level of responsibility or accountability is inherent in
the job.

How safe and comfortable the setting is where the job is
usually performed.

To what extent the job requires supervision or management of others.

Sometimes these factors are weighted unevenly, on
the basis of their importance to the particular company.
Accountability or supervisory responsibility may, for example,
be given twice the emphasis that relative safety of the work
environment receives. Such weighting influences the number
of points assigned to each job.

The factors are, in turn, subdivided into several levels that
correspond to increasing amounts of sophistication or difficulty. A number of points is set for each level; the more difficult
or complicated a job is with characteristics at a certain level, the more points awarded. For example, a job requiring a
graduate degree receives more points than one needing only a
bachelor's. A position requiring close daily supervision is rated
with fewer points than one characterized by a great deal of
expected initiative and only a quarterly review of performance.
A manager who oversees a department of 200 workers is rated
much more highly than a professional who supervises only one
assistant or a secretary.

Job evaluation appears logical, perhaps even semiscientific.
Through quantification, it provides a convenient way to represent a series of collective judgments about a job's characteristics and worth. But many systems of job evaluation have a
serious flaw: They are biased toward rewarding management
skills. The ways in which points are allocated almost inevitably
make it difficult for employees in nonmanagement positions to
receive anywhere near the maximum number of points. Some
systems even limit nonmanagement positions to no more than
50 or 60 percent of the maximum number of points.

Because many managers are unfamiliar with the details
of these job evaluation systems, a description of how they can
cause problems is provided in the Appendix. The Appendix

also relates how a team of senior employees in a rapidly growing biotechnology firm eliminated the bias from their compensation system before it could lead them to become overstaffed with managers. Their scientific curiosity caused them to challenge some features of job evaluation systems that others take for granted or assume are being taken care of by their compensation specialists.

When the pro-management bias of job evaluations is brought up with many executives, their first reaction is typically one of acceptance. Frequently, they do feel that senior management positions are the most strategically important in their firms, and they are happy that this is reflected in their compensation procedures. What they are less comfortable with are the ways these systems treat employees in the middle ranks of their companies. And they are often very concerned when they start to see the connection between what appears to be their overlayered organizational structure and the methods that are used to set salaries.

Job evaluation points quickly translate into salary dollars. When the point allocation is biased toward management jobs, the message is: To get ahead in this company, become a manager. In some very traditional manufacturing operations, this message makes sense. But it is much less relevant for companies employing many staff professionals, engineers, and scientists. The greatest value of these "knowledge workers" lies in their individual contributions, not their supervisory skills.

This compensation-fueled desire for management positions sends another message: Keep high performers loyal and motivated by providing abundant management jobs for them to move into. For some, this is fine. But for too many employees, individual capabilities and the requirements of management positions do not match. This reality has not escaped many companies, and they take it into account when they design these jobs. More often than not, these "management" jobs have a limited number of direct reports, so as to allow plenty of time for individual contributions. Eventually, these companies find reasons to reorganize and add an additional layer of managers. This layer allows for the closer supervision that these half-managers, half-contributors sometimes need. And it provides another rung in the advancement ladder, as the half-managers move upward to jobs worth still more evaluation points.

Several technology-based companies have addressed this problem by creating customized job evaluation systems that are less biased, but often this is expensive and time-consuming. Others have worked around some of these problems by creating two career ladders: one for managers and one for technical staff. While these changes are often useful for middle-level jobs, usually only the management ladder reaches the highest salary levels. Few senior executives have reached their jobs via the technical ladder. And the nonmanagement career path usually is limited to bona fide scientists and engineers, leaving lawyers, personnel specialists, salespeople, and strategy planners no option other than management advancement. This situation leaves many companies with no alternative but to create more management positions.

Until companies change the ways they set salary levels, so that having fewer people to supervise does not always equate with less responsibility and pay, the drive for greater compensation will continue to inflate the management bulge, making it very difficult for a company to be streamlined.

One-Way Career Development

Just as job evaluations often imply that the only route to increased earnings is up the management ladder, career development practices likewise breed tall management hierarchies by sending the message that getting ahead means moving in one direction on the organization chart—upward.

The assumptions behind upward career development made more sense in the 1950s, when seasoned managers were relatively scarce, markets were growing rapidly, and having "management-in-depth" was an enviable position. This era of the Organization Man also was when many companies installed fast-track training and promotion programs for their most promising new recruits.

These fast tracks, staffed by well-educated but minimally

experienced new hires, indirectly led to increases in management layers. Setting someone on a fast track implied making a series of closely spaced promotions, often in several areas of the company, as a way to rapidly develop management talent and give the up-and-comer high visibility. To survive the rapid coming and going of fast-trackers—and still keep the business on an even keel—companies created new management positions to supervise them. But the rapid turnover rate of these recruits necessitated narrower spans of control, and their limited experience in each of their assignments led to additional headquarters staff units to monitor their work and detect their errors. This shifted the balance of power in some companies from line management to staff departments. Because each job change usually implied an upward movement, some companies also found it necessary to add additional layers, or half layers, to accommodate the fast-trackers.

For some rising managers, the fast track involved several employers. Unwilling to wait for openings as corporate hierarchies began to clog up, these managers job hopped to advance their career and salary. This contributed to a high turnover, often in key positions, and eventually resulted in such jobs being more narrowly defined, with more of them created.

Eventually the merry-go-round had to slow down. Recessions, a glut of talented baby-boom MBAs, and the maturing of many growth markets lowered the speed on corporate fast tracks. But the organizational results of this period have disappeared more slowly.

Fast tracks and upward career progressions have contributed to the midriff bulge in many companies' organizational structures. Spans of control at the bottom and top of many corporate hierarchies are relatively broad. This is especially true in manufacturing firms, where a first-line supervisor may oversee 12 to 30 workers and the chief executive may have 8 to 12 direct reports. But in middle-management ranks, the pyramid commonly narrows to 3, 4, or 5 people reporting to a manager, and the number of management layers increases.

Why? Companies that tell employees the best careers are those which advance steadily up the hierarchy build disappointment into their organizational structures. Hierarchies inevitably narrow, and well-performing but unpromoted employees are likely to leave or become demotivated if their expectations of rising to the top are not met. One way to reduce turnover or postpone disappointment is to add extra rungs to the ladder. While companies are seldom restructured explicitly for this purpose, the driving force behind many reorganizations is the desire to build in room for good performers that might be needed for the company's next growth spurt. While there is nothing wrong with preparing for management's future needs, there are ways to do it with fewer adverse side effects. We will consider some of these alternatives in later chapters.

Upward career paths also have less relevance for many knowledge workers, although companies frequently continue to manage these people in the traditional way. Professionals, such as planners and engineers, often can make a stronger long-term contribution by having careers of well-planned lateral moves through different divisions instead. Businesses as diverse as Citicorp, Club Med, and 3M have found such rotation a key to remaining competitively innovative.

Corporate Cultures Based on Mistrust

The third factor that contributes to excess headquarters staffing is much less tangible than compensation or career development. But it is just as strong, and is far more difficult to eliminate than fast tracks or malfunctioning compensation systems. That factor is the set of beliefs firmly embedded in American corporate culture:

> It is better to win than to lose.
> It is better to control than to be controlled.
> It is better to hide mistakes than to admit them.

These beliefs do not appear in any company's policy manual, but most managers seem to learn them early in their careers. Harvard behavioral scientist Chris Argyris has confirmed after many years of research that these, and similar statements, make up the assumptions that influence how most managers relate to one another. When these assumptions are acted upon, the behaviors they produce seem common to business regardless of size or industry, so it is fair to call them pivotal values of American corporate culture. Note, however, that these assumptions—and therefore also the culture—are based on mistrust.

Argyris has examined the adverse consequences of these assumptions. Among the most serious is the tendency many managers have to protect themselves by making it difficult for others to bring up information that contradicts a position they have already taken. Many subordinates realize that reporting such contradictory information goes against the company norm, so they censor themselves or recast the information in the best possible light—information about, for example, a declining market share that may diminish their boss's public delight with continued sales increases.

A tendency to hide unfavorable information often occurs in companies that are quick to reward success and equally quick to punish failure. The net result is managers who are not very good at learning from their mistakes; they bury failure rather than learn from it. This tendency to hide failure often is ignored in times of growth and earnings increases; unfortunately, by the time economic conditions turn less favorable, it is often too late. Situations as diverse as the Challenger space shuttle disaster and the American automobile industry's decline in competitiveness illustrate these consequences.

Argyris calls these aspects of corporate culture "undiscussibles," but many companies have realized the problems inherent in such self-protective behavior. Rather than change the situation that leads to this behavior, executives try to short-circuit it. They create special staff watchdog units to allow alternative channels of communication to the senior management. These units are commonly part of planning departments, the controller's staff, an information systems group, and sometimes the human resource function. This short-circuiting is often the real reason many outside consultants and researchers are hired. All these means are used to combat the tendencies of managers to highlight good news and hide the bad, to underestimate expenses, and to overestimate customer demand.

These watchdog methods are expensive, however, both in money and in the slowed-down decision making that occurs with groups of checkers and auditors who watch the checkers. The most common response is to add additional layers of management, supported by groups of headquarters staff policemen. Since these additions, at best, only temporarily circumvent the problem rather than change the climate that produces it, they easily become counterproductive. Win-lose managers find ways around the system, so frustrated executives respond again by continuing to bloat the corporate bureaucracy. Gamesmanship prevails, and new products take even longer to reach their customers, who by then may have become ex-customers.

Sometimes the consequences are more tragic. We may never know for sure why Korean Airlines Flight 007 left its planned course and flew into Soviet airspace in 1983, but some pilots of that airline have suggested that a company management practice could have contributed. They dismiss the possibility of an intentional overflight or spy mission. They feel it was much more likely a navigational error, such as entering the wrong coordinates into the 747's guidance system. The pilot of Flight 007, they say, appeared from radar records of his flight path to have discovered the mistake but, rather than return and correct, decided to fly on using the less reliable method of compass and star watching. Why did he not choose the safer course of returning and fixing the problem?

A Korean Airlines pilot suggests this was because of the company's policy of severely punishing pilots who make such mistakes. He cites examples of pilots who were disciplined harshly when it was discovered that they had made similar navigational mistakes. The policy leads pilots to fear punishment and embarrassment more than the risks of flying without properly set instruments. This corporate culture encourages hiding mistakes, even though it can lead to far more serious errors. And, unfortunately, no amount of additional staff or increased management layers can change the ways this culture may encourage people to act.

An Intolerable Situation

Up to this point we have considered a dozen forces working to build and maintain a corporate bureaucracy. They work from both inside and outside the organization, and they are strong and persistent. It has taken several strong shocks to the U.S. economy to loosen their grip, but recently an increasing number of American companies have noticed the problems they create and have begun to attack them.

Until the early 1980s, the bulge in the corporate pyramid generally was tolerated. It was assumed to be a necessary cost of doing business in a time of increasing complexity. But a combination of factors early in this decade forced many companies to reexamine their approach to management staffing. The recession of 1981–82 was deeper and broader than many previous downturns. The customary costs of business came under detailed review. Work-force reductions were common, as in the past, but for the first time they involved significant numbers of white-collar workers. Included among these white-collar layoffs, again for the first time since the Depression, were sizable numbers of managers and well-paid headquarters staff people.

This recession signaled not just another shift of the business cycle, but a growing awareness of how mature the U.S. economy had become. The growth rate of many basic industries had declined and in some cases become negative. Competition was oriented more toward fighting for someone else's piece of the pie, rather than stimulating an expansion of the pie. And increasingly the challengers came from abroad with well-honed marketing skills developed in highly competitive local markets.

These overseas competitors discovered that many American companies were quick to analyze but slow to react. They found them more attuned to the needs of smooth factory production than to changing customer requirements. They also found an unexpected ally in our overelaborated management structures and systems. In the early 1980s, Ford Motor Company needed a dozen levels of management to produce cars competing with those Toyota built with only seven layers of management.

In the dark days before Ford's turnaround and Chrysler's successful rebirth, many business commentators speculated that the future American economy would be based on food growing and hamburger preparation. But other, more perceptive, observers refused to equate maturity with decline. They identified some alternatives to the staff-driven, layered structure of organizing and managing business operations.

Emergence of a New Philosophy of Management

By the mid-1980s, academics and management gurus had rallied to the support of American management. "Managing Our Way to Economic Decline," a landmark *Harvard Business Review* article by Robert Hayes and William Abernathy, helped sound the alarm. *Theory Z* and *The Art of Japanese Management* dissected key features of the new competitors' organizational designs and management styles. And *In Search of Excellence* achieved best-seller status while reminding executives that all that was good in management did not necessarily come with a "made in Japan" label.

While a weakened economic situation provided the initial impetus for management cutbacks, the emerging collection of new management philosophies provided its justification. These authors and others stressed a return to basics and management through people rather than by numbers. The new center of attention was the factory floor, not the senior analyst's carpeted office. The new watchword was "lean and mean."

Thomas Peters suggested, "There is, then, a lot that can be said for simply cutting staff. We find so many companies that do so much better with so many fewer people. Our journey through the terrible recession of 1981–83 was peppered with stories of company presidents who had cut their staff, often by up to 80 percent. The only noticeable difference in output, they'd tell us time and again, was *better* staff work."

Peters' examination of America's best-run companies found eight characteristics many shared. While he described each as an independent attribute, there is one characteristic that seems to have a pivotal role in making excellence possible. This is the one he terms "simple form, lean staff." Four of his other attributes make it possible to be simple and lean:

> Stick to the knitting.
> Have a hands-on, value-driven management.
> Invest in people to improve productivity.
> Closely control only the critical activities; decentralize the rest.

And Peters' three other attributes happen most easily in companies with restricted staff groups and management layers:

> Be action oriented.
> Stay close to customers.
> Innovate by providing operational autonomy.

Supported by business books and popular articles, and with some recent recession-driven practice in making management cutbacks, many executives approached downsizing with renewed vigor. Headquarters staffs were slashed and entire layers erased from organization charts. And many mid-level workers lost their jobs. We'll look at the forces behind this phenomenon, and many of its unexpected consequences, in the next chapter.

Chapter 2

Demassing:
A Blunt Response

More than one million U.S. managers and staff professionals have lost their jobs since 1979.

This Conference Board estimate covers a period of sharp economic downturn, but more than half of these job losses occurred following the 1981–82 recession. Data collected by the Bureau of Labor Statistics are no more comforting. They indicate that unemployment among managers and administrators is at its highest level since World War II. And government statistics do not even include the thousands of professionals and managers who have stopped job hunting because they took early retirement or decided to go into business for themselves. One head of an executive search firm estimates that over a third of U.S. middle-management positions have been eliminated during this period; other reports suggest that from 1,000 to 2,500 management jobs per company have been lost in many *Fortune* 500 businesses.

In most of Europe, such actions would be unthinkable. French and German social structures are tighter and business communities are smaller and more ingrown. In countries such as the Netherlands, most corporate executives know each other in much the way people do who live in small towns. In many parts of the world firing people because of poor performance is a concept only slowly being adopted. But firing middle managers and professionals because the company unintentionally overstaffed—this is unheard of in most economies where jobs are protected by custom or law.

In the United States, psychological inertia is usually stronger than social structure. Guilt has been one of the biggest barriers in the past to managers laying off other managers or high-level staff. As difficult as it has been for many executives to close down factories when foreign competition seemed undefeatable, or to terminate large teams of engineers at the end of a contract, firing numbers of their peers and subordinates has usually been near impossible. It has often been easier to mandate cutbacks that were implemented by managers several layers away. But it has taken severe outside pressures to overcome the guilt executives feel about terminating people whom they have worked with for many years, have seen every day, and perhaps have grown close to.

In this chapter we will consider what these pressures are, and will look at practices such as job buy-outs and outplacement, which make it easier to succumb to those pressures. These pressures and practices are helping executives make organizational changes that might have been unimaginable only a few years ago. We will also examine the consequences—both intended and unintended—of these major mid-level reductions, called "demassing" by the booming outplacement industry. But first let's define demassing and consider some of the forces behind this phenomenon.

What Is Demassing?

Double-digit work-force percentage cuts can be brutal to an organization. So can reductions of 5 to 9 percent when they are made over a short period of time. *Demassing* is the word coined to characterize these removals of large chunks of managers and professionals from their organizations. Characteristics of many demassing programs include:

Relatively large reductions (5–15 percent and more of the middle-level work force).

Widespread cutbacks that affect many, if not all, divisions and departments.

Deep reductions that usually cover several levels of the organization.

Priority on lowering costs by lowering head count.

Emphasis on completing the program as quickly as possible.

Demassing has hit corporate headquarters in all types of businesses. International Telephone and Telegraph matched the sale of large segments of its operating units with a reduction of almost 70 percent of its 900 New York headquarters employees. Exxon has sold its headquarters building in New York City and is reducing staff there from 1,400 to 320. General Electric's purchase of RCA is expected to result in the elimination of all 500 of RCA's head office jobs.

Cutbacks at Eastman Kodak Company went well beyond its Rochester, New York, home office. About 13,000 employees from all levels in Kodak's worldwide operations found their jobs eliminated, either after they accepted a voluntary separation offer or were let go. Salaries of some executives who stayed were also reduced.

Several years ago, the Brunswick Corporation's new chief executive, Jack Reichert, was advised by his investment banker to abandon his sports and recreation businesses, which had become too mature and too cyclical. Unwilling to become a corporate restructuring chameleon, Reichert decided instead to abandon an overgrown corporate structure. Soon afterward Brunswick shed the chief operating officer's position, the entire group level of management, almost 60 percent of its headquarters staff, and three divisional organizations. The results were red ink turned to black, increased sales, and speeded up decision making. And more Brunswick managers came to believe Reichert's philosophy that wealth is created at the operating level, not at headquarters. Brunswick's strategic position had not changed, but its ability to cope with it had improved significantly.

This wave of management reductions has not been limited to companies in mature industries. Many high-technology businesses have been affected as well. Tektronix planned a work-force reduction of 10 percent along with an equivalent salary cut for all officers. Hewlett-Packard offered 1,800 employees an early retirement program. One of its competitors, Victor Technologies, found that it had built an elaborate regional organization bigger than its sales could support. The result: a layoff of several hundred employees. Xerox's disk drive subsidiary, Shugart, closed down its operations after prolonged poor competitive performance. Some observers blamed Shugart's performance on increased competition, others on an organization which did not allow new products to get into production quickly enough. This cutback came not long after its parent, Xerox, eliminated several thousand managerial and administrative employees in a multiyear "leaning" effort.

Nor have media companies been spared the managerial streamlining. Two of the major television networks have new owners dedicated to running lean operations, while the third has new management; all three are reducing the size of their work forces. The often glamorized, sometimes aloof and free-spending television bureaucracies have run headfirst into declining revenues and soaring programming costs. Even CBS' in-house medical unit was disbanded. Among the three networks combined, there were several thousand layoffs. In publishing, Time Inc., spent $13 million to save $12 million annually by reducing 5 percent of its positions. Jobs as senior level as assistant publisher were eliminated. And few of those laid off will be able to move to jobs on Madison Avenue. The advertising industry is facing its own turmoil with shrinking margins and a wave of mergers leading to lost jobs.

Japanese companies, mistakenly thought by many to be havens of lifetime employment, have also been facing work-force reductions. A combination of competition from other Asian nations and declining sales growth owing to a strong currency have forced layoffs in the Japanese mining, shipbuilding, and steel industries. In a subsidiary of Hitachi, several thousand jobs were eliminated. At Sumitomo Metal Industries, capital spending has been cut by a third and the work force

by more than 20 percent. Profit declines among some consumer electronics makers are causing even some of Japan's
best-known businesses to make retrenchment plans.

Forces for Continuing Retrenchment

Ironically, the mid-1980s were a period of high overall employment, low interest rates, minimal inflation, a strong stock market, and an economy showing signs of continued growth—and
yet companies laid off thousands of managers. In the past such
factors implied a time of healthy corporate growth. What happened?

Unlike other upswings of the business cycle, the economic
recovery of the mid-1980s did not halt the cutbacks in managers or staff specialists. If anything, the pace of these cutbacks accelerated in the second half of the decade to affect
an increasing number of industries. A number of persistent
trends in the business environment promise to sustain this
pace. Let us review nine of the more significant ones.

Strong Overseas Competition

Companies in Brazil, Korea, and Taiwan are joining those
of Japan and West Germany to provide strong price and quality competition in many industries once dominated by American firms. Global competition is showing every sign of intensi-
fying well into the 1990s, forcing many U.S. companies to compete by cutting payroll costs and, in some cases, abandoning
entire industry sectors. As many of these overseas-based companies establish manufacturing operations in the United States,
they provide close-at-hand examples of high-performing, lean
organizations. When Marvin Runyon moved from being a Ford
vice president to head Nissan's new Smyrna, Tennessee, plant
he found it was possible to run his automated assembly plant
with only five management layers—several fewer than was
common to do the same job in Michigan.

Back in Detroit, business as usual has hardly been the rule

at Ford. For 29 consecutive quarters, each period closed with fewer salaried employees on Ford's payroll than the previous quarter. Cutbacks like these helped improve its net income to the point where it reported 1986 earnings that exceeded those of General Motors, a company with twice Ford's sales revenues.

Globalization of American Companies

Another response of American companies to the globalization of the marketplace has been to set up overseas operations to manufacture goods for U.S. customers. Initially, these companies exported production worker jobs, but as more growth begins to take place outside the United States than within, supervisory and management jobs are also exported. Growth in staff positions is also increasing abroad. India's highly trained and cost effective technical talent is making Bangalore a center for computer programming and technology management. Both the French Alps and the Riviera are becoming attractive locations for electronics R&D, as several global-minded U.S. companies have found. Some Caribbean islands and China are also becoming centers for data processing. As satellite-linked computer networks increasingly become multinational, it is possible to have design engineers in several different nations working simultaneously on a project by keeping them updated via their desktop terminals. The combination of advanced communications technology and low-cost overseas professional talent is making it possible to decentralize operations once thought to be headquarters bound. It also has encouraged many corporate recruiters to cast a wider net for professional talent than ever before.

Decline of Manufacturing, Growth of Service, and Innovation

While it is unlikely that the United States will abandon its factories for an economy based on fast-food merchandising, software production, and corn growing, the upheaval of the last decade suggests that some aspects of the economy are more globally competitive than others. Among the strongest sectors are R&D-based new-product development and distribution and retailing.

Each of these strong sectors cuts across a variety of traditional industry definitions, but each has a common prerequisite for success: minimal corporate bureaucracy. Technology-based innovation thrives in a flat organizational structure with few rules and controlled entrepreneurship. The razor-thin profit margins of most retailers create an environment hostile to management layers and expensive staffs. And some industry watchers predict at least 10 percent of these retail management positions will be gone by 1990. Department store chains such as the May Company and Macy's have already reduced staff and reorganized.

Many factories will remain to produce the innovative products that flow through a slimmed-down distribution network. But increasingly these will be showcases of computer technology and automated manufacturing, with work forces of broad-gauged technicians, not hourly laborers. Few levels of supervision will be needed as self-managing teams handle many routine decisions at shop-floor level. Automated logistics management and computer-aided design equipment will eliminate the need for many traditional plant staff jobs.

Declining Energy and Commodity Prices

Sharply falling prices for oil, some chemicals and minerals, even silicon semiconductor chips for microprocessors have led to major staff reductions in these industries. While some of these price depressions reflect temporary or cyclical conditions, the pressure they have put on many commodity-based companies to reduce their administrative scale of operations is likely to linger after prices have stopped falling. Even if those prices rebound, many commodity sellers have realized how low their revenue can go and how little overhead they must be prepared to support.

Some of the largest reductions have occurred in the oil business. For some of the large international companies, the pruning back is driven by both OPEC price fluctuations and unsuccessful attempts to generate earnings from diversification. An Exxon employee relations vice president admitted that the bulk of Exxon's cuts involved middle managers and professionals, some as a result of the elimination of synthetic fuel and office automation businesses as well as from a belt-tightening in the oil business. At Phillips Petroleum Company, which in one year reduced total employment by 12 percent, supervisors and managers were cut by 21 percent.

Exxon's cutbacks focused on organization as well as staffing. Fourteen major operating organizations were consolidated into nine units, and a layer of management was removed from its international operations. Now Exxon's foreign affiliates report directly to the United States, instead of through overseas regional offices.

Computer chip makers, such as United Technology Corporation's Texas-based Mostek Corporation, contributed to this state's managerial recession. When its electronics parts became price-sensitive commodities, Mostek laid off 2,600 employees. A fifth of these were managers.

Deregulation: Phase Two

For many companies, the deregulation trend, which throughout the 1980s has been reshaping U.S. airlines, financial services, phone companies, trucking, and railroads, is starting to enter a second, more difficult phase. Deregulation's early promise of expanded growth opportunities has been replaced by a later phase of often brutal competition and price cutting driven by excess capacity. Many companies that operate in deregulated business environments made limited initial staff cutbacks to become leaner and meaner. But as competition intensified, these companies deepened the cutbacks in order to survive. The resulting industry shakeouts, mergers, and bankruptcies continue to drive staff streamlining and other cost-cutting efforts.

At times it is the attacker as well as the defending company that makes cutbacks. MCI Communications Corporation reduced its overall work force by 15 percent as it shifted its strategy from increasing its market share to increasing its profits. MCI, the second largest U.S. long-distance telephone company, faced increased competition from its original competitor, AT&T, as well as from several smaller new entrants into this deregulated industry. MCI's layoffs covered all levels of their work force, including senior management positions.

Even more severe reductions have taken place at MCI's chief competitor. Thousands of management positions at AT&T have been cut from its well over 250,000-person work force. Compounding the cutbacks resulting from a need to lower costs because of heightened competition, AT&T is also consolidating several of its major operating units. These in-house mergers, of groups totaling more than 100,000 employees, can cause as much disruption and job switching as does the merger of two independent companies.

Acquisitions and mergers are common during the second phase of an industry's deregulation. Texas Air Corporation's purchase of Eastern Airlines resulted in a major streamlining of the surviving Eastern executives. Eastern's complement of corporate officers was reduced from 47 to 16. Nine senior vice presidents were demoted to vice presidents, and most former vice presidents took on lesser titles. Northwest Airlines survived the Northwest-Republic consolidation, but their higher labor costs meant they would have to lay off almost 1,000 employees and relocate many others.

Pressures for Earnings Growth in Mature Markets

We have already considered the maturing of many American markets and industries. As, in the jargon of strategic planning, more "growth stars" become "cash cows," investors' expectations change. They look more for regular earnings growth than for skyrocketing stock price appreciation. For many companies in stalemated strategic positions, these earnings increases can come only from continued cost (that is, headcount) reductions.

In a large and profitable manufacturer, the first move of a newly appointed CEO was to announce a 5 percent across-the-board staff reduction. His primary motivation was to make sure his first year as chief executive was not marred by the company's first decline in earnings. Another business, the spicemaker McCormick & Company, cut back four percent of its work force as part of a plan to boost profits and speed new product development.

Much of the U.S. chemical industry has been plagued with overcapacity and foreign competition. While many companies are trying to shift from selling bulk commodity products to specialty chemicals and the results of biotechnological research, there's often still a need to scale back operations. The Olin Corporation eliminated 700 salaried jobs in implementing a plan to close or sell uncompetitive businesses.

Stock Price–Driven Strategic Planning

One response many companies made to their stalemated growth prospects was to shift attention from market share to stock price as the key indicator of performance. This "value-based planning" has led to a breakup of many conglomerates when they determine that the price-earnings multiple of their stocks is being held back by one or two lackluster divisions. Called "industry restructuring," these moves have resulted in a wave of shutdowns, divestitures, leveraged buy-outs, and other ways of taking companies private. Many of the spun-off or bought-out divisions, now free-standing companies, find they must reduce management and staff overhead significantly to remain viable when weaned from their corporate parent. And many of the former parent corporations find that restructuring leaves them with a smaller business to support staff overhead, also resulting in downsizing. More than one chief executive has found that going lean means losing his or her staff of economic advisors as well as a private jet.

Part of the Control Data Corporation's restructuring effort was to spin off to public ownership its Commercial

Credit Company subsidiary. Sanford Weill, Commercial Credit's new chief executive, soon put together a plan for streamlining its organizational structure to save $4.5 million annually. Ten percent of its Baltimore headquarters staff jobs would be cut to increase efficiency and eliminate some duplication of effort.

Merger and Acquisition Frenzy

The most commonly observed result of industry restructuring is the boom in mergers and acquisitions. Company combinations, whether they be General Electric's acquisition of RCA or the merger of railroads that form CSX Corporation, almost inevitably result in staff and management redundancies. Merged companies seem to differ only in how and when they deal with surplus staffing. The rise of the junk bond–supported corporate raider has also led to increased downsizing. Sometimes these corporate raiders take over and slim down a company, while other times businesses try to avoid these unwanted suitors by cutting costs to shield their autonomy through increased earnings and higher stock prices.

The earlier examples of Eastern and Republic airlines illustrate the downsizing that results from consummated mergers. But often just the threat of a takeover can have the same result. An attempt by GAF Corporation to increase its ownership in Union Carbide Corporation, coupled with the threat of massive expenses related to the Bhopal disaster, pushed Union Carbide to eliminate about 15 percent of its white-collar work force. For CBS Inc., expenses related to buying back a portion of its common stock to fend off Ted Turner's attempted acquisition forced it to reduce its work force by over 1,000 employees.

The banking industry has also seen an acceleration in merger activity. The experience of Crocker National Corporation illustrates what sometimes happens. Crocker was acquired by Wells Fargo and Company in what was at the time the largest bank merger in history. Wells Fargo, a legendary cost cutter, hoped to increase Crocker's annual profits by a factor of four, just by reducing expenses. The effort began as soon as the sale was final, and nearly all Crocker's executives and almost 1,600 managers immediately were told to find work elsewhere. Additionally, plans were made to cut back twice that number of Crocker positions during the next two years.

Privatization

This is a practice that has been receiving increasing attention in many Third World countries, whose economic infrastructure had to be created by the government. At the prodding of the World Bank and other international financial institutions, some developing countries are turning control of their national enterprises over to the private sector. Called "privatization," this action is intended to keep their oil companies, airlines, state-owned factories, and telephone companies more attuned to the marketplace than to bureaucratic procedure. It is a phenomenon not limited to the developing world, though.

The U.S. government is starting to identify parts of itself that can be spun off to private ownership. The director of the Office of Personnel Management has proposed that many of the 600,000 federal jobs that duplicate ones in the private sector (ranging from data processing to vehicle maintenance) be spun off into businesses partially owned by the former government workers who filled them.

This type of privatization has also been a key element in British industrial policy. Recently, formerly government-owned companies making fast cars (Jaguar) and supersonic planes (British Aerospace) have gone public. This is a trend likely to persist into the 1990s in the United Kingdom, as well as in the United States and other countries. Successful implementation of privatization projects frequently mandates management and staff streamlining as goals shift from providing employment to increasing earnings. In preparation for an anticipated privatization, British Air cut its work force by 40 percent, including reductions of both executives and middle managers.

The nine economic factors just reviewed are the driving

force for demassing in a variety of companies and industries. For some of these businesses, demassing has been seen as the only way to ensure the company's survival, as well as ensure the jobs of those who remain. But for other firms, demassing has been a convenient rationale for postponing earnings declines as a result of poor management decisions. One executive even admitted privately that his main purpose in announcing an across-the-board staffing cut was to get poor performers off the payroll, a result he was not able to build into his annual performance appraisal system.

Reducing the Guilt

For whatever reason, more executives than ever before are summoning the willpower to demass their companies. The severe guilt that used to accompany such moves has been lessened by the existence of (1) outplacement services, (2) job buyout programs, and (3) the "bandwagon effect."

Outplacement services have made it easier for many executives to say good-bye. These services provide executives with a way to temporarily extend their concern for terminated employees beyond their last day at work. Paid by the firm, outplacement services for laid-off managers typically include some immediate counseling after the termination notice, followed by several months of coaching and follow-up. Lessons in job hunting, career replanning, interview techniques, and résumé writing are frequently provided. Some services also provide job seekers with office space, telephones, and limited secretarial help to facilitate their searches.

Harvard Business School human resources expert D. Quinn Mills calls outplacement an example of a company acting in its enlightened self-interest. Outplacement can help the morale of the remaining employees, and might also reduce some of the negative community impact that layoffs often have. Quinn sees services like these eventually being extended to nonmanagers, too.

The industry that provides outplacement services has been growing understandably fast. Outplacement has increased about 35 percent annually since 1980. From the 43 firms who offered these services in 1980, the industry has quadrupled in number and grown in size to over a quarter billion dollars billed each year. The outplacement industry originally was founded to provide customized counseling and placement help to senior executives whose companies wanted to remove them gracefully. Coupled with generous termination settlements, these services helped calm many troubled waters. Psychologically, they provided a safe place for discharged executives to release their anger at their former employer while reformulating their career plans. Demassing large groups of middle managers in recent years has turned many of these personalized outplacement services into assembly-line operations, however. Group lectures have replaced individual counseling, and private temporary offices have deteriorated into soundproofed dividers on long tables.

While middle-level termination settlements typically are less generous than those provided to released top managers, a variety of job buy-out programs have joined with outplacement services to facilitate demassing. The two most common programs are early retirement offers for long-serving managers and lump-sum cash payments for more recently hired ones. The widespread use of these options has eased the consciences of many executives as they have authorized cutbacks. They feel that the people leaving the company are at least getting "something" for losing their jobs—maybe not as much money as if they had been able to stay, but a more generous settlement than that provided to workers in some near-bankrupt industries. They also find that some of these offers make good economic sense for the company. A number of firms, such as Du Pont and Time Inc., feel that these buy-out programs have relatively fast payback periods. Chapter 7 will consider the economics of these programs more closely.

A third factor helping some executives yield to economic pressures and initiate demassing is harder to quantify. It is the bandwagon effect that comes from so many companies in so many industries cutting back on middle management. Demassing is no longer a phenomenon limited to the very troubled steel or automobile industries. Everyone seems to be doing it. And when this happens, it is harder for some companies to face their corps of investment analysts without at least having studied the possibility of eliminating some staff.

The social barriers to downsizing have weakened, too. Criticisms from public officials of corporate bureaucracy, congressional concerns about industrial competitiveness, and bestselling books exhorting lean and mean management have pushed executives committed to lifetime employment back into a corner. On the other hand, some top managers have even become eager to talk publicly about their staff reductions because it "demonstrates their resolve to keep a short rein on costs." Demassing is clearly in style, and fashion has contributed to its momentum.

Unintended Consequences

Unfortunately, in spite of practices that alleviate guilt and soften the blow of job loss, companies are finding that demassing can lead to many unwanted consequences. The comfort of safety in numbers has not kept executives from hearing comments similar to these:

> Maybe we did manage to strengthen our bottom line, but at the cost of many stunted careers and hurt people. At times I wonder if it was really worth it.

> Too many of the managers we've kept don't seem to be working up to their potential. Many seem chronically insecure—even though we've told them they're too good for us ever to let go. I don't think our credibility with them is too high. And the team spirit we depend on to move products out the door in crunch times ... it really seems to have disappeared. Nobody trusts anybody anymore.

Our last layoff seemed like a misguided attempt to stem the negative tide starting to engulf the company, rather than to face the reality of where our real problem lies: our dearth of new products and fresh ideas.

We were surprised by how many senior circuit designers took us up on the early retirement offer: twice as many as we predicted. Some of our new product work is at a standstill, and we're making plans to hire away some experienced engineers from a competitor.

Nobody is going to stick his neck out to promote a new idea here anymore. Security seems a lot more important, and most of us feel that keeping our jobs means hunkering down and focusing only at the work in front of us.

Let us consider the issues behind these too commonly heard laments.

High Human Costs

Some of the language used to describe demassing programs sounds like a replay of former Secretary of Defense Robert McNamara's numbers-driven attempt at victory in Vietnam. The phrase "head-count reduction" is used instead of the Vietnam-era "body count," but the same depersonalization is implied. The word *demassing* itself sounds more appropriate in a physics classroom than a corporate boardroom. It and the popular *R.I.F.* ("reduction-in-force") are neutral enough terms to make some managers forget that they describe large-scale firings of their co-workers. One management observer has even heard personnel departments referring to remaining employees as "backfill," a term more commonly used in building roads and sewers.

We often use words to distance ourselves from unpleasant happenings. Self-delusion may be necessary to get through a difficult time, but its continued use creates more problems than it solves. The danger in thinking of people as backfill, as Thomas Horton, president of the American Management

Association, has noted, is that sooner or later we may start to treat them that way.

There are many human costs to demassing. Many companies have been able to restructure their organizations and improve their financial performance, but for a price. One frustrated former member of a headquarters staff has noted the trauma felt by many of the several hundred employees who were terminated. He has expressed considerable disappointment that more efforts were not made to help those laid off, especially those who—like himself—are over fifty. The head of the nation's largest outplacement business, William Morin, is concerned that middle managers are becoming unemployed in such numbers that even the best outplacement advice may not do them very much good. He says, "Unfortunately, a lot of people are going into jobs they have no interest in. That's a crime and a waste of skills." The reality seems that, for many people losing jobs in declining industries, the likelihood of returning to similar work in a large company is almost nil.

A former Exxon employee said it seemed that, "Management broke the unwritten promise that Exxon would take care of its employees. . . .When I left, I felt I was going from the womb into the piranha tank." Self-esteem is sometimes shattered, even though the only performance mistake many former employees feel they made was to look after the company's welfare more than their own. The disappointment of losing a job, sometimes summarily, and the bleak prospects some people feel they have of finding ways to reuse their skills, can lead to depression, drinking and drug problems, family difficulties, and other damaging mental and physical disorders.

The consequences of being dismissed can be financial as well as psychological. For many laid-off managers, severance payments run out before they find new jobs. One study by the American Society for Training and Development indicated that a third of the displaced managers over 35 years old find jobs that pay less than what they previously earned; these laid-off managers often needed five years to get back to their former pay level.

Missing Real Problems

Companies can also pay an unexpected price for entering a period of continuing, large employee cutbacks. Some, such as AT&T, have special difficulties when they try to formulate a much needed new strategy while simultaneously attempting to significantly lower their employment. A middle manager in AT&T's finance division admitted that he found it hard to focus attention on the global strategies of James Olson (AT&T's chief executive) while he was worried about losing his job. Continuing concerns about job security, coupled with shifts in overall business strategy, can quickly reduce the employee commitment that is critical to turning plans into results.

The problem of insecurity for those still on the job is eventually correctable, usually as time passes and the new strategy settles into place. AT&T, it is important to note, is going through more change in a few years than most companies experience in their entire history. But there's another type of problem that can have long-term adverse effects. It occurs when executives substitute demassing for a direct assault on the real problems of their businesses.

Making major work-force cutbacks is a dramatic sign that the company is changing. But these cutbacks do not always address the appropriate problems. Weak competitive performance can be a result of high management overhead being built into product prices. But it can also be caused by inferior quality, lack of a differentiated product line, poor market positioning, an attempt to sell outdated technology, inadequate logistics and customer support, and a failure to negotiate the best prices for raw materials—just to indicate a few possibilities. Companies in which management expenses are a relatively small proportion of their total product costs can sometimes get more value by obtaining better results from their middle managers and staffs than they can by reducing the size of their staffs.

For some companies, the greatest danger of demassing

is the false sense of security it provides. Valuable time may be lost if top management feels declines in earnings will be arrested by early retirements and reorganization, when the real future problems will result from a lack of new products in the development pipeline. Competitors may steal much of that company's market share by introducing new products while the company is still recovering from the demassing.

Revolving Door Syndrome

An AT&T manager tugged at his few remaining hairs. An electrical engineer by training, he was pleased when, a year earlier, he was rotated into a top-level manpower-planning slot. He had close access to the vice presidents running his part of the company. Most of his time went into preparing for a major work-force reduction in his division. But by now his early excitement at being charged with such a critical task had deteriorated into complete frustration. A look at his planning numbers revealed the problem. As fast as he was able to identify people who could be let go in one part of the division, requisitions would come to him from other parts asking for approval to hire people vitally needed to keep AT&T's development groups up to date in new communications technologies. Even after he weeded out the additions, he could barely keep the overall work force at its current size, let alone achieve any of the headquarters' mandated net reductions. After a few more months enduring the life of Sisyphus, he requested a transfer to a less complex job: managing one of these advanced communications technology groups.

Other human resource planners in fast-moving business environments share this AT&T manager's revolving-door dilemma. As fast as managers are laid off, new ones seem to be needed. Sometimes this is because, though people are let go, the work they did remains. It happens when the focus of demassing is on body-count reduction, assuming the organization and the work will somehow take care of themselves. They seldom do, however, and the companies that approach downsizing this way find it hard to stay slim after the immediate economic pressure lets up.

The other revolving door in demassing results from using untargeted early retirement and job buy-out plans. Since these offers must be made to groups of employees, not individuals, companies often have difficulty predicting how many will accept. Some companies have faced the embarrassment of letting people go and then finding they have to hire them back or employ them as consultants to keep key projects moving along. Sometimes new employees need to be hired, adding the expenses of recruitment, selection, orientation, and training to personnel budgets that were originally intended to be cut.

Squashing Innovation

Innovation is a complex and delicate process to manage. It often thrives in corporate settings relatively free from excessive management layers. It requires an organization quick to take action and test new ideas, not one that overanalyzes them with a large bureaucracy. Many recent demassing efforts try to deliver such an environment, but streamlining alone is not enough to promote innovation. In fact, it may keep innovation from happening.

Encouraging innovation also requires that corporations tolerate diversity and nurture mavericks. As we've seen, demassing programs can leave companies with an atmosphere of mistrust and insecurity, atmospheres hardly conducive to employees deviating from the straight and narrow. Downsizing may unclutter the organization chart, but it may also eliminate enclaves that harbored some creative contributors. One of the several thousand managers who lost his job in General Electric's major cutbacks has warned that employees may tend to spend more time concerned about their future employment prospects than they spend innovating and growing the company's future business.

Studies of companies that have been especially good at making money from innovations indicate that such businesses often have two organizations functioning at once. One form is that which is described on the official organization chart; it distributes power and authority in a way oriented toward smoothly running the already established business. But in many companies a second, shadow company also exists. The orientation of this shadow company is toward the future, toward planning and developing products that will provide the next decade's positive cash flow. Its employees may hold two positions simultaneously—their official job and another role in what may be a hidden or semiofficial skunkworks.

Unfortunately, when staff reductions take place, decisions about who stays and who goes are more often based on official jobs. People's role in the shadow organization tends to be ignored. Even though it is becoming popular for executives to look the other way while bootlegged projects are undertaken, many of these half-sanctioned efforts to develop new products are unintentionally disrupted by major cutbacks. Care needs to be taken so that getting back to "today's" basics does not ignore what it will take to develop tomorrow's.

While many stock-market analysts have praised the cost-cutting efforts of Eastman Kodak's downsizing program mentioned earlier, at least one has warned that saving money will not be enough to restore the company to its earlier growth pattern. He feels Kodak will need a better flow of new and innovative products. An analyst who follows the chemical industry felt that the Celanese Corporation had gone as far as it could go in downsizing. While several years of reducing capital spending, cutting its work force by almost half, trimming R&D, and selling off businesses based on innovative technologies have helped the company's income and stock price to soar, these actions may also have cut short its life as an independent business. As if to underscore the analyst's concerns, at the end of 1986, Celanese directors agreed that the company be purchased by the West German chemical giant Hoechst AG.

Most innovations originate in one form or another with customers. But companies with cost-cutting myopia are likely to miss these. Apple Computer is a company that went through a severe downsizing, shedding a fifth of its work force and a co-founder, without crippling its ability to innovate. By reorganizing to balance its focus on creative product development, with close attention to the uses its customers make of the products, Apple was able to strengthen the market position of its Macintosh personal computer. Under Lee Iacocca, the Chrysler Corporation has shown a similar ability to safeguard innovation while streamlining, as it introduced the minivan and brought back the convertible.

Creating New Problems

In addition to the unintended consequences of demassing already discussed, large-scale cutbacks create other problems. The most immediate of these is reduced morale among the survivors. People charged with doing the actual firing may feel guilt and depression, while the colleagues of those people who left may need to get over their resulting feelings of grief and loss. Some, but not many, companies are aware of these problems and have instituted programs to help these employees. Companies that do not plan for these groups risk building up feelings of permanent insecurity among their middle-level managers. Surveys by Opinion Research Corporation indicate a significant drop in feelings of job security among middle managers. For example, in a 1982 survey, 43 percent felt very secure in their jobs; four years later, only 27 percent felt that way.

Special counseling and programs that try to redirect attention to the work at hand can be useful, but companies that do not carefully evaluate their staffing needs often subject their work force to successive waves of downsizing. These waves of firings turn today's survivors into tomorrow's victims, and they limit the credibility of any morale-boosting attempts.

Fear and apprehension take their toll, as managers spend considerable time anticipating layoffs before they occur. Morale and initiative-taking are weakened long before top management finalizes any layoff plans. At times executives realize this but, instead of providing information about the company's situation and the plans to deal with it, they try to maintain employee spirits by denying that anything is wrong. This approach seldom works, and it can lead to even lower morale as managers' visions of worst-case scenarios fill the void created by the absence of authoritative information.

Because demassing frequently has been based on a need to make deep cuts in payroll costs, rather than on a campaign to weed out poor performers, good as well as weak contributors have lost their jobs. These across-the-board cutbacks can leave some strong managers, laid off because there was no more work for them, with undeserved doubts about their own abilities. It can also leave remaining good performers unsure that continued hard work is the way to survive and advance. The chief economist of the American Society for Training and Development, Anthony Carnevale, has suggested that for these managers, developing better political skills may replace their former concerns with improving productivity.

Some of these are short-term problems and can be alleviated through combinations of clear communications, consistent management, and individual counseling. But there are also long-term consequences of demassing that can tick quietly like a time bomb.

Broken Bargains

Many companies have been scrutinizing and rewriting their policy manuals and employment applications to ferret out implied promises of job security, termination benefits, or lifetime employment. While this might make good legal sense, overemphasis on this type of preventive action misses the point about what is happening to many employment relationships.

For many mid-level employees, psychological contracts have served the same purpose that employment agreements have for senior executives. They are the understandings, both explicit and implicit, that exist between employees and employers. They are shapers of people's beliefs and expectations, and they can be powerful motivators (and demotivators).

The key word here is *expectation*. Plant-floor workers at GM have been conditioned by years of cyclical cutbacks in production to have limited expectations about job continuity. This has helped prepare some of them for eventual plant closings and the need to build a career in another industry. These workers have very different notions of what to expect from their employer than do middle managers, who might have received their college education from General Motors Technical Institute, worked only at GM throughout their careers, and have felt they had every reason to believe there would be a job at GM for them as long as they performed adequately.

This expectation is far more widespread than just at GM. A 1986 survey, conducted by Louis Harris and Associates, of middle managers at 600 large corporations questioned whether they assumed, when they started working for their current employer, that they could stay as long as they liked, assuming they were doing a good job. More than half of these managers believed they could.

According to management psychologist Harry Levinson, people tend to select a job based on their expectation that the company will help them meet their psychological needs. Over time people stay, in part, because a comfortable match has been made. When the rules change in the midst of people's careers, as they have in many banks, insurance firms, and telephone companies, people react in many ways. Initially, they feel anger and frustration because a bargain seems to have been broken. Some people adapt quickly to the new situation; perhaps they never were really comfortable with the old rules anyway. Others try to resist, becoming part of Roger Smith's bureaucratic and unresponsive "frozen middle management." This resistance seldom is viable in the long run as it usually leads to frustrated managers and poorly performing companies. Most people eventually adjust to the new reality, one way or another, though the adjustment is not usually a very comfortable process.

When what people are adjusting to is a realization that good performance, long service, and corporate loyalty no longer ensure job security, the consequences to employers are not particularly favorable. This message has been driven home by waves of demassing. The "new contract" being offered can narrow the scope of the employer-employee commitment to the short term and the immediate work at hand. It will also be harder for loyalty to remain a "bankable" commodity. Sixty-five percent of the managers in the survey just mentioned felt that most salaried employees are less loyal to their employers than they were ten years ago. Now it is easier to call a management position "just" a job. Rex Adams, Mobil's Vice President of Employee Relations, fears the management and professional work force of the late 1980s will include many "mercenaries" more interested in building résumés than companies. This means turnover will increase, but so will total employment expenses. And eventually the number of management layers will also increase, by the process outlined in the last chapter, leaving some companies right back where they started.

The future does not have to be this bleak. Many companies still have time, before feelings harden and attitudes resettle, to keep their mid-level work force from converting to a group of loosely affiliated hired guns. In later chapters we will consider some actions that can be taken. But first, it is important to remember that employees have ways outside the job to meet their inherent need to be dependent upon someone else. Some people are able to find this security in their families and other relationships. Demassing, however, can also lead workers to rely more on unions and the government for help, especially when the causes of employee cutbacks are unclear and felt to have been done unfairly.

The "Blue Collarizing" of Middle Management

Most warnings about the "radicalization" of the middle class have proved false. While it is unlikely that a political movement such as West Germany's Green Party will take root in the United States, it is likely that some attitudes will shift. It is possible that some laid-off managers, as well as those still employed but anxious about job security, will abandon their traditional middle-of-the-road political stance. Others may be a little less quick to defend the free market system. Many managers will be less willing to trust senior management and assume that the company is committed to their long-term well-being.

Increasingly, managers are feeling caught in the middle. They lack the job guarantees and severance agreements provided to many union workers. They also lack the bargaining clout of executives to negotiate employment contracts and golden parachutes. Traditionally, they took care of job security by getting a job with an established blue-chip company, but they find this tactic is no longer very effective. Where do they turn?

Here is one scenario, not favored by many executives. The new leadership of unions such as the Communications Workers of America, the United Automobile Workers, and even parts of the Teamsters takes advantage of the organizing opportunity offered by disenchanted middle managers. Their promises are of job security coupled with large cash settlements if layoffs are necessary, limits on "excessive" overtime and relocations, union-supervised job posting and career planning, job rights defined through tightly written and followed position descriptions—all in addition to collectively bargained salary and benefit packages. An increasing number of white-collar workers, the scenario assumes, find that these promises, along with a less tangible offer of long-term loyalty, fill a void created by their employers.

The other part of the scenario involves some state legislatures and possibly Congress, who are less concerned with ensuring international competitiveness than with reducing middle-class unemployment. By enacting European-style employment legislation, these legislative bodies can place restrictions on management to terminate or move employees. In addition, the extra costs such restrictions would bring about could outweigh the earlier benefits companies received through large-scale payroll-reduction efforts.

While neither part of this scenario is very likely, neither

is impossible. Together, it represents what may happen when society's outer limit of toleration for continued demassing is reached. The regulatory responses within this limit will still be unfavorable to many companies. They will most likely be directed toward limiting management's freedom to staff and organize, because this freedom will be judged to have been abused.

Avoiding the Body-Count Mentality

Many problems have resulted from using a body-count mentality for large-scale cutbacks. Companies whose primary downsizing objective is short-term cost reduction often take as big a slice as possible from the payroll. Their primary reduction tool has too frequently been an across-the-board, often untargeted layoff completed as quickly as possible.

As we have seen, reductions achieved in this manner can also have unwanted, unproductive consequences. The costs of these consequences are borne by the companies making the cutbacks, as well as by the people losing their jobs. Fortunately, not all companies have taken this approach to downsizing. Some have done a more effective job in managing the size of their organization on an ongoing basis. When they have downsized, they have done it in ways that minimize human costs and maximize long-term economic benefits. In the next chapter we will review some of these practices. They can be useful for companies still needing to prune back management bureaucracies. In addition, companies that have already demassed might find these practices a guide to helping them stay slim.

Chapter 3

Planned Downsizing: A Sustainable Alternative

Concern about the unintended consequences of demassing has left some thoughtful executives feeling caught between the proverbial rock and a hard place. They are reluctant to make deep, quick cuts in their organization's size because of the disruption, the human costs, the damage to their innovative ability, and the lost loyalty that may result. Perhaps they are not even certain that excess staffing is their highest priority problem. But, they also feel legitimate concerns about how the number of management layers has grown and how staff experts have proliferated. They want to avoid the difficult situations faced by AT&T, General Motors, and many others. Maybe they have recently purchased another business, and they realize they will receive few benefits from the acquisition until they eliminate duplicate staffing. Is there a middle ground available, they wonder.

Increasingly, they are agreeing with views expressed by management experts such as Michael Tennican, a Senior Vice

President of Temple, Barker & Sloane, Inc., who oversees
the firm's corporate planning and development consulting
practice. Tennican criticizes American industry's over-reliance
on cost-cutting as a means to achieve revitalization, calling
it "indiscriminate, impermanent, and ultimately ineffective."
He maintains that it does not do an especially good job of
discriminating between activities with high and low values to
a company's customers. Moreover, he argues that its results
are impermanent because organizational slots emptied in cost-
cutting programs tend to be refilled when profitability pressures lessen. In Tennican's opinion, a single-minded focus on
cutting people and costs is ultimately ineffective in removing
the underlying barriers to efficiency, such as fragmented jobs
and narrow spans of control. Cost-cutting, by its very nature,
will have only a short-term impact. In order to revitalize American industry, companies must expand their markets, develop
better products, provide better service, improve their workers'
morale, and modernize their plants.

Some companies have been able to address these concerns
while charting a course between demassing and doing nothing.
TRW, with its long-term strategy of simplifying its organization
and reducing its manpower, is one such company. Dana Corporation, which has worked hard to keep its management size
in direct proportion to its production work force, is another.
Xerox has obtained some hard-won experience in how to keep
its headquarters lean. Even in the roller coaster price-driven
oil industry, two companies have made fewer reductions than
most: Schlumberger and the Shell Oil Company. Both of these
energy businesses have European parents, which, given the
labor regulations there, may explain the care they have taken
to keep constant control over their staff size. Shell has followed
the injunction of IBM founder Thomas Watson, who warned
that prosperity can be more dangerous for a company than
depression. According to John Bookout, Shell's chief executive, "We didn't let staff get out of hand during the upswing.
We didn't cut like others in the downswing." These, and
companies like them, have long practiced "planned downsizing."

Five Lessons

The experiences of these and other successful downsizers suggest some lessons for others. Some companies that have done a good job of managing their size up to this time may not perform as well if business conditions change significantly. Few companies are good at all aspects of managing their size, but it is possible, in identifying the practices that work for some, to discover some general principles for all. Here are five of these principles; they form the basis for the topics covered in the rest of this book.

Start before you have to.
Prepare for the down side.
Use a rifle, not a shotgun.
Continually manage size and shape.
Go after more than costs and jobs.

Too many companies have found that they had no choice but to demass, because they waited until they were forced to prune their overgrown organizations. For companies that face a sudden bankruptcy threat, demassing might be the only alternative, but overnight moves from riches to rags happen to few vigilant businesses. Foreign competition and new products introduced by domestic competitors usually provide warning signals before they make a meal of a company's market share. Takeover attempts and raider's attacks come with less notice but, as many executives have commented, if a company's stock is traded publicly, the business is up for sale every day the market is open.

Being forced to make deep, quick staff cuts leaves the business open to all the negative consequences of demassing. It is possible to recover from some of these consequences, but others will have lingering effects that may cancel out much of the payroll savings. Sharp cuts like these drastically limit an executive's options for dealing with a bloated staff and management. On the other hand, streamlining a company over a longer time span opens up many possibilities for reducing staff without firing people. Chapter 7 discusses the alternatives available to planned downsizers. But to utilize these options, a company must move before it is forced to.

If a company can take action on *its* schedule, not on a junk bond–supported raider's or a short-term focused stock analyst's, there is time to prepare the company for the new style of management that downsizing will require. Running a lean and mean business is not a natural act for many executives. For some companies, it may be riskier than maintaining a bloated payroll. Reducing the number of managers while keeping the same degree of oversight is not impossible, but it does require a good bit of planning. Avoiding a move from "analysis-paralysis" to "out-of-control" requires some careful consideration of what it takes to operate a downsized company. Downsizing has a down side, but it can be managed. The prerequisites for doing this are discussed in Chapter 8.

Avoiding some of the pitfalls of demassing requires pinpointing excess staff and management layers, rather than holding all units to the same across-the-board reduction target. Use a rifle, not a shotgun. Pruning a management hierarchy is different from reducing the scope of a headquarters staff. And different considerations come into play when a company cuts back on internal auditors than when it downsizes an in-house publications unit. How to treat each of these situations differently is the subject of the next three chapters.

Achieving one-time employment reductions is often difficult and painful. But the experience of many companies has shown that these cutbacks do not necessarily sustain themselves. To stay streamlined, changes also need to be made in organizational structure, compensation systems, career ladders, hiring and training practices, and at times the overall corporate strategy. Chapter 9 outlines the steps to ensure that the hard-won gains from downsizing remain.

Finally, the hoped-for results of downsizing should be planned for at the outset. Too often, only near-term headcount reductions are sought, at the expense of long-term efficiencies. Other benefits, such as speedier product development, are left to chance. Let us start by considering some of these high-payoff objectives.

Broadened Objectives

Companies have a number of stated objectives for downsizing, but the one they pay most attention to is head-count reduction. Other objectives, such as speeding up decisions and improving line management morale, are frequently tossed out as justifications for the cutbacks and then forgotten. Few companies have figured out what the *mean* part of the "lean and mean" state to which they aspire really signifies.

Companies good at getting the most mileage out of management and staff reductions—the ones we call "planned downsizers"—have broader objectives than job elimination. For them, the overall goal is to build the most efficient and effective organization they can, and then to put practices in place that will keep on delivering this kind of organization. They seldom use the meat cleaver to slim down, because one of their objectives is to come out of the downsizing with a strong and committed work force. When they plan downsizing, these companies choose among a wide range of objectives and tactics. These objectives include:

□ *Lowered costs.* Lowering costs implies minimizing non-salary as well as salary expenses. Many planned downsizers search hard for alternatives before reducing employment to cut costs. Some manufacturers have been able to save more money by adding staff to their purchasing department and obtaining savings through shrewder purchasing methods and materials management. When they need to cut payroll, targets are expressed in terms of employment dollars saved, not in number of people terminated. Total costs of employment are examined for saving possibilities, including salary and benefit reductions, elimination of overtime and vacation carryovers, and conversion of full-time jobs to part-time.

□ *Faster decision making.* Achieving this commonly sought objective means specifying in advance which decisions are to be made, how long they now take to be made, and what the target times are for making them in a more streamlined structure. Otherwise, this objective becomes pie in the sky, not an aspect of a business whose performance is actually managed. Companies such as Ford and Pacific Telephone have gone to great lengths to chart out steps in making important, recurring decisions. Then these flowcharts are closely examined to identify shorter paths. Out of this examination come targets for pruning: extra management layers, unneeded committees, excess staff inputs, and the like.

□ *Quicker response to competitors' actions.* Improvement in this aspect means shortening the path among those who first hear of a competitor's move, those who decide what to do about it, and those who implement the decision.

□ *Less distorted communications.* A combination of management-layer reduction (see Chapter 6) and investment in computer networks (Chapter 9) can help here.

□ *Greater action-orientation, less analysis-paralysis.* This objective usually implies reducing the role of the headquarters staff in decision making, or using something like IBM's "contention system," which requires constant collaboration of staff and line management to reach major decisions. Achieving this objective usually implies changing the mix of skills among managers as well as their number.

□ *Quicker diffusion of new ideas.* Making a company more innovative is an important objective, especially for businesses facing stalemated positions in maturing markets. To become more innovative, give fewer people veto power over new ideas. As we have already discussed, while moderate organizational streamlining can be helpful, demassing can encourage a new corporate culture inhospitable to innovation.

□ *Facilitating synergies within the company.* The easiest way to encourage synergy, structurally, is to reduce the number of divisions and departments that need to interact, then limit the hierarchy in each that could stand in the way of such interaction. As with innovation, downsizing is not enough to encourage increased cooperation across organizational lines. Coordinating mechanisms such as carefully chosen committees and task forces, as well as incentives and rewards for behaving this way, are needed.

□ *Higher general manager morale.* Better morale can come when staff groups that tend to second-guess line managers are reined in (assuming the individual managers are able to solo without their "support"). Reducing the overall number of managers can, to a point, increase the morale of those remaining by giving them full-time management jobs. We will cover this in more detail in Chapter 6.

□ *Focusing on customer needs, not internal procedures.* This re-focusing requires both limiting the hierarchy between key managers and key customers and managing the operation with a short rule book.

□ *Giving authority to managers closest to customers.* This objective can also be a result of reducing management layers and delegating decision making on matters of immediate concern to customers to those who deal with them most frequently.

□ *Easier ways to pinpoint individual responsibility.* This objective should be a natural result of a streamlined organization and a test of that structure if it is sufficiently streamlined. Responsibility for economic performance should not be lost among overlapping layers of managers. Key managers should have both performance targets and the resources needed to achieve them.

□ *Increased management productivity.* On a manager-by-manager basis, this usually happens by increasing the number of people reporting to each. Company-wide management productivity can be tracked by watching for improvements in "management value added."

Return on Management

Too few companies directly track how much value their management adds to their business. The value-added concept is an underused way to set overall downsizing objectives and also keep track of progress toward meeting those objectives. Its calculation is not extremely difficult, as some seem to assume. Paul Strassmann, a retired Xerox vice president for strategic planning, has developed a ratio he calls Return on Management (ROM). It is analogous to Return on Investment (ROI), and is also a measure of management productivity. He defines ROM as "management value added" divided by "management costs." "Management value added" is simply the difference between the total value a company adds (calculated the way economists customarily do—the difference between what companies sell their goods and services for and what their total costs are in producing them) and the portion of that value added which reflects a company's total operating expenses (which include labor and the capital expenditures involved in business operations). "Management costs" are the combination of (1) managers' salaries, bonuses, and benefits, (2) capital expenditures related to management (computers, and the like), and (3) the services that managers purchase (travel, consultants, and so on).

Strassmann has found this a useful indicator. The productivity of a management structure can be overlooked when global indicators of productivity tell a good story. The Strategic Planning Institute reports a situation whereby traditional measures such as revenues per employee and value added per employee both increased by 33 percent over a two-year period, while at the same time ROM *decreased* by 1.5 percent. This decrease can be an early warning of trouble to come.

According to Strassmann's calculations, the ROM for all of American industry is 1.2, not an indicator of very high productivity. Thirty-five percent of all U.S. companies have a ROM of less than 1.0. This means that for many, management is paid more than what it delivers as value added. The link between these measures and an organization is that companies with the highest ROM are the ones with limited vertical integration. Strassmann says, "They buy more and more of their overhead from outside. One of the big problems with low-performance organizations is that they're trying to own too much of their overhead. That approach creates hierarchy, because each group of experts enters into the game of getting their cut of the budget."

Match Organization with Strategy

We have considered a range of objectives beyond the simple head-count reduction that can be achieved, at least in part, by taking a planned approach to downsizing. The benefits they provide can have long-term significance, but achieving these objectives must be a managed activity. Becoming better at product innovation or faster at making key decisions are not qualities that happen just by accident. Because the management effort for any one of these objectives can be considerable, some basis is needed to select those with the biggest payoffs.

The best reference point for deciding what the outcomes of downsizing should be is the company's strategic plan. Typically, this plan will focus on an extended period and be oriented toward investing resources in areas of the company's most sustainable advantage over its competitors.

For example, a large supermarket company was concerned that its return on equity was lower than that of a number of its competitors. Its executives felt this was reflected in a lower stock price than was warranted, given the company's strong competitive position in many of the regions it served. This bargain stock price might, they feared, attract unwanted suitors. These key managers also worried about the company's ability to maintain its lead over the competition, because its competitors were, increasingly, smaller companies and owner-operated stores. They all had less management hierarchy, which allowed store managers to respond more quickly to changes in what customers wanted. In this larger company, on the other hand, decisions about product selection, store layout, and pricing were made at a large central headquarters.

The first alternative was a large, across-the-board personnel cut. This would provide an immediate boost to earnings and possibly help "clear away some of the cobwebs" at headquarters. After much debate, this option was rejected. It was viewed as too heavy-handed by many of the new, rising managers, whose loyalty the company needed to retain. The supermarket had historically treated its employees paternalistically; top management felt this mutual commitment on the part of workers and management was something it needed to build on to outperform their aggressive competitors.

Instead, the supermarket put its attention on the wide range of businesses and activities that over time had come under its corporate umbrella. A list of the "businesses" they were involved with were full-service supermarkets, discount food warehouse stores, drugstores, food packing and manufacturing (to make their private label brands), and trucking and warehousing (to get the food to their stores). They also had a large headquarters staff, where the bulk of the employees designed stores and managed construction (this company built or remodeled several stores each month), planned and decided what food to sell at what price, and purchased food (to sell in the stores).

When they looked at these businesses and activities, they asked themselves which they were really best at. They considered which gave them the greatest advantage over their competitors. Because many of these divisions were interrelated, it took some careful analysis to break apart this company's "value chain." But when they looked at the individual performance of each activity, they realized there were two things they did exceptionally well:

1. They knew how to buy food at wholesale prices.
2. They were very good at merchandising food in their stores.

They were not doing a very good job running pharmacies—the synergies between them and the supermarkets never emerged. They also made little money in their food plants when they realized they could purchase private-label goods from other manufacturers at about what it cost them to make their own. They had a great deal of money invested in their logistics operations, which penalized their return on assets, but they were supposed to be in the food business, not in trucking.

This analysis led the supermarket executives to plan a downsizing program that would be implemented gradually. They planned to sell off the drugstore and manufacturing businesses when good purchase offers were obtained, with relatively few employees laid off. The company started to convince the managers of its trucking and warehouse operation to use a leveraged buy-out loan secured by long-term contracts with the supermarket to buy this business from the company and run it as an independent entity. Again, plans were made to reduce the company's work force considerably, but with few workers losing their jobs.

At headquarters, the streamlining targeted the store-design group for elimination. Services just as useful could be purchased from outside contractors, and they helped their laid-off employees get work with some of these contractors. The skilled food-purchasing group was protected from cutbacks, while the unit that set prices and planned the details of store operations was gradually disbanded as soon as the individual store managers could be trained to handle that work on a coordinated but decentralized basis. This action required an increased budget and staffing for the headquarters' management development function. Eventually, they found they could eliminate a layer of line management as these better-trained store managers required less supervision. The net result of these changes was a streamlined company in which top management could spend its time on the activities with the greatest payoffs.

Other companies have discovered the virtues of closely linking their downsizing to their strategic plan. Donald Kane, General Electric's manager of organizational planning, considers across-the-board cutbacks to be the height of idiocy at GE, because the company depends on countercyclical trends in many of its businesses to maintain overall corporate performance. This does not imply that GE has been free from downsizing; its experience has been quite to the contrary. But it does give more attention to linking the size of its organizational units with the needs of its individual businesses than do most companies. GE has not faced the problems of a large steel company, where the chief executive was accused by one of his top managers of using a machete to attack a cancer. Another manager at that company was concerned that the blunt approach to streamlining may have adverse effects on the quality of the company's products—in a marketplace where quality is one of the few strategic advantages left.

Eastman Kodak has also taken a planned, objective-based approach to streamlining. To maximize the benefits from the painful reduction described in the last chapter, it has given major attention to quicker decision making about new products. This has helped Kodak get a digital medical-imaging device to customers much sooner than it would otherwise, an event which may help reduce the concerns of the industry analyst mentioned in Chapter 2.

The Bottom Line: Better Performance

This chapter has encouraged a planned approach to downsizing, one that is closely keyed to a company's strategic plan rather than one in reaction to a management fad. Such planning avoids the unintended consequences of demassing and serves as the basis for building a lean organization than can stay lean.

Do streamlined companies really perform better? A multi-industry study that looked at organizational structures and economic performances of well-managed businesses points clearly to a yes. This research effort, conducted by A. T. Kearney, Inc., examined 26 companies including Allied Corporation, Coca-Cola, Dana Corporation, Digital Equipment, General Electric, Hewlett-Packard, IBM, Johnson & Johnson, Merck, 3M, Nucor, Schlumberger, and Xerox. The study matched these corporations and other relatively lean firms with others in their individual industries, tracking them over a five-year period, to determine the connection between organization and business results. Compared to their industries, these 26 firms did much better. Table 3.1 shows the average annual

Table 3.1. Average annual increases, 1979–1983.

	26 Leanly Managed Companies (in percent)	Industry Average (in percent)
Sales growth	11.5	5.3
Earnings growth	9.6	1.4
Market value growth	20.0	2.3

percent increases, from 1979 to 1983, as compared to composite industry averages.

How different from their industry peers were the organizations of the 26 corporations? In both management layering and number of staff people not directly involved in production, the differences were considerable. Table 3.2 looks at these measures of management efficiency.

These measures imply that lean companies, on average, were able to get almost twice as much management work out of their managers. They were able to operate with organizational structures that were, on average, only two-thirds as tall as those of their competitors. As we will consider in Chapter 6, the taller the organizational structure, the more likely decisions will take longer and information will be distorted.

Table 3.2. Measures of management efficiency.

	26 Leanly Managed Companies	Industry Average
Average maximum number of salaried levels	7.2	10.8
Average number of direct reports per manager	4.8	2.6

Regarding nonproduction staff, the Kearney study showed that the number of staff per million dollars of sales varied widely, depending on which industry was considered. They found that the leaner, better performers averaged one-half staff person per million dollars in sales less than the industry averages. This difference is not as inconsequential as it may seem; for a billion dollar company, it implies managing with 500 fewer people. When the average salaries paid to this many people are considered, the cost is almost equal to the average net profit most corporations earn on a billion dollars of revenues.

Many of the lean companies in this study have controlled their management size carefully over many years. Most corporations are less streamlined, and are starting to find that demassing alone cannot reshape the way they organize managers and staff. To reshape an organization, executives must carefully examine the work done by each manager, and consider how it can be changed. The purpose of the next three chapters is to suggest ways to accomplish this planning and reorganizing. Because staff work often seems more mysterious and harder to get your hands around than line management, we begin with that task.

Chapter 4

Pinpointing Excess Staff

Only weeks after James Renier took charge of Honeywell's computer operations he trimmed more than 1,000 middle managers and staff from the payroll. He summed up his downsizing philosophy simply: "There are two ways of managing: One requires a lot of useless staff, and the other lets people do their jobs and tell you what expertise they need. If you've got a staff that is either trying to do the line job or has turned into a large group of scorekeepers, you had better get rid of that staff."

Corporate Staff,
A New Endangered Species

At some companies, entire staff specialties—like corporate economists—have become endangered species. Xerox eliminated its chief economist position, although its last incumbent still provided counsel to the company as an outside advisor. Citicorp's central economics unit of 150 employees has gradually been phased out, mostly through decentralization to other divisions. As part of a 25 percent reduction in the size of W. R. Grace's headquarters, the entire economics staff was cut.

The W. R. Grace reductions were motivated by earnings

declines. Acquisitions and mergers also fuel staff streamlining. When "Hubie" Clark bought Envirotech Corporation for Baker International, he also inherited its 154-person corporate staff. Wanting to maintain Baker's lean headquarters philosophy, he allowed only three Envirotech people to remain at headquarters. Twenty others were reassigned to positions in the operating units, and the rest were fired.

Headquarters staff units such as these have been frequent targets of work-force reductions and reorganizations. At times these cuts have reflected the needs of a company's strategic plan, but increasingly corporate staff people are finding their jobs at risk because their contributions are hard to quantify or defend.

This chapter and the one that follows suggest some ways to pinpoint staff downsizing opportunities, assuming a review of company strategy suggests such cuts are appropriate. Too many companies embark on overhead reduction efforts loosely targeted at middle management. These projects too often fail to distinguish between the problems caused by excess staff professionals and those caused by too many management layers. Each situation requires a different diagnosis and a special treatment. This and the next chapter consider the problems related to staff size, while the chapter that follows them deals with management layering. Eight alternatives for measuring staff performance are suggested here, while some guidelines for continuing direction of staff work are presented in the next chapter. But before we look at ways to trim staff, it is useful to understand exactly who the staff people are, where they come from, and what they do.

Who Is "Headquarters Staff"?

Corporate headquarters staff: These are people who advise, support, guide, and help senior executives control the work of a company's operating managers. They may also provide a variety of services to employees throughout the business.

The military is usually credited with creating the distinction between "staff" (thinking) and "line" (doing) work. The headquarters general staff, kept safe from enemy fire and able to see the "big picture," was to do the thinking and planning. This left the troops, facing the enemy on the "line" of battle, free to do the actual fighting. Perhaps this differentiation began when some astute general realized that there was a scarcity of soldiers rating high on both brains and brawn. More likely, the distinctions took hold when generals realized they needed help coordinating the logistics and battle plans of widely scattered armies. Legions protecting the far-flung Roman Empire were organized in this fashion in the first century A.D. Kings and popes relied on councils of closely trusted advisors throughout the Middle Ages and beyond. The success of the strong Prussian general staff in the nineteenth century helped ensure the popularity of the line-staff distinction in the military; it was quickly imitated by the most advanced part of the contemporary commercial sector—the early railroads.

The building of the railways throughout the United States and Europe in the middle of the nineteenth century required a more elaborate form of organization than was provided by the craft guilds and family-owned businesses that controlled most of industry then. The unprecedented complexity of constructing and operating the early railroads caused their founders to look to the military for personnel experienced in operations that spanned a large geographic area and required healthy doses of coordination and communications. They brought with them the style of organization to which they had become accustomed. Geographical divisions were created to oversee the building and running of trains and track. Back at the home offices, smaller policy- and procedure-setting groups of more analytically inclined employees planned the timetables and locomotive maintenance programs for the divisions. Teams of inspectors from headquarters regularly traveled throughout the railroad systems to evaluate compliance with their policies and procedures.

The railroads, in turn, served as an organizational model for the development of many large-scale industries. By the time General Motors, Du Pont, and Sears adopted their divisional structures in the 1920s and 1930s, the concept of a headquarters staff was well established in many U.S. companies.

A common way of distinguishing staff from line in modern corporations is to define line functions as those concerned with *designing, making, selling,* and *servicing* whatever a business has to offer. All other units, with the exception of the executive superstructure, are staff. This approach has the virtue of simplicity, but the distinction must be applied with some flexibility. Some companies with a relatively stable configuration of prod ucts view engineering and product design as primarily staff work. Other firms, such as those in pharmaceutical manufacturing or biotechnology, have their business results and stock prices directly determined by the new products in their R&D pipelines. For them, it would be difficult to argue that product design is a mere support or advisory service to their line operations.

In other companies, the line-staff distinction is even less clear. Most observers slot a company's legal department firmly in the staff category. But MCI's legal unit in the 1970s was its key competitive weapon against AT&T. Its lawyers, not its sales force, were the way MCI could enter future markets. These attorneys also served a product design-R&D function, since they helped shape the nature of the deregulated services that MCI would offer its customers. This was certainly line work.

Likewise, the McDonald's Corporation's famed Hamburger University is not a typical headquarters support service. Its staff, and those who prepare McDonald's detailed instructional manuals, have a significant line role in the success of the company. McDonald's makes money when its franchisees make money. Its market strategy is based on quality and consistency of service and product. Because of the franchise arrangement, headquarters lacks direct reporting control over the people who produce the product and service. But control of the content of its franchise-mandated training programs allows the headquarters staff, at arm's length, to standardize these people's behavior to execute its worldwide market strategy.

At American Airlines, the information services department, which runs and updates its SABRE reservations system, is a key element of its competitive strategy. This department made possible the introduction of the first frequent-flyer program; its increasing sophistication and well-managed data base allow American to maximize airplane revenue by carefully rationing its number of deep discount seats. It is doubtful that computers would have served as a strategic weapon if American had managed its information function as a traditional backroom support staff.

As corporate strategies change, so can the definition of staff work. Throughout much of its history, the American Can Company's primary business was container manufacturing. Appropriately, its MIS unit was a staff function. By the mid-1980s, through a major program of divestitures and acquisitions, American Can had restructured into a major provider of financial services. At the conclusion of the restructuring the company changed its name to Primerica. In its turbulent new businesses, information management plays a much more critical role in its economic success. MIS now has less of a supporting and more of a line "manufacturing" type role in Primerica's new business constellation.

The staff-line distinction is still useful, especially when determining how many managers of each group are necessary. But the choices must be made with care. A key consideration is the strategic role of a suspected staff unit. If that unit adds as much value in the company's competitive arena as do some of the traditional line responsibilities, it may deserve to be considered an operating function and managed accordingly. One clue to a staff unit's potential for competitive value added is to find out how close to the customers the operations of this staff group are.

A Popular Villain

In addition to being hard to categorize, corporate staffs have acquired an unfortunate reputation for making mischief and retarding performance. The Dean of M.I.T.'s Sloan School of Management, Lester Thurow, has pointed out that, while the total U.S. economic output rose only 15 percent from 1978 to 1985, the number of accountants on corporate staffs increased by 30 percent. He found this staff increase even more puzzling because this was a period during which many companies invested heavily in automating their accounting functions. He concluded that spending money on productivity improvement for some staff functions can have the opposite effect; for the accountants, its net result was to increase the frequency and number of the accounting reports they generated.

Jack Reichert, Brunswick's president who cut his headquarters staff almost in half, criticized accountants more bluntly: "We've been rewarding bookkeepers as if they created wealth. U.S. business has to make more beans rather than count them several times."

Accountants and other staff professionals have become popular villains. It is now obligatory to blame at least part of America's competitive economic decline on the "analysis-paralysis" brought on by too large or too powerful staff units. Staff groups are also seen as adding extra steps to the decision-making processes, steps that take time and slow the company's reaction to competition. They are also blamed for over-analyzing some situations—the problem being not the quality of their analysis but the tendency of their executive clients to substitute analysis for action.

Many executive decisions, especially decisions that set a company's future direction, must be made with incomplete information. The consequences of these decisions can provoke feelings of anxiety in even the boldest CEO. That anxiety is compounded by win-lose corporate cultures, which require correct decisions to be made all the time. A common way to deal with these pressures is to postpone the decision. Large, bright, and eager analytical staffs have provided more than one executive with an escape valve. Sometimes the extra analysis is helpful. Even if it does not reveal new insight, the analysis may provide time for a consensus to emerge that makes a decision easier to implement. But, as executives in the auto, oil, and steel industries have found, there are some problems that cannot be "analyzed out of."

At times, headquarters staffs have been accused of sins much worse than excessive analysis. Their ready access to senior executives has given rise to fears of the Rasputin syndrome. Grigory Rasputin was a Russian monk and mystic who exceeded his position as religious advisor to Czar Nicholas II to provide advice on the management of the Russian Empire. His ability to captivate and mystify his monarch has been compared to that of some contemporary practitioners of esoteric strategic planning techniques. Unfortunately, Rasputin's efforts to prop up his weak "CEO" led to his intense unpopularity with the czar's "group executives," and these noblemen eventually arranged his "downsizing."

Good operating executives focus on the needs of their factories, sales forces, suppliers, and—most significantly—customers. This means there is less time to be concerned with headquarters politics and currying favor with top brass. That is all well and good but at times those who are distant from headquarters can become suspicious of those who are closer. Some line executives become concerned that staff people may too easily abuse their easy contact with top management; others are more concerned about the monopoly some staff people have when they are a chief executive's only source of information about a critical issue. Often the worst fear line executives have is that well-placed staff people may form alliances with other line executives—against their capital appropriation requests, against their needs for a bigger sales force, or even against their promotion prospects.

Even staff people who have been able to avoid being overly political have found themselves attacked for what they are not. Arch Patton, a retired consultant and expert on executive compensation, has been critical of American companies that have given too much pay and importance to staff professionals at the expense of line managers. He thinks too many companies have emphasized "thinking" jobs over "doing" jobs, resulting in second-class factory management and performance. He quotes a Japanese electronics executive: "The United States puts its best minds to work in staff jobs and has for years. Bright people have gotten the message. They avoid line jobs. Japan, on the other hand, wants its brightest men in line jobs." Patton has noted that compensation surveys of the 25 highest-paid jobs frequently list more staff than line positions.

Ironically, some staff jobs have suffered from the opposite criticism. In some companies, staff jobs are reputed dumping grounds for poor performers—safe places to put these people out of harm's way. Personnel departments especially have suffered the reputation of being places to send line managers who have gone "soft." Fortunately, the expectations for line managers have changed, and the human resource function has been professionalized to an extent that there is little room for noncontributors. Outside the United States, though, this holding area for marginal performers is still common. This situation is illustrated graphically in the headquarters building of a Latin American energy company. Lacking company retirement plans and unable by government decree to fire anyone, the firm has established a special administrative unit which occupies an entire floor of its headquarters. This unit serves as home for weak performers, because the oil company assumes it is better to keep these people concentrated in one place rather than scatter them throughout the business where they may get in the way of operations. This practice seems to work for that company, though it is questionable whether the policy should be emulated.

One final concern expressed about headquarters staff is potentially more serious. "What has always frustrated me about staff is that the people you want solving problems end up administering," says Charles Knight, Emerson's chairman. Over time staff work seems to evolve into management work. Some astute companies take this as a signal to rotate the staff member or to rethink the unit's responsibilities, but too many companies just tolerate it. The results are confusing, blurred, or multiple lines of authority as well as lowered management morale.

Some chief executives have done more than tolerate this practice, however. They have consciously built their management systems around such blurred lines. Most well known of these executives was Harold Geneen, International Telephone and Telegraph's chief executive for two decades. Geneen's numbers-driven management style was shaped by a relentless search for "unshakable facts." He used infamous periodic meetings with his management group to probe deeply for difficulties and potential performance problems in ITT's operations. He used staff groups to serve as checks and balances on his line managers. Geneen mistrusted any single source of information. He established a second channel of information by having his divisional controllers report directly to the chief controller at ITT headquarters, not to the general managers of the divisions in which they worked. He also set up a worldwide matrix of "product group managers"—staff analysts who tracked product sales and development across divisions and subsidiary lines. They provided a third data pipeline that Geneen could use to verify the correctness of the data he received from his line managers. Overlaid on all of these cross-checks were special task forces set up to deal with emerging business problems. These task forces sometimes competed with each other and with divisional management to provide solutions.

The Geneen system made life for line managers like working in a goldfish bowl, where their actions were constantly monitored by closed-circuit TV and sonar. Many staff people received performance bonuses keyed to how many problems *they* had solved and how many line management mistakes *they* had detected. This created a global tournament over which Geneen presided. He was happy with the contention the system generated because it put him at the convergence of multiple streams of information. It played to Geneen's strong ability to master countless details, and it put him at the center of all major and many less-than-major decisions.

After Geneen retired in 1979, it was difficult for a successor to maintain that delicate balance between staff and line. It was also difficult to maintain the business results that the company had achieved during Geneen's tenure. In recent years, ITT has exited from many businesses, including more than half of its worldwide telecommunications activities, where it once had unquestioned strength. The French purchaser of this business, Compagnie Générale d'Electricité, believes ITT's telecommunications performance was retarded by remnants of Geneen's top-heavy management structure. Its first step was to lay off many of the headquarters staff who came with the acquisition and to prepare plans to eliminate several thousand additional staff and managers.

We have covered a broad range of problems that companies have experienced with headquarters staff. Some of the foregoing criticisms are warranted, although the responsibility for these problems seems to be most fairly shared by both staff and the managers they report to. Both have contributed to making headquarters staff a popular villain and, in some companies, a logical target for downsizing.

The Two Types of Staff

Some staff problems have arisen because of overly ambitious people in those positions, others from executives inappropriately using staff people in operating rather than advisory capacities. But many difficulties arise from genuine confusion about the staff role. Before making plans to cut back on staff, it is important to distinguish among the types of staff and the varying roles each plays. Each type requires a different approach to managing its performance and a different way of determining its appropriate size.

Henry Mintzberg, a management professor at Montreal's McGill University, has developed a framework for distinguishing between two types of headquarters staff. One type makes up a company's technostructure—the group of analysts, planners, and regulators whose primary purpose is to *assist* management control and to standardize the work of other employees. Let's call it the "control staff."

Control staff performs functions such as strategic planning, financial management, internal auditing, materials management, industrial engineering, and regulatory compliance monitoring. These people are the writers of the policy and procedures manuals. At the plant level, they are the industrial engineers, production schedulers, and purchasing agents.

In Mintzberg's system, the others are "support staff." They exist to provide services wherever needed in the company, ranging from operating the company cafeteria to getting out the payroll. The employee counseling center, the mailroom, the computer center, and some R&D labs are operated by support staff. They also receive visitors, guard the factory gates, and clean the floors.

The labels "control" and "support" apply to specific responsibilities, not necessarily to entire departments. Care must be taken in using them, however. In some companies, the primary role of the legal staff is to serve as watchdog, a control function. Other companies, with less demanding legal and regulatory situations, encourage their counsels to take a stance more of providing services for their internal clients. Public relations units are often charged with establishing rules that line managers must follow when talking to the media and in maintaining company-wide graphic design standards. These are control staff jobs, though the same units provide editorial services, publish annual reports, and write the employee newspaper.

The human resources department plays a divided role. It has both control and service responsibilities. It establishes and enforces a wide range of personnel rules and helps ensure compliance with many government regulations. It helps control labor costs through union negotiations and contract monitoring. And it is often expected to represent management's wishes to the employees.

But this department is expected also to represent employee concerns. Providing this service well is often a key to maintaining a union-free environment. The HR department conducts attitude surveys to keep line managers informed about employee morale. It monitors changes in the labor market to help anticipate future worker shortages. It helps managers attract new recruits. It helps employees deal with alcohol and drug abuse. It advises managers on how to improve performance and productivity. And sometimes it helps executives change the corporation's culture. These are all support staff functions.

The human resources department often is also responsible for providing training and orientation. Is this a job of control or support staff? In most companies, training is operated as a service to line managers and, occasionally, as a way to help employees advance their careers. But some firms, IBM being the one most frequently cited, actively manage their training programs to serve a control function. They use orientation and training to socialize new recruits and inculcate the company's values and procedures. Training in these companies is mandatory, not an optional bonus. When done regularly and well, training can eliminate the need for some control staffs (more on this in Chapter 8).

Each type of staff has a different way of relating to the rest of the company. A control staff has clients (usually senior executives). It guards their interests by doing things that affect the work of the staff's "targets of control" throughout the business. A support staff tends to have managers rather than clients. Its efforts are directed at serving internal customers. Figure 4.1 indicates these relationships.

Control staff units are populated by knowledge workers and professionals. Often these professionals have dual loyalties. They respond both to the needs of their employers and the influence of their professions. Later we will consider the importance of managing these two tugs on their attention. Much of the post-World War II growth in staff size has been in these units, and many of the problems reviewed earlier about headquarters staff have been concerns about control staff.

The size of many support staff groups has also grown, though possibly at a slower pace. As many of them try to stay on top of the latest developments in their individual fields, they expand the scope of services they provide. Because many of these functions are centralized at headquarters, their budgets are allocated by formula to operating divisions and they receive less scrutiny than do the individual operating budgets. This has allowed their size to escalate as long as overall corporate earnings have increased. William Johnson, IC Industries' chief

Figure 4.1. Two types of corporate staff.

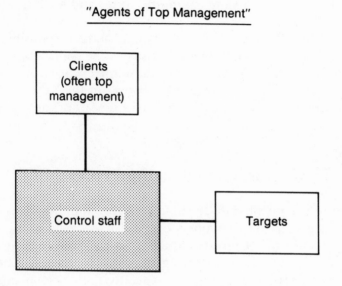

"Agents of Top Management"

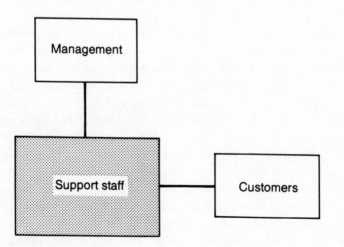

"Mini-businesses"

executive and a strong believer in a lean headquarters staff, feels that if these are not closely watched, they will grow and centralize, in turn slowing communications and leading to new errors and inefficiencies.

Why all this attention to labeling staff responsibilities? Because each type poses different issues to be considered when downsizing. Without considering these differences, as is common in demassing, it is possible to throw out the baby with the bath water. The baby, in this case, is often a critically needed control staff position.

Downsizing the Headquarters Staff

Downsize a control staff by first carefully limiting its scope. Make sure it hasn't expanded because it is really doing line management work. Consider which of its control functions can safely be delegated to operating executives. Redeploy headquarters control staff people to the divisions and plants to help line managers with their new responsibilities. When John Welch became General Electric's chief executive, among his first downsizing targets were what he called the "checkers on checkers"—the layers of control staff units whose main job was to review the work of other control staff people.

Focus on ways to measure and improve the productivity of those who remain. Use computers and telecommunications technology in ways that decrease a staff's size, not that expand its scope. And, sometimes most important in companies prone to demassing, identify which few control staff people are going to be most critical to the company's future management. Protect them. You do not want to create the situation the American Productivity Center has warned against when divisional vice presidents become judge, jury, and executioner.

As we have noted, some staff departments include both control and support staff components. Before these units are streamlined, their functions may need to be separated. For example, when Xerox examined its headquarters marketing unit, it found the unit performed control staff responsibilities in setting pricing policies and also served as a support staff in the corporate advertising and sales promotion areas. The control staff work was delegated to a committee of line managers, which was likewise charged with maintaining needed corporate consistency. The advertising and promotion activities remained centralized because they required specialized talent as well as company-wide coordination, but they were moved to a new home. The marketing unit itself was abolished.

Pure support staffs are often easier than control staffs to slim down. It is usually simple to reduce a staff department's size by contracting outside for those same services. This is not as easily done for control staffs. Training courses and food management services are easier to contract for than internal audits and purchasing. It is also often easier to live without some staff services than without some control groups. Some support staffs are also easier to decentralize to profit centers, where customers can more easily decide what they need and how much they can afford. When headquarters at the Allied Corporation was slimmed, the divisions, called "companies," were told to absorb their support staffs or lose their services. Some support staffs also need protection from downsizing, however. These are usually departments closely tied to a line function that helps differentiate a company from its competitors.

At times, support staff builds up its own management hierarchy. It becomes, in effect, a miniature production operation. The tactics described in Chapter 6 can be applied to lower the cost of managing such operations.

Evaluating Staff Performance

Staff size would be easier to control if it were simpler to measure how well staff units are doing. In general, the best people to evaluate support staff are the customers they serve; later in this chapter we will consider some methods for doing this. Control staff results need to be judged by the clients, usually a company's senior executives. But making these judgments is much more difficult than similar decisions about service providers.

Objectives can be set for control staff, but it is often hard to link these objectives with a company's economic performance. And often, the most significant feature of good staff work is that it has kept something bad from happening to the company. How can we measure bad things that do not happen?

Many executives rely on their personal judgment and the word they hear from the company grapevine. The performance-review sessions they hold with staff managers frequently take on a very different tone from those they hold with their line executives. With operating executives, these discussions can quickly zero in on last year's economic results and next year's plans. Numbers showing budget performance and profit contribution are all out on the table. But with staff, the economic issues are more of overhead control than of profit contribution, and while budget performance can be evaluated, the real issue often is how to determine the appropriate size of the budget. And this is where the performance review can get stuck.

These sessions are also difficult because of the dependency, often unadmitted but usually felt, many executives have on their staff experts. In some cases, sessions to plan a staff's activities for the upcoming year start with the executive admitting: "You're the expert. Tell me what we should be doing in. . . ." The well-meaning answer to "what we should be doing" may be more than the company can afford or can really use. Less frequently, the executive feels comfortable enough about the staff manager's responsibilities to start with: "Here's what we need from you and your group."

In spite of these difficulties, downsizing forces executives to make judgments about staff performance. At worst, these evaluations are subjective and political; at best, they involve an assessment of the current and future value each staff function adds to the company. A variety of methods have been used to plan staff downsizing. Some are more comprehensive than others. Some are based on careful anticipation of a company's future business needs and the kind of organization it must shape to be successful. Others are quicker and dirtier, oriented more toward cutting costs than building the organization.

In the sections that follow, eight approaches to staff downsizing are reviewed. These targets for pruning are based on answers to the following questions:

1. Is the staff doing what it is supposed to?
2. Is it keeping to its budget?
3. Is it improving its productivity?
4. How much would be spent if its function had to be restarted from scratch?
5. How do its size and cost compare with the equivalent staff in other companies?
6. How do the details of its performance compare with other staff groups?
7. How do its customers think it is doing?
8. How much do its activities really cost?

Meeting Objectives

Probably the most common way of measuring how well a staff unit is serving a company is by assessing its achievement of set objectives. Extending the management by objective (MBO) process to staff units has been a common practice for a number of years. Goal achievement often triggers bonus awards and other forms of incentive compensation, giving some professionals more of a feel for a business's risks and rewards. However, missing a goal, especially when related to schedule deadlines, seldom receives more sanction than "please try harder next year."

The main problem with using MBO performance to select staff for downsizing is that objectives themselves may not necessarily reflect the issues most critical to a company. As suggested earlier, staff performance objectives lack a common bottom line with other units of the business and frequently are very inward looking. It is possible for a staff unit to meet all its objectives and still play only a marginal role in a company's

economic future, while at the same time another staff department could miss several MBOs but still make a more solid contribution to the business.

For this reason, objective achievement is usually a weak
means of pinpointing cutback targets. It is a common tool for
managing the actual reductions, however. Reduction targets
are frequently specified in total dollars saved, and we will consider their use in the section that follows. Too often, though,
these targets are expressed more narrowly as payroll dollars or
head-count targets. Both can cause problems.

Asking all managers to cut head count by X percent is
usually an inefficient way to downsize. It is wide open to game
playing, such as firing several recent hires or support staff
people while leaving tenured, high-salaried low performers in
place. Often, the most convenient people to let go are the
ones who are affected by downsizing. Focusing on head count
puts management's attention on the wrong issue. It selects
downsizing targets based on the relative ease of terminating
one person over another, rather than by first considering in
detail what staff work needs to be done and what work is
adding limited value. One chief executive lamely explained
that a 5 percent reduction of staff in *each* department was a
way to give his managers practice in laying off people, because
he expected much deeper cutbacks in the near future.

Setting objectives keyed to payroll ("a company-wide
reduction of 15 percent" or "every department will cut its payroll budget by 11 percent") is a little better. For departments
in which 80 to 90 percent of the costs are salary related, there
is not much else to cut. But for other situations, the guidelines
may be too narrow. Like head-count measures, payroll objectives put initial attention on people rather than on the work
they do. It is possible to cut a big chunk out of a department's
payroll without really improving its effectiveness or its net contribution to the business. Later we will consider techniques that
deal with these issues.

Games can also be played with payroll budgets. Their size
can go down while the expenditures for contractors, consultants, computers, and overtime can increase to the point of
zero net savings. Cuts may be made too deeply, and newcom-

ers might eventually be hired to do the work of those laid off, bringing with them the harder-to-measure but just as real expenses for recruiting, training, and diminished productivity while these new hires come up to speed.

Payroll cutback targets can be supplemented with other guidelines that are more performance related. For example, an engineering manager can be asked to "reduce the staff involved in new product design so the development cycle is reduced from X years to Y months." Or a marketing staff can be told to "cut in half the time it takes to respond to competitors' price changes." Achieving both objectives may require staff cutbacks, but at least they focus on the ultimate benefits the company wants to achieve.

Keeping to the Budget

At times, the potential benefits of downsizing are primarily cost reductions. Then it can make sense to express the objectives in terms of budget dollars saved. In addition to "is it doing what I asked it to do?" staff units frequently are judged on the basis of whether they are costing what they are supposed to cost. Budget preparation is the tool most frequently used to regulate staff size. But just keeping within budget, like completing all assigned objectives, is not necessarily a good indicator of which staff departments are candidates for downsizing.

What if the company can no longer afford the budget? Then the annual budget-preparation process turns into a form of decentralized downsizing. Rather than expecting senior executives to identify detailed cutback targets, all staff managers are charged with submitting budgets at some level below their current year's. Shortly after General Electric acquired NBC, a 5 percent across-the-board reduction was ordered for all departments. Requests such as these are usually called "edicts" by the managers charged with implementing them when they must explain what is going on to those affected. These broad cutbacks are often useful when top management is faced with having to reduce costs quickly without the time to analyze operations in detail. It is a blunt tool, most appropriate in times of financial emergency.

Downsizing by considering ways to reduce a department's budget does offer some advantages over head-count or pay-roll-reduction targets. A unit's entire budget is open for examination. Jobs may be saved by reducing money spent on travel, rent, or equipment. Overtime and part-time help can be cut before regular employees need be terminated. Computer services may be purchased at less cost than buying the actual machines.

A New Jersey–based pharmaceutical manufacturer used a modified version of this process to cut several hundred thousand dollars out of each of several headquarters staff groups. Faced with an upcoming loss of patent protection on one of its main money-makers, top management set cost reduction targets for all non-R&D headquarters units. But rather than specifying how the money was to be saved, the company encouraged each department head to convene committees that would represent a cross section of workers in each department. The department heads were told of their department's share of the cut and were given several months to plan ways to achieve it. The human resource planning function provided data to the committees and also helped facilitate their meetings. All aspects of each department's operations were examined from the ground up—the first time this had happened for most of them and the first time that all levels of employees were invited to dissect the budget and spending history. Employees were told that the company was firmly committed to budget cutting, but not necessarily by firing people. The committees took this policy as a challenge, and eventually developed enough cost-cutting recommendations that the reduction goals were met without any terminations. But steps were recommended that lowered compensation for a number of employees.

After the committees considered all the obvious nonsalary costs, most found that their departmental targets were impossible to achieve without doing something about payroll size. A detailed work-flow analysis identified a number of responsibilities that could be handled with fewer people. It was suggested that several jobs be combined. Some employees chose to work part time, while restrictions were imposed on overtime and hiring to fill vacant positions. Several employees were down-graded in salary level, and bonuses and salary increases were eliminated for a time. Across-the-board pay cuts for all levels were also considered, but these were not needed.

The remarkable aspect of this pharmaceutical company's approach was its employee involvement. Without it, and the strong feelings of team spirit that it helped produce, many of the suggestions for work rearrangement would have been impossible to plan. In addition, worker willingness to take pay cuts to save jobs would have been impossible.

Unfortunately, this company's story does not have a completely happy ending. The company's skill in human resource management was not matched by capabilities in managing the timely development of new pharmaceuticals. Another, more severe budget crunch arose several years after the first reductions, and a number of headquarters staff people were let go. Still, the company's earlier termination-free cutback experience helped employees better understand the situation and the need for more drastic action. Morale was maintained because employees did not have lingering resentments that co-workers were losing their jobs while executives still flew first class and were paid sizable bonuses.

The experience of the pharmaceutical company suggests that, while extensive employee involvement can help identify opportunities for saving single-digit (or mid-teen) percentages of budget costs without layoffs, deeper headquarters staff budget reductions usually imply job losses. Employee involvement is critical to another aspect of belt-tightening, though—the achievement of continued productivity improvements.

Doing Better Than Before

Manufacturing executives have become accustomed to managing their operations in a way that chases costs down an experience or learning curve. For many repetitive operations, achieving these efficiency gains is critical to staying competitive. However, few executives monitor the cost experience of their staff operations as closely. Especially for support staff, it is reasonable to expect productivity increases that, if monitored and managed, can keep ahead of rising labor costs. Achieving these increases, just as in the factory, does not happen by magic. Goals have to be set, staff ideas must be solicited, feedback and incentives need to be provided, and gains must be shared. Productivity improvement needs to become a way of life, not a one-shot campaign. And even in many companies that do an excellent job of managing their factories, these productivity techniques never seem to migrate to the offices and executive suites.

The productivity of control staff is harder to manage, but it is not always impossible. The first step is to strip away some of the excuses used for "why they are so different." Some control staff people will complain that their productivity cannot be improved because so much of their work is on "one of a kind" projects. This may be true, but even these assignments require many staff people to employ similar techniques that can be done more efficiently. Few staff, even those constantly at work on "special assignments," need to reinvent the wheel each time.

Other staff people will proclaim they are professionals who can hardly be expected to be managed along the same lines as mere workers and managers. Perhaps these people need to be reminded of the productivity revolution now affecting lawyers and doctors. Faced with increased competition among attorneys and severe health-cost containment pressures, members of both professions are reconsidering the traditional ways of getting work done. They are investing in automation, creating new subprofessional jobs to do the work for which they are overeducated, and stressing problem prevention over litigation and surgery. Some of these lessons may well be translated to headquarters staff.

Zero-Based Evaluation

Zero-based budgeting offers a way to rethink the size and purpose of headquarters staff. It implies building the budget for each staff function from the ground up, since it starts with the assumption that the activity does not exist. Often several scenarios are created, based on different assumptions about what is happening to the business and what types of staff will be needed. One may project business as usual, another may consider staff requirements if several large and unrelated acquisitions are made, and a third might assume a major decentralization program. The costs of each are calculated, and the results framed in what are called "decision packages." These packages specify the pros and cons of each option and help link the levels of service provided by each staff unit with their individual costs.

Levi Strauss and several other companies have used zero-based budgeting to plan headquarters cutbacks. President Carter attempted, with mixed success, to introduce it as a way to control growth of the federal government. His results were limited, partially because the budgeting method was applied on top of, rather than in place of, many existing budgeting procedures. But the method was also susceptible to political manipulation. Bureaucrats created budget alternatives that lumped together critical functions with more marginal ones, leaving their superiors little choice but to approve the package.

Zero-based budgeting is difficult. The analysis required to do it well makes it a time-consuming process that does not reflect the urgency with which many companies must downsize. But in some situations, especially when a company's future is uncertain and there are no obvious next steps to take regarding staff functions, it can be helpful. It provides a fresh perspective, which is often superior to the way many companies plan changes in staffing levels—by just incremental changes from the status quo. When done well, the zero-based approach forces a reconsideration of *everything*. Units are spotted that had served a useful purpose but now preside over solved problems. And it is more likely that creative new staff configurations can be invented than when incrementally oriented methods are used.

A key to successful zero-basing is not using it on every staff department at once; it is too easy to drown in paper and analyses. Instead, pick one or two functions worthy of fundamental rethinking. Also, do not make this an annual exercise. It disrupts ongoing operations to have to rethink their *raison d' être* every 12 months. It is also hard to keep inventing fresh alternatives that frequently.

One especially worthy aspect of zero-based evaluations is the make-or-buy analysis. As mentioned earlier, it is often possible to contract in the external marketplace for support staff work previously done in-house. Common targets are building maintenance, cafeteria operation, and security guards. But, as we will consider in Chapters 8 and 9, work such as industrial engineering, systems analysis, medical services, and in some cases entire factories can be purchased as needed. Some headquarters functions, such as legal and public relations, usually have long-established ties with outside service providers. Regular reviews should be made of what work needs to be done in house and what can more economically be handled outside. The large internal legal staff that made good economic sense when bills from law firms were skyrocketing may not be as cost effective in a time of negotiated fees and heavy competition among firms. Likewise, significant changes in the labor supply in key professions and trades necessitates reconsidering how many people in these fields need be on the payroll.

Production executives often conduct this kind of analysis of operating departments in their companies, but much less frequently do they seek and evaluate outside alternatives to headquarters staff. Often, the senior executives to whom they report are preoccupied with other aspects of the business. Given the disincentives most job-evaluation systems put in the way of staff managers to reduce the number of people reporting to them, it is not always reasonable to expect them to initiate this kind of study. Regardless, a make-or-buy analysis is a useful yardstick for evaluating cost effectiveness and can be an alternative means of preventing bloated staff organizations.

With the exception of make-or-buy studies, the techniques reviewed so far are all inward looks at staff performance and size. They can frustrate executives looking for confirmation of an appropriately lean staff. Many such executives want outside norms or standards to help them make this judgment.

Norms and Ratios

Executives love to compare their operations with those of others. Financial accounting has given line managers many sophisticated and comparable yardsticks: annual sales revenues, net earnings, return on assets, price-earnings multiples, market-share indices. Keeping score with measures like these is ingrained in management behavior, so it is logical that managers hope to use similar indicators to determine if they have overstaffed their overhead units. It is common to hear informal guidelines such as:

> One human resources staff per 100 employees is about right.

> Total headquarters costs should never exceed 1.5 percent of revenues.

> Computer-related expenses should remain below 1 percent of sales.

Several industry and professional associations maintain extensive data bases so their members can know where they stand in relation to similar companies. Frequently, the first request a client makes of a consultant is to provide a set of ratios for determining if the company's staffing is appropriate. While these can be helpful indicators, more often than not they are deceptive. Paying too much attention to such ratios can cause an executive to ignore the real staffing issues.

To illustrate these difficulties let's consider how staffing ratios were used by a corporation in the chemical industry that we will call Company X. This company is relatively large, with sales in the billions and employees in the tens of thousands. It has always been profitable, with growth in sales revenue each year since it began operations. But recently its top management raised a concern about a leveling off of growth in several of its core businesses, and it wanted to be prepared by ensuring that its overhead expenditures were no larger than absolutely necessary. Because labor costs made up 80 percent of this overhead, the director of Company X's human resources department was charged with conducting a cost analysis. To demonstrate impartiality, he started with his own function, and he decided to compare its size with that of several peer companies.

First he calculated the ratio of his human resources staff to the total Company X employment. This was not as straightforward a task as he thought, because Company X had recently acquired several subsidiaries, which accounted for about a quarter of its total employment. Each subsidiary had its own personnel department, which duplicated some functions provided by his central organization. Gradually, functions were being transferred to his staff and the subsidiaries' overhead was being reduced. After calculating the ratio several ways, the director decided that the simplest approach would be to lump all employees and all human resources staff together. He felt reasonably comfortable doing this, but he started to realize that ratio analysis provides a *static* picture of a *dynamic* situation.

The director wondered how other companies handled this situation. One of his peers in a similar company said he was glad to share data, but he had to confess that, because of recent acquisitions and a plethora of unincorporated subsidiaries, he had no real idea of how many human resources staff he really had. The data he was able to provide were for headquarters staff only. While the Company X director thought this was better than nothing, he started to wonder if he was comparing apples to oranges. A series of calls by one of his staff to several companies in this industry yielded the information shown in Table 4.1.

The six companies selected for this comparison were chosen carefully. The human resources director started with companies in his industry, assuming they would have similar organizations and staffing mixes. He picked three companies that he knew his chief executive regarded as the best managed in the business, and he added one of Company X's chief competitors. He also selected a company that was frequently

Table 4.1. Comparative employment of human resources staff.

Company	Total Employment	Total HR Staff	HR Staff/ 100 Employees
A	85,000	366	.43
B	22,000	156	.71
C	42,600	379	.89
D	6,800	80	1.18
E	38,200	466	1.22
F	8,900	169	1.90
		AVERAGE	1.06
X	29,500	407	1.38

cited in the business press as a paragon in human resources management.

Unfortunately, his assumption that these companies were similar was only partially correct. Even though all six were in the chemical industry, several were moving in divergent strategic directions. Two were changing their product mix from commodities to specialty chemicals. Another was exiting from manufacturing and evolving into a distribution and sales company. And one company had started a diversification program by acquiring firms outside the chemical business. These strategies all had implications for each company's mix of employees, and they created differing work loads and priorities for their human resources departments. Company X's human resources director wanted to avoid comparing his firm with industry averages made up of data from hundreds of companies. But he created other difficulties by using a handpicked group of companies, because that sample was too small for such strategic differences to cancel each other out.

Still, the director felt that these were the best quantitative reference points available—which was probably a correct assumption. His real concern began when he compared Company X with its peers. Its staffing ratio, 1.38, seemed on the high side when the average among the six companies was only a little more than 1.0. He also noted with alarm that three of the firm's peer companies managed their personnel programs with less than 1 staff member per 100 employees, and that one of these companies had a ratio three times as "good" as Company X.

Discouraged because he always thought he ran a lean operation, the director started to plan ways to shrink his organization by 25 percent so as to bring it closer in size to that of its peers. In the face of such "hard" data he felt he had little choice, given the cost-cutting objectives of his numbers-oriented top management.

Was he making accurate judgments? Not completely, for several reasons. Data such as these can suggest useful questions to ask about an operation, but it is risky to use them as the basis for final decisions about the need for and size of cutbacks. Let's consider the situations of the individual companies in more detail, using some information not provided by this quantitative survey.

Company A has the most impressive staffing ratio. But it also has the largest work force—-almost triple that of Company X. This allows Company A to achieve some economies of scale in the personnel function; it often takes as many benefits planners and procedures writers to deal with a work force of 10,000 as to handle 100,000. Company A, through an expensive investment in management training that does not show up in these ratios, has been able to decentralize some routine human resources staff responsibilities to its line managers and thus limit the number of its central staff.

Company B manages its human resources function with almost half as many staff per 100 employees as does Company X. But a closer examination reveals that its scope is much smaller. In Company X, the human resources department is responsible for plant security, receiving visitors, staffing the company cafeterias, and running the medical department.

None of these activities is included in Company B's human resources organization. Its medical department is grouped with plant safety and product toxicology functions into a separate environmental assurance department that reports directly to its CEO. Its cafeteria services are staffed by outside contractors.

Company C also has a below-average staffing ratio. But based on the number of equal employment and sex discrimination lawsuits that have been filed against that firm, it is not clear that it has enough staff in all areas. This company does little in management training, and its lack of a systematic approach toward developing an awareness of employee attitudes has led to its top managers not noticing a steady decline in factory-worker morale. Meanwhile, an industry union has targeted several of its plants for organizing campaigns. It is unclear if Company C will have the number of skilled labor relations professionals on its board to allow it to fend off the union drive.

Companies D and E have very similar ratios but very different situations. Company D's employees are concentrated at one location, making personnel administration simpler than for Company E, which has a larger work force scattered over dozens of facilities around the world. Company E's range of programs is also much more limited and less sophisticated than Company D's, which has used automation to reduce the size of its clerical work force.

Finally, Company F is the one famous for its excellent programs. High quality, unfortunately, is frequently expensive.

Considering the details of each company's situation, it is apparent that ratios can hide as much as they reveal. Factors such as investment in automation, decentralization philosophy, and geographic dispersion of plants have significant impact on a staff function's appropriate size. The missions and objectives of the staff units can vary greatly. Some human resource functions are engaged in major catch-up management development efforts, some in union decertification campaigns, others in expensive culture-change programs. Others are run on a more steady, do-just-what-is-required basis. Some companies have severe EEO or pay equity problems that require expensive staff help. Other firms have these issues well under control and are able to spend less in that area. While we have used the human resources department as an example, similar issues emerge when considering similar staffing ratios and norms for other staff areas. The detailed factors differ, but the same principle holds: Simple examination of ratio indicators alone will not identify the factors that produce the numbers.

What good then, if any, are these quantitative norms? They are good starting points for a more detailed analysis. They can establish the boundaries of the ballpark in which a company should operate. To the extent a company is two, three, or more times more staffed than its carefully chosen peers, these norms may be indicators of excess costs. If a company is significantly understaffed when compared to others, the norms might show that some needed work is not getting done. Regardless of what these comparisons indicate, their use should always be followed by the question why. These norms are blunt tools. More detailed analysis is needed to carve out the specific targets for reduction.

Benchmarking

Benchmarking is a more precise way to compare one company's staff operations to those of others. This method goes beyond simple ratios of staff size or cost to examine a staff's most significant performance attributes. These attributes are compared, not to composite industry averages, but to the performance of a company's toughest competitors. Denver's Intra-West Bank is coping with deregulation by tracking the costs of 16 competitors as a guide to determining its staffing levels. Xerox has made significant changes in the organization and size of its manufacturing and engineering staffs as a result of benchmarking. This approach gathers data for comparison from both competitors and noncompetitors. Benchmark indicators can go into great detail: the number of drawings an engineer in a Japanese competitor can produce in a year, the number of square feet employees occupy, the amount of time a key process takes. Measures of staff activity have been key indicators as Xerox played strategic catch-up with the Japanese during the first half of the 1980s.

Xerox, probably more than any other corporation, has made benchmarking a way of life. It is not an activity done by a cloistered group of headquarters analysts, but rather, each division and department manager is expected to use benchmarking on an ongoing basis. The process has been eye-opening for many managers. Its results have frequently forced them to set higher targets for efficiency improvement, 30 to 50 percent plus, which they might have resisted had they not been aware of how the other side operated. Benchmarking also provides some staff managers, for the first time, with a way to measure their operations against the competition. This instills in the staff side of the business some of the competitive spirit common in line operations.

Xerox has also been creative in gathering information to use as benchmarks. When information about competitors was not easily available, they went to great lengths to identify the best-run companies in noncompeting industries. To develop benchmarks for their logistics and distribution function, Xerox examined the details of L. L. Bean's warehouse system. Though data about the internal workings of some Japanese competitors were difficult to obtain, Xerox was allowed easier access to the operations of their affiliate, Fuji Xerox.

General Motors and several other companies have found that joint ventures, especially those run by the Japanese, offer good sources of benchmarks. And GM has not had to go all the way to Tokyo for those reference points. Its Fremont, California, plant with Toyota (run by New United Motor Manufacturing, Inc.) has provided lessons in organization as well as revenues and profits. Many companies have set up partnerships with large overseas firms as well as with domestic high-technology businesses noted for their lean, entrepreneurial style. These partnerships serve as windows on a new technology or market, but can also provide challenging benchmarks to help improve staff performance.

Some companies with large operations scattered around the world have been able to develop their benchmarks internally. IBM has been able to take advantage of its size through what it calls a Common Staffing Study (CSS). Intended to help monitor and improve the efficiency of IBM's nonmanufacturing staff, the study characterizes a function's productivity at one point in time and then periodically repeats the measures. The functions include personnel, engineering, and finance and the procedure involves four steps:

1. IBM-wide descriptions of generic tasks are prepared by each staff group. At one point, IBM identified 160 such tasks in 14 common staff departments.
2. IBM identifies what it calls "modifiers." These are the factors in manufacturing that cause indirect work. Over 100 of these modifiers have been catalogued. For example, IBM has found that increases in a plant's work force usually cause subsequent increases in the secretarial work force. Likewise, the size of the personnel department is determined by the number of people it serves.
3. Exhaustive annual surveys are conducted at plants and other locations to determine both the resources needed to do the tasks and the modifiers that may affect them.
4. Statistical analyses are conducted at IBM's Armonk headquarters of all survey data. The key ratio for each activity at each location is people per unit of modifier. While both secretaries and personnel staff may increase as a plant expands, the analysis may show a steady secretarial increase but an incremental increase in personnel professionals. This could suggest optimum plant levels to keep personnel from growing just beyond the threshold where additional and costly indirect staff must be added.

Comparisons are then made among plants and between current and previous year's reports for each plant. Locations doing especially well managing a particular activity are given visibility and recognition. Other facilities are challenged to do as well as they have. This internal competition helps keep the rolling productivity averages moving upward year after year. The data also serve as useful inputs to IBM's manpower planning. IBM has found that techniques such as CSS are vital to maintaining its full employment tradition.

As would be expected at IBM, the data and analyses are maintained in computerized files. They are accessible by all locations to help them conduct "what if" analyses and plan staff productivity improvements. IBM's method works well if a company has a large, geographically scattered operation with similar functions carried out at several locations. If a company's scope is smaller, it is possible to pool data with a group of firms, possibly creating a network that links suppliers and customers.

Customer Ratings

A number of companies have found benchmarking and make-or-buy analyses to be useful tools in managing their staff size. A few have profited from zero-based analysis, and many have made use of comparative norms and ratios. Downsizing objectives are becoming more common on senior managers' MBO lists, and many are using the annual budget process also to plan staff reductions and improve productivity. But, unfortunately, all these techniques ignore a very important source of data about how well a staff unit is doing: what its customers think.

Earlier we discussed the importance of identifying the customers and clients for each staff function. Staff units are corporate early-warning systems, and part of their value is the perspective they bring from their professional specialties. But staff people are often most useful when they keep in mind that their primary purpose is to advise, serve, and support other parts of the business. The managers of these other parts are, in effect, the customers.

An increasing number of companies have built the evaluation of staff performance by line managers into their regular management practices. For example, the division heads at

Emerson Electric have been asked to grade the performance
of its headquarters staff. Weyerhaeuser Company has asked its
division heads to do a zero-based exercise in which they each
assume they are running a stand-alone business. The object
of this is to identify what staff they could do without. Acme-
Cleveland has held staff "fries," where the line managers who
pay for overhead allocations hear the justifications of those
staff budgets as part of the annual review process.

Many other firms have involved line managers through
one-time "participative" downsizing exercises. Called by various names including profit-improvement planning and administrative, overhead, or staff-value analysis, these efforts are
used to make significant reductions in overhead costs in a relatively short period. Rather than focusing on the overall budgets of staff departments, these techniques pinpoint the costs
of the end products the departments produce. By costing the
products rather than the people, a company depersonalizes a
process whose outcome, however, still frequently means people
lose their jobs.

Let's first consider the steps to pinpoint reduction targets,
then look at some of the difficulties companies have had with
these exercises. Done carefully, the study phase of staff value
analysis can easily take six months. Unfortunately, many companies that are concerned about the impact of the analysis on
morale and ongoing work try to compress it to less than half
that time.

First, staff departments considered for reduction are identified. It is useful to simultaneously examine as many departments as possible, because their work is often interrelated. For
each department, a concise statement of its purpose is developed and the six to ten key activities that support this purpose
are listed. The list should cover all activities that go on in the
department. Then the products or services that each activity
generates are specified. These might range from preparing
2,000 lunches each day to circulating a monthly budget variance report. Some "products" may be less tangible, such as
"facilitating six SBU annual planning sessions" or "providing
advice about liability risks associated with new products being
developed."

These services or products are the heart of staff value analysis, so it is important they be specified precisely. The receiver(s) of each product is (are) also identified at this stage. At times, some products will be sent to other staff departments before they go to their end users; other products will require input from different staff groups before they are ready to be handled by the department being studied. All these linkages and interconnections should be specified, because the next step of the analysis involves estimating the total costs to produce each product.

This is often the most difficult analytic task. Most accounting systems are set up to provide information by organizational unit or expense type; few track the cost of staff work products, especially when their "production" crosses departmental lines. Fortunately, most of the cost of staff work usually is salary related, so product cost can be estimated by approximating the time each staff member spends on a product per year. This number is then multiplied by the salary and benefits paid to each employee. To this are added any expenses directly attributable to individual products, such as travel or equipment. Indirect or hard-to-allocate by-product costs, such as telephone and secretarial services, are averaged by employee and then added to the product totals. The result is a complete breakdown of each staff department's annual expenditures by service or product provided. Developing these estimated costs is more difficult when inputs from several other departments are involved, however. Care must be taken to avoid double counting, so that the grand total of product costs equals the budgets of all departments being studied.

When this product-cost information is assembled, alternative ways to reduce the cost of each product can be considered. Options to analyze include:

1. Completely eliminating the product or service.
2. Leaving the product or service alone and looking elsewhere to cut costs.
3. Reducing the quality of the product. Sometimes called "de-goldplating," this step may involve tolerating more mistakes, using form letters instead of customized

ones, obtaining less data before producing a report, or
responding less quickly to internal customer requests.
4. Reducing the quantity of the product. This might mean
   providing fewer and shorter reports less frequently or
   preparing reports that indicate only exceptions to policy, rather than providing exhaustive reviews of everything that happened.
5. Making major changes in the way a product or service
   is provided. For example, this step might involve using
   outside contractors, investing in labor-saving automation, or combining the product with others.

These are only general suggestions; specific plans need to
be prepared for each product. The intent is to find creative
ways to reduce the demand for each staff product or service.
In some cases, several alternatives might be developed for each
product, each offering different potential savings. Of course,
reducing the demand for some staff services, especially those
provided by a control staff, may be popular with line managers,
but it could be unwise for the corporation's welfare. So along
with reduction suggestions, consideration must be given to the
potential adverse consequences of eliminating or reducing each
product.

Figure 4.2 indicates the rough priorities in which each
reduction suggestion would be considered for implementation.
First priority goes to the easy decisions—those whose implementation brings high dollar savings at minimal risk to the
business. High-risk alternatives with minimal gains are ignored
or considered only if the company is forced to make severe
cutbacks.

To increase the number of alternatives, companies may
request they be developed to achieve a high cost-savings target, often ranging from 40 to 60 percent. These "stretch" targets force consideration of major cuts, not only incremental
improvements. Targets often must be set this high to produce
final, implementable savings of 15 to 25 percent.

At times, to help soften the blow of potential reductions,
some companies will allow small expansions or additions of new

Figure 4.2.   Prioritizing staff products for possible elimination.

Risk	Small	Moderate	Large
High	Last to be cut back	Fourth	Third
Moderate	Fourth	Third	Second
Low	Third	Second	First to be cut back

Amount of money to be saved

products or services to be proposed as long as each department achieves a net reduction. These concessions may be useful substitutes for products or services eliminated, but more often than not this is a gratuitous part of the analysis.

Who does the analysis and makes the final decisions? This varies by company, but often a task force is set up to oversee the work. Its membership can include both providers and consumers of staff services. Managers of the staff functions being reviewed may be asked to identify the products and costs; then they work with line managers from the major consumers to target the products for reduction or elimination.

As might be expected, discussions in these task force meetings can become heated, with line managers pushing hard for overhead reductions and staff heads feeling compelled to defend their operations. For the process to work, it usually requires strong support from the chief executive. A set of well-thought-out procedures for the analysis and rules for the discussions are also critical. Some companies find a tight timetable also helps keep the study from getting bogged down.

The result of these meetings is a list of agreed-upon products and services to be cut back, ranked according to attractiveness (amount of money to be saved). This list goes up the chain of command for modification and final decisions. The larger the number of decisions, the more weight is given to the opinions of the line managers. Decisions tend to be oriented toward finding the simplest way to achieve the greatest reduction. Some executives try to shortcut the process by asking their line managers to rank the staff products from most to least valuable. A composite list is then made, and as many of the low-rated products are slated for cutbacks as needed to achieve the executive's cost-saving target.

Often, there are roles for outside advisors or consultants in this process. They can help keep the task force discussions on track, and they sometimes can serve as referees. At times, these advisors can help with quality control and provide formats for task force members to structure their analysis.

Staff value analysis offers a number of advantages. It solicits the views of the internal customers about the quality and importance of the staff work. It is participative to the extent that the providers and consumers nominate the targets for reduction. By concentrating attention on products and services, it is less blunt than across-the-board downsizing and more precise than comparing staffing ratios. Staff value analysis requires less analysis and paperwork than zero-based budgeting. And it can, if managed well, provide relatively fast decisions that lead to significant reductions in staff costs.

But the speed with which the analysis is carried out can have some disadvantages, too. It limits the fact-gathering, which itself may have to be based on marginally accurate estimates. Insufficient time for building a consensus or developing creative options can lead to solutions that become unstuck and feelings that some decisions were "railroaded." Moving very fast usually implies limiting the number of participants in the process, which in turn means that potentially useful ideas from the lower levels of the organization are seldom solicited. Time pressures can also make the process more political than analytical, and can turn some task force meetings into "horsetrading" sessions more appropriate for congressional committees than corporate meeting rooms.

Processes like these involve tradeoffs between cost-reduction benefits and potential mishaps if a critical staff job is eliminated. Unfortunately, the benefits can be quantified in dollars, while the risk assessments tend to be expressed in feelings. The tangible dollars saved frequently sway a decision more than unsubstantiated worries.

Some companies have dismissed these criticisms, saying that if cuts are made too deeply they can always hire the staff back or restart the shutdown activity. Maybe so, but the whiplash involved could have a negative impact on both employee morale and management credibility.

Techniques such as staff value analysis assume that organizations can be improved by hacking away at less needed activities. That may be true for the short run, but this assumption flies in the face of work by many modern organization observers, who stress that companies are more than lines and boxes on a chart. They maintain that the interactions among information systems, employee capabilities, management style, rewards and incentives, *and* structure are what lead to good or bad economic performances. These interactions are so complex that it's very hard to change one without eventually affecting the others. So for the effects of a downsizing to be sustained, executive attention must go to a broader range of issues than that which usually appears on a rank-ordered, value analysis worksheet. But for companies seeking short-run or one-shot solutions, these value-analysis and profit-improvement techniques may have significant benefits.

Other companies, such as Xerox, have found ways to use internal customer ratings of staff to promote continuous performance improvement. Xerox uses benchmarking to help maintain efficiency and limit size. It also charges each staff function with the responsibility of tracking the requirements of its customers (other Xerox departments and employees) and its effectiveness in meeting those requirements. As problems are identified, corrective plans are developed.

These surveys may be related to staff managers' annual objectives, the achievement of which can determine compensation changes. When outside vendors are hired by Xerox to provide services such as health care and employee relocation assistance to Xerox employees, their contracts require that they periodically measure the customer satisfaction of these employees. Xerox has put considerable thought into the development of these systems. They realize that the most important constituencies of some staff, such as college relations managers, are outside the company. So they regularly survey the heads of college placement offices for feedback on their managers' performance. These regular evaluations parallel the extensive customer-service measurements Xerox has for monitoring how outside customers perceive Xerox's products and services. They help break down the barriers between line and staff people by emphasizing the services both provide.

Ongoing use of internal customer surveys such as these is not limited to multinational, high-technology companies. Domino's Pizza Distribution Company insists that all headquarters staff functions act as though they were in business to provide service to others. To provide feedback, every user of the accounting department, for example, rates it on a scale of from one to ten. Comments must be provided to justify the ratings given. All employees of Domino's are eligible to receive a bonus check every month. The size of the bonus pool is determined by company performance; an individual's share is set in part by his customer-service ratings. Company president Donald Vlcek discovered a side benefit from the rating process: It enables him to operate with a lean management structure because the ratings cause problems to surface early and encourage staff and line people to work together to solve problems quickly. Fewer "coordinators" and "policemen" are needed in this highly self-regulating environment.

How Much Does It Really Cost?

Activity cost measurement is the final technique we consider in this chapter. This technique offers a way to obtain more precise estimates of how much various staff activities actually cost. The information can then serve as a basis for a careful reorganization planning.

The process begins with someone assembling information about the reporting relationships of all the managers and supervisors in the company to be studied. As with the staff value analysis, activity cost studies are most useful when they cover as many staff groups as possible. Unlike the staff value analysis, the activity cost data are collected about line work as well as staff. This information also includes the salaries, or sometimes the total compensation, of all workers in positions studied.

While this information is being assembled, a directory or dictionary of work activities is also compiled. This roster of work done by all organizational units includes the definitions of 150 to 250 of the most common activities. One such directory for a manufacturing firm included activity names such as:

Accident investigation	Material handling
Capital expenditure planning	Payroll accounting
Community relations	Performance evaluation
Competitive analysis	Pricing
Cost accounting	Production scheduling
Data entry	Product planning
Equipment design	Recruiting
Forecasting sales volume	Sales order processing
Invoicing customers	Secretarial
Machine setup	Vendor expediting
Managing and supervising	Work measurement

The directories are customized to include areas of most concern to the management overseeing the study. The listings are intended to cover all but the most trivial aspects of a unit's operations. These lists are typically more detailed than the lists of end products or services developed in the staff value analysis.

Each manager or supervisor uses the directory to record the time spent, either weekly or monthly, on each activity that requires at least 5 percent of his or her time. At times, the manager also records this information for the individual contributors reporting to him or her, though more accurate information is sometimes obtained when staff professionals provide their own data.

Finally, an analysis is conducted to match an individual's salary with his or her distribution of time. Most easily done by computer, this process provides the total payroll cost associated with each activity. It also provides an indication of how scattered some staff work has gotten. Companies with large personnel departments are surprised to find managers throughout their organization spending considerable amounts of time on personnel administration tasks. Or they may discover that four different groups are each spending time gathering data and producing reports for their own use, when that job could be done more quickly by the accounting department using its centralized data base. The duplication of effort from this misplaced work is often very expensive, as this analysis indicates when the equivalent person days are totaled. Considerable savings can sometimes be made by eliminating this duplication without giving up any activities or staff products. This information, it almost goes without saying, can be of considerable use in evaluating a department's annual budget request.

Sometimes staff work is excessively fragmented. Often, when a great many people are each spending a small amount of time doing something, the "something" doesn't get the concentrated attention it really deserves. Activity cost summaries surprise some executives when they see how many authors a capital budget or a corporate plan actually has. Activity cost studies help pinpoint areas in which healthy decentralization has turned into expensive fragmentation.

Activity cost analysis produces a data bank of activities and their costs that can guide downsizing efforts. A listing of the activities that account for 80 percent of a payroll usually illustrates the 80:20 rule: 20 percent of the activities in a company frequently account for most of its costs. By having a clear idea which activities are most expensive, it is easier to find high-leverage reduction targets. Often, just listing who is doing what is valuable in considering more economical ways to restructure work. This is information that never appears accurately in position descriptions.

The next step in using this analysis is for senior managers to assess the relative importance of each of the moré expensive activities. They can make some of these judgments themselves; for others, they need input from the internal customers of the staff products.

These data also provide a basis for restructuring individual jobs. An analysis of the activities done by, for example, a highly paid integrated-circuit designer may well indicate a considerable amount of time going to jobs that could be done just as well by lower-priced talent. By assigning some engineering assistants to these jobs, the expensive designer can be freed up to concentrate on work with a higher value added. The total number of such expensive employees can be reduced, their output increased, or the pressures to hire more of them lessened.

Activity cost analysis has been popular with many banks and insurance companies. General Electric has made use of it in all its business sectors. When GE examined the results of 85 studies that looked at the activities of over 75,000 salaried employees, it found opportunities for $100 million in savings. Follow-up reviews indicated that more than half of these opportunities were taken advantage of.

As with the seven other techniques we have reviewed here, activity cost analysis has strengths and weaknesses. Both it and staff value analysis are narrow in the way they collect data, but each along different dimensions. Because activity cost analyses typically consider only payroll numbers, other costs such as computers, subcontractors, and travel are not factored into the study. If the bulk of a staff's budget is salary, this is of minimal consequence. But this is not always the case. Staff value analyses tend to analyze only the costs of end products, even though these costs are estimated in ways that take into account all the intermediate products that went into producing them. Activity cost analyses pick up these internal activities, which in some cases may be substantial. In staff work, some products build on inputs to others, and the real cost-reduction issue is how to provide the inputs more cheaply, not how to eliminate one or the other product.

The healthy skepticism many managers give position descriptions should be carried over to activity cost analysis. Even though the data are expressed in numbers instead of words, they can be just as inaccurate and subjective. Without resorting to time-and-motion studies, it is useful to audit or have managers carefully confirm the validity of the time breakdowns that go into the analysis.

Earlier, we criticized staff value analysis for sometimes moving too quickly. Activity cost studies, if not closely managed, can produce the opposite result. Unless an action plan is developed to make early use of the volumes of data and reports, the only outcome will be to raise expectations—or worries.

Something Is Missing

It seems clear that the biggest difficulty in pinpointing targets for staff reduction is evaluating how well the units are performing. In this chapter we have outlined eight common approaches to evaluating staff performance. Some are more comprehensive than others. Some provide only rough assessments, while others probe the details of how staff units really spend their time and what they actually produce. And some are elaborate and time consuming, while others are quicker but built on many guesstimates. Several techniques, such as zero-based budgeting and staff value analysis, lend themselves to one-time use, while others are most effective when part of a company's regular management practices (benchmarking, consumer surveys, and productivity improvement planning). In

Chapter 9 we will suggest how ongoing attention must be given to managing staff size, lest the gain and pain from these one-shot efforts be wasted.

But none of these techniques is perfect. Each seems to lack a useful feature that another has, and often they work best in combination. Their inadequacies also indicate that something is missing. The next chapter outlines another way of thinking about headquarters staff functions by suggesting ways to better compare the apples and oranges of staff work.

Chapter 5

Managing Staff Strategically

Few companies manage their staff functions with the same care and attention they give their line operating units. While priority must always go to customers and products, in many companies insufficient attention has been paid to controlling staff size and scope. As we have seen, this too often results in high overhead, slow decision making, overanalyzed decisions, overengineered products, and weakened general managers. The techniques discussed in the previous chapter can help pinpoint specific instances of excess staff and identify how well individual staff groups are functioning at a given point in time. But to understand how staff work should change over time, a more dynamic perspective is needed.

The key to this broader viewpoint is to treat staff activities more like real businesses and less like business appendages. The first step is to break a staff department down into the activities it undertakes or the products and services it provides. The discussion of customer evaluations and activity cost analyses in the last chapter covers ways to do this. Consideration then needs to be given to managing staff units strategically. This means paying attention to:

1. Competitors (including alternative ways a company can do what staff units do).
2. Customers and the value staff units add to them.
3. Industry dynamics.

Staff Departments Have Competitors

Staff units have several types of competitors. In corporations prone to downsizing, some of the competitors are other, more valued activities within the business. In some firms, these activities might be in sales or marketing when all available resources are directed to launch a new product. This was the case when the Coca-Cola Company introduced its new formulation of Coke, and funds became scarce in many nonmarketing parts of the company. During Chrysler's turnaround, and in many companies with heavy debts after a leveraged buy-out, the competitor might be the finance department, as it gathers cash to meet high loan payments. When CBS, Owens-Illinois, and Union Carbide needed to fend off acquirers with the heightened stock prices that improved earnings provide, the competitor became the company's bottom line, as every possible measure was taken to generate immediate profits.

These competitors are usually difficult for staff departments to fend off. Defense from budget cuts provoked by such competitors usually is limited to the "little jewel" strategy: Pare back activities until only the most essential remain. Fortunately, not all competition is as difficult for staff to cope with. Corporate staffs also share competitors with other parts of the business. These include:

Their customers.
Other staff groups looking to expand their range of services.

Substitutes for the services and products they provide.
Some of their suppliers of goods or services.

These factors are similar to the forces Harvard Business
School professor Michael Porter feels drive external competition in most industries. Headquarters staff units face potential
competition from groups within the company, especially line
managers. To the extent that what has been staff work, such
as strategic planning or handling of day-to-day labor problems,
can be taken on by line managers so as to do without or at least
reduce the size of the staff unit. This is a popular way to run
a downsized company, although it has its costs and pitfalls, as
we will consider in Chapters 6 and 8.

At times, consolidating the work of several staff groups
into a single, smaller unit makes sense. This can be the method,
for example, when the public relations department takes over
the work of marketing support and investor relations groups,
or when several manufacturing support units are streamlined
into a materials management function. In some companies,
equal employment or labor relations problems can be managed by the legal department. A number of corporate medical
departments have expanded into what was formerly a personnel function, as they add employee assistance programs to their
roster of services.

There are three general substitutes to many staff units.
The simplest approach is to keep the products or services they
provide, but procure them from outside sources. Make-or-buy
analyses have convinced many companies that it is cheaper to
obtain cafeteria management, payroll preparation, and security and janitorial services from companies that specialize in
providing these services. At times this approach is valid for
professional services such as legal and business planning, too.
Often, the quality of the services may be better when provided
by these specialists.

The second form of substitution involves reducing the
demands on the staff units so that they are able to limit the
range of things they do. Techniques such as activity costing and
value analysis are useful in determining where demand may

be reduced. Reports could be issued less frequently, under-used studies could be eliminated altogether, or the range of training provided by the human resources department could be narrowed.

Finally, there are times when the suppliers of inputs to staff departments may be able to take over staff functions. This is a variation on the forward-integration strategy that some businesses follow, and it is especially valid when staff departments are adding relatively little value to the inputs they receive. A computer center may evolve into an information services function that uses the data it once processed for the personnel and finance departments to produce some final com-pany-wide reports in these areas. Or an environmental scan-ning unit in the planning department, whose primary function was to package and distribute externally published information about future trends affecting the business, might be replaced by contracting out with think tanks or outside experts.

These competitive environments call for a strategic approach to managing staff activities if benefits are to be maximized. A strategic approach is one concerned with how a staff's resources should be positioned over the long haul. It looks at staff departments not only in terms of how they fit into the organization, but also how the issues they are concerned with affect, and will continue to affect, the business. This is a dynamic view, not a static one. A strategy for managing staff is concerned with the same objective that an overall business strategy is: how best to concentrate a company's resources for the greatest long-term advantage.

To illustrate these concepts, let's look at one staff function in a hypothetical company. Assume this company makes parts and subassemblies for airplane builders such as Boeing and McDonnell-Douglas. It is a company with many competitors, but only a handful of customers—a situation that requires con-stant attention both to controlling costs and to differentiating itself from its rivals. Let's examine how this company strategi-cally manages its information services function.

To start, let's specify the key activities of the informa-tion services department that may be comparable to discrete businesses. In this simplified example, assume there are three of these activities:

1. Systems planning.
2. Systems development.
3. Systems operations.

In essence, this staff unit's work involves running a traditional computer center (systems operations) and providing two interrelated support services. Systems planning is the activity that sets the specifications and plans the design for this manufacturer's computer-based systems. Systems development either writes or acquires the software needed to implement these plans; the software is then run on equipment that is operated or maintained by the computer center. While these activities are interconnected, each stands alone for purposes of analysis.

This concept may be more obvious when the competitors, and potential competitors, of each activity are considered. See Table 5.1 for a breakdown of these activities and the potential competitors. A glance at the sources of competition suggests that this information systems department indeed faces significant potential competition.

Let's consider each activity in turn. In this company, sys-

Table 5.1. Sources of competition for an information services department.

	Systems Planning	Systems Development	Systems Operations
Customers	Yes	Possibly	Yes
Other staff functions	Yes	Possibly	Possibly
Substitutes	No	No	Yes
Suppliers	Possibly	Yes	Yes

tems planning is primarily a control staff activity. It sets, or attempts to set, standards in the area of information system design, so that the company maintains comparable systems. Unfortunately, a number of its internal customers, the targets of these controls, resist these standards. Some even propose standards of their own. Some of the heavy users of computing, especially the accounting department, feel they can do a better job in this area. Systems planning also studies activities throughout the company to determine how they might be automated. This is another area in which the customers, including other staff functions, also feel they can contribute. There is overall agreement, though, that some group must be charged with doing systems planning; as an activity, it does not have any obvious substitutes. The company has used consultants in the past to assist here; greater use of them is another competitive alternative to keeping this staff activity in-house.

Systems development, which primarily involves computer programming, has fewer but stronger competitors. Many sources of software exist, and many firms are available to develop customized programs. While there are few immediately available substitutes for software, this company's technological planners see a time coming when much more software will be built into the computer, and programming itself will be done by computers, reducing the need for a large programming staff. The dispersion of programming skills throughout the company and the availability of more off-the-shelf software increase the potential for greater competition from customers and staff counterparts.

The centralized computer center—the heart of the department's systems operations activity—is the most threatened by competition. Outside suppliers (computer service bureaus and time-sharing hookups) and substitutes for the company's large mainframe (increasingly powerful desktop microcomputers) are its major competitors. Widespread use of personal computers by the company's staff and line departments makes the systems operations staff particularly vulnerable to competition.

Value Added to Staff Customers

Two principles that have long been used in developing strategies for externally-oriented businesses can also be helpful when managing staff. They involve a consideration of how much value each product is adding to a company and an examination of how far along the product is in its life cycle (its "maturity"). These principles can be adapted to plan staff activities instead of products. They can provide suggestions about how big a staff group should be, how fast it should grow, and where it should be placed in the organization. Let us start by considering the value added.

Specifying a staff's value added is not as easy as determining the value a company adds to a product it makes and sells. The latter can be found with a straightforward calculation. Assessing staff value added, as discussed in the last chapter, is less precise and more subjective. Sometimes it is possible to rank activities based on how well their users have rated them. This can be helpful, but for some kinds of staff work the internal clients are not sophisticated enough to make judgments about what they or the company really need. One way out of this dilemma is to force users and providers to judge the value added, based on what they feel would happen to the company if a particular activity was *not* there. Views of outside experts can also be helpful here. To simplify the process, judgments can be made from one of four categories. Each is a possible answer to the question, "What would be the consequence of eliminating this particular staff activity?"

1. There would be a critical negative impact on the business which would be hard to recover from (high value added).
2. There would be a significant loss, but one that the company could recover from (significant value added).
3. There would be hindrances only to day-to-day operations (moderate value added).
4. There would be few or no problems caused (low or no value added).

Which category a particular activity belongs in can be a matter of considerable debate. This debate, and the perceptions it generates, can often be more useful than the outcome. The value of such planning exercises is more often in doing them than in the answers that come from them. In slotting activities, it is sometimes helpful to specify what the value added currently *is*, and what it *should be*. It is important to keep in mind, however, that a particular staff product (such as a monthly budget variance report) may be of only low or moderate value added for some companies, but of significant or high value added for some others (such as those on the brink of bankruptcy).

Going back to the information services example, the value added of its three activities varies, based primarily on the number of alternatives the company has to do what each provides. The systems planning activity offers significant value added because it is the hardest to do without. But there are many ways the work of systems operations can happen, and the company's dependence on a mainframe computer center even seems to be bucking the tide of information-systems decentralization made possible by personal computers. So this activity is rated as having only low to moderate value added. The value added of the systems development activity is more solidly in the moderate range, considering again the alternatives available to get this work done.

Assessing Activity Maturity

Market planners have developed a method to track the development of products through the stages of their life in the marketplace. This method provides an idea of when to invest in R&D to produce a new product and when to offer low-price promotions to keep an older product moving. It allows planners to manage a unified portfolio of products, each with different strategies and different customers. Just as products and markets tend to evolve along a life cycle, so does staff work. It is possible to use this evolutionary perspective to have a better understanding of how big a staff department should be, how fast it should grow or shrink, and where it should most logically be placed in the company.

Each staff activity is part of an "industry," made up of related activities, competitive activities, customers, and suppliers of inputs. To make a judgment about the value added by a particular staff activity, it must be viewed in relation to the priorities of the business. The heart of a strategic analysis of staff work, though, is a consideration of how each staff activity compares to others in the outside world (or to the dynamics of the industry to which it belongs). Remember the concept of "maturity" mentioned earlier. Characterizing a staff activity by its stage of maturity gives clues to its appropriate size and place in the company. Four distinct maturity phases can be identified: embryonic, growth, mature, and aging. Based on an activity cluster's characteristics, a staff activity can be considered to reflect one of these stages.

Embryonic staff activities tend to be new issues, not just for the company but for industry or society as a whole. They can range from techniques to detect carcinogens in the workplace to the best ways to integrate female talent into the corporate hierarchy. Their impact on the company is often hard to determine, and there usually are only a few sources of expertise in dealing with them. The "product line" available for each is narrow, and the providers of that expertise may come and go quickly. Often, the technology needed to handle embryonic activities is very limited or even nonexistent. Much of the published information on these issues is found in obscure professional journals. Some ideas are talked about widely, then forgotten; others have more staying power. In the late 1970s, computer-integrated manufacturing, artificial intelligence, and employee assistance programs had many characteristics of embryonic issues. But a few years later, each took off and became growth areas for corporate staff attention.

Growth staff activities are ones that have established their importance on a company's agenda. Spending on them increases more rapidly than do expenditures in other areas of staff involvement. Depending on their popularity, a variety of products and services relating to them emerge. Premium prices are often charged and in-house talent becomes more available to deal with them. Depending on the nature of their audiences, best-selling books appear (ranging from John Magee's writings on inventory control in the 1950s to William Ouchi's work on Americanized Japanese management in the early 1980s).

By the time the "definitive" book on a particular subject appears (such as Michael Porter's *Competitive Strategy*), the issue is usually a mature one. Its overall impact on a company may be sizable, but it is also definable. Total corporate expenditures on a mature issue tend to grow no faster than for most other staff areas, although they frequently require greater annual budgets than when they were in a growth mode. A clear and sometimes diminished selection of outside sources of expertise and services are available. Price competition becomes more common among those that remain, and companies that need outside assistance often find themselves in a buyer's market. With publication of the definitive book, if one is written, the knowledge to cope with this issue is standardized and spreads easily in-house. Corporate concern is shifted away from "staying on top of things" in favor of efficiency and cost cutting. The work in this area becomes fairly routine and dispersed throughout the company. As implied earlier, the strategic planning function is now considered mature. Many activities of the controller, legal counsel, and public relations department also fall into this category.

Aging issues are so much a part of corporate routine that it may be forgotten that considerable staff efforts still go into them. They seldom receive attention from senior management. To the extent that outside providers are used, there may be a diminishing number of them from which to choose, or they may have become very fragmented and localized. But, unlike the situation of humans in their life cycle, it is possible for staff activities to reverse the direction of their movement. Rubbish disposal, which was generally judged to be an aging staff concern, has reverted to an embryonic or growth issue for the many companies whose waste includes hazardous chemicals. The company travel office, a service so ordinary that many companies let outside travel agents provide its services, has grown in importance and become a less mature service now that deregulation has dramatically changed the airline industry. In-house travel services are becoming common, and are sometimes even treated like miniature profit centers.

The three activities of the information services department of the airplane parts maker have differing maturities. Its systems planning activity is closest to the growth stage. Its usefulness has been established, but knowledge and techniques for accomplishing the activity are still being developed. A number of external consultants are available, but they tend to charge more for their services in this area than do those in the software writing business (corresponding to this company's systems development group), which is more of a mature activity. Systems operations fits better into the late mature-early aging stage, especially in this company with its emphasis on traditional, centralized batch processing.

The Strategic Turf

Few management consultants, when presented with two factors that characterize a situation of interest to executives, can resist the temptation to construct a matrix. Figure 5.1 shows the matrix resulting when the concept of value added is linked with that of maturity. Its 16 positions represent the possible combinations of these two variables. The shaded box represents the most common strategic position of typical staff work: mature activity of moderate value added. Relatively few staff activities are, or should be, in the high value added row or the embryonic column.

The matrix defines the strategic turf of staff work. After the work of a staff department or several departments is broken down into individual products or activities, those activities can be displayed on this chart. Decisions about which activities are candidates for downsizing can then follow.

Companies that have done a thorough study of their activity costs (as described in Chapter 4) already know their *total* expenditure on each activity. Activity cost studies usually indi-

Figure 5.1.   Strategic turf of staff work.

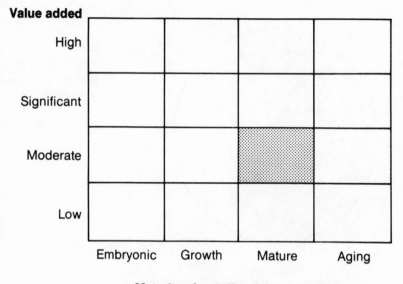

Value added

High

Significant

Moderate

Low

Embryonic   Growth   Mature   Aging

Maturity of a staff activity or product

cate that considerable amounts of money are being spent on staff work outside the organizational unit directly responsible for it. Sometimes this happens because of planned decentralization, sometimes because of duplication of efforts, and often because of the time it takes other departments to respond to requests for information from staff units (filling out forms, going through planning and budgeting exercises, and the like). Regardless, a pie chart showing the total cost of a staff activity can be drawn, with the size of an activity's circle in proportion to its budget. The shaded area represents the portion of the cost incurred by the department responsible for it and the unshaded portion represents the costs borne by other parts of the company. For each activity, the pie chart provides a visual clue to how much money each activity is costing the company and which areas are prone to misplaced staff activity. Figure 5.2 shows such a breakdown.

With these pie charts, it is possible to set norms for how a company *should* expect its staff dollars to grow and be dis-

Figure 5.2. Breakdown of a company's expenditures on a typical staff activity.

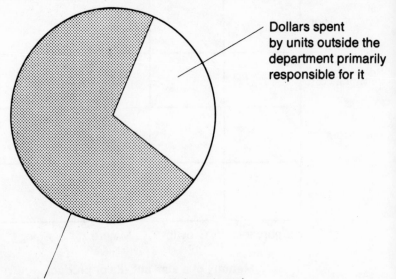

Dollars spent
by units outside the
department primarily
responsible for it

Dollars spent by designated staff department

tributed during the course of a staff activity's life cycle. Figure 5.3 illustrates one evolution that many companies hope will happen. Of the four stages, the embryonic phase is smallest in size. Only a small proportion of its pie chart is shaded, indicating that many embryonic activities are too new for one logical home base to be assigned. As the activity grows in importance—and in total expenditures—the breakdown of expenditures changes, with the lion's share going to a primary staff unit. When that activity reaches the mature stage, total company expenditures are usually greatest, while the activity starts to be decentralized throughout the business. From early to late maturity, the pace of decentralization increases and total company-wide expenditures start to decline. Finally, the aging activity comes to the point at which total expenditures are less than during its growth stage, and much of the work is done throughout the company, instead of being concentrated at headquarters.

Figure 5.3. "Ideal" distribution of expenditures for a staff activity over its life cycle.

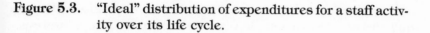

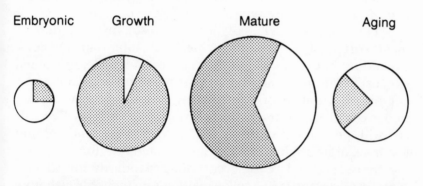

Note: Shaded area represents expenditures made on an activity by the primary staff unit responsible for it; unshaded area represents expenditures made by units in other parts of the company.

"Natural" versus "Usual" Evolution

The "natural" pattern of evolution implied by this discussion does not happen automatically. For staff activities to grow and have their expenditures distributed along these lines, their evolution needs to be managed. This is seldom the case, however. Top management's attention is usually focused on other matters, and few companies have powerful organizational planning units that monitor these developments. This neglect means that the pattern shown in Figure 5.3 is less common than many executives want it to be. Instead, the typical development path for many staff activities has budgets growing continually throughout the mature stage, sometimes even into the aging phase. Rather than reducing the scope of work as the activity matures, staff units often expand and become entrenched in a headquarters group. All too frequently this situation persists as the activity enters the aging stage.

It is not difficult to understand why this happens. Managers of staff departments have few incentives to decentralize mature activities and pare down aging ones, even if there is a possibility these actions will allow them to pick up embryonic or growth activities. The compensation and career advancement of these managers too often depend on increasing the number of people reporting to them. These interests, coupled with the benign neglect shown by many senior executives, lead to the more typical pattern of evolution.

This "unmanaged" situation can result in staff departments, originally designed with clear-cut, important missions, expanding into areas where they add considerable, unneeded expense. One manufacturer originally set up a headquarters engineering unit to prevent cost overruns on a new factory under construction. It did this job very well, and was "rewarded" with permanent status. Unfortunately, over time the unit lost track of its original mission and devoted its efforts to growing by issuing and revising corporate standards for all new construction efforts. But following these increasingly elaborate specifications resulted in overengineered and overbuilt plants that frequently cost more than budgeted. A central engineering group in another company was originally established to do work that exceeded the capabilities of engineers in that company's divisions. Eventually, the group expanded its charter and started to review and redo the engineering done in the divisions, most of which was easily within the capabilities of the company's technical staffs. The end result of both these typical types of staff scope evolution was increased costs, deteriorated morale, and decisions that took longer.

When studies are made of typical headquarters staff activities, the "portfolio" that emerges frequently looks like that shown in Figure 5.4. The circles on the matrix are clustered in the upper right-hand corner of the matrix, indicating that most of the company's staff expenditures are for activities in the mature or aging segments of their life cycle. It is also common for these activities to be placed on the upper, rather than the lower, half of the matrix. Much staff work, especially that done by control staff, is considered indispensable. The consequence of this ratings inflation is potential overinvestment in some of these activities. This overinvestment occurs either at the expense of higher corporate overhead or because insufficient attention is given to activities that should appear in the middle and in the upper left-hand cells.

Figure 5.4. Typical portfolio of activities in a staff department.

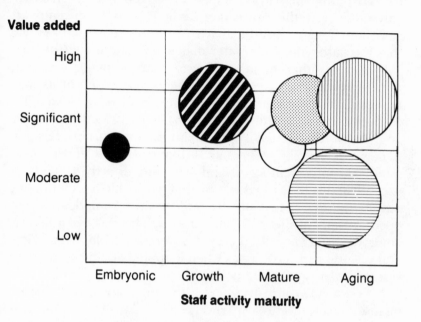

Grow or Downsize?

The strategic management perspective we have been applying to staff activities suggests a way to decide which activities are candidates for pruning and which might be considered for expansion. Expansion, though, does not always have
to mean increasing the head count. In the automobile industry, the engineering design function has usually been considered as one that provides significant or high value added. The
introduction of computer-aided design and manufacturing has
helped move this mature discipline to more of a growth state.
But it also has allowed Chrysler to cut its engineering group in
half while speeding new-product design. Expansion like this is
referred to as expansion of capital investment, not of staffing.

As staff activities mature, make-or-buy decisions become
more appropriate. These can work in both directions, of
course. Sharply increasing legal bills and an over-supply of

legal talent have encouraged many companies to save money by expanding their in-house legal departments. Much of the "mystique" left the profession, as it shifted from a growth activity to a mature staff activity. And it became a staff activity that was susceptible to greater management and control.

On the other hand, during a time of major organizational streamlining, General Electric looked closely at its market research and economic forecasting activities for possibilities of outsourcing. At the same time, GE illustrated that it was applying a differential approach to planning for staff work. A new top-level job was created—that of chief scientist. Given senior vice president status and reporting directly to the chief executive, this individual was made responsible for identifying new businesses that could be built upon technologies developed in General Electric's laboratories. This was essentially an embryonic staff activity. Few rules were available, which General Electric had recognized when it appointed an experienced research manager to the position.

As we have already seen with corporate travel departments, outside events can reverse the maturity, importance, or appropriate size of staff activity. Deregulation in the telephone industry has drastically changed the formerly aging activity of telecommunications management. Previously, this low-level job involved only interfacing with a nearby Bell System representative. Now, with alternative service providers, new technologies, and potential for multimillion dollar savings through capital investment, companies have increased the staff size and value added of this growth activity.

As some staff specialties mature, they fragment into subspecialties in different phases of evolution. The esoteric computer center of the 1950s (stage: embryonic) became the growth information services activity of the 1970s. The staffing levels of these major departments increased accordingly. Technological changes in computer networking and the widespread use of personal computers scattered this activity throughout companies as the staff activity of information services units matured in the 1980s. While these outside influences are causing some companies to halt the growth of their central staffs, others—such as American Airlines, Fidelity Investments, and Wells Fargo & Company—simultaneously have set up chief information officers (CIO) patterned after GE's chief scientist. In these companies, this individual is charged with bringing order to technology- caused chaos. But, even more important, he or she is expected to help turn the information-processing activities into a source of competitive strength, a more embryonic staff function. To do this, the CIO is often given responsibility for some maturing staff activities, with the task of melding and revitalizing them. At Wells Fargo, the CIO is in charge of strategic planning and the personnel function, in addition to its computer systems. At General Foods, the CIO follows the forward-integration strategy discussed earlier and also controls the critical market research unit. Aetna Life and Casualty Company has its CIO also running the mailroom, publications department, and even the corporate art gallery. These consolidations of mature staff functions are one way some companies are controlling their size while increasing their value added.

Identifying targets for downsizing is the most common reason companies go through this sort of analysis. In general, the more mature, moderate, or low value-added activities are the primary candidates for cutbacks. Figure 5.5 summarizes how activity size can be managed for each cell of the matrix. The general guidelines suggest:

- Embryonic activities—very small staff units, often just a part-time responsibility.
- Growth activities—rapidly growing staff groups for higher valued activities, more stable staffs for less important activities.
- Mature activities—stable, eventual gradual decreases in staff size should be possible.
- Aging activities—streamlined staffs, possibly reduced to a small core group or completely eliminated.

While applying these generalizations is better than using the meat cleaver, across-the-board method of staff reduction,

Figure 5.5. Rough guidelines for managing staff activity size.

Value added

	Embryonic	Growth	Mature	Aging
High	Moderate growth	Rapid expansion	Maintain	Gradually reduce size and consolidate
Significant	Monitor for new investment	Moderate expansion	Gradually reduce size and consolidate	Streamline
Moderate	Monitor for new investment	Maintain	Streamline	Prune back; consider for elimination
Low	Prove viability or eliminate	Streamline	Prune back	Consider for elimination

Staff activity maturity

it is important to keep in mind that they are still generalizations and that exceptions will certainly occur.

If we apply these guidelines to the information services function discussed earlier, there are several changes that could be made in its three key activities. Systems planning is the most likely candidate for moderate expansion, both in the size of its operations and in its scope. Because the dynamics of its "industry" are more in the growth phase than the mature phase, it probably makes more sense to strengthen the unit and keep its control and standard-setting functions centralized. It is also important to ensure that most of the company's expenditures in this area be centrally managed, not dispersed throughout other staff functions.

Systems development (primarily computer programming)

is a more mature activity that provides less value added than systems planning. Its budget is almost twice as large as that for the planning activity. Because a number of ready-to-run programs are available in many areas of interest to this aircraft parts manufacturer, and because there are several outside contractors able to customize these programs for less than this company now spends creating its own software, the development activity is a good candidate for streamlining. Its overall budget can be reduced, and a greater portion of it spent on outside services.

The systems operations activity is even more marginal to the company. Its low value added, combined with its aging position in its life cycle, suggest that this unit be considered for pruning or possible elimination. Eventually, this company may want to make greater use of mini- and microcomputers, which will make it possible to completely decentralize the computer center and sell the mainframe equipment.

These changes are summarized in Figure 5.6, which shows both the current positions and the suggested changes in the information services department's portfolio of staff activities. It also shows a new activity, which may be funded in part from the savings achieved by cutting back on expenditures in systems development and operations. Headed by a chief information officer, this discrete activity, like its counterparts at American Airlines and Wells Fargo, is charged with finding ways to use information technology as a competitive weapon. The CIO function is embryonic in nature—companies are just beginning to learn how to use this type of position—but it shows promise of providing high value added. At our aircraft parts manufacturer, this activity may focus on developing computer links with some of its key suppliers to help speed the ordering of raw materials while reducing inventory. It may also explore installing a computer network to link this components supplier to several of its major customers. This network could be the means for cementing better relations with these customers by encouraging their design engineers to use the company's computer-assisted design technologies early in the planning stages for new airplanes.

Figure 5.6. Example of an information services department portfolio of staff activities.

How the Department Looks Now

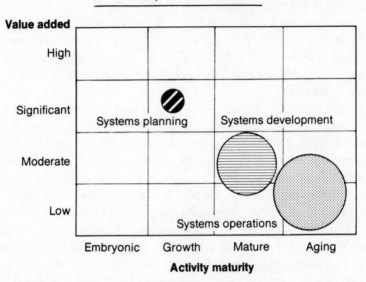

How It Would Look with Possible Changes and Additions

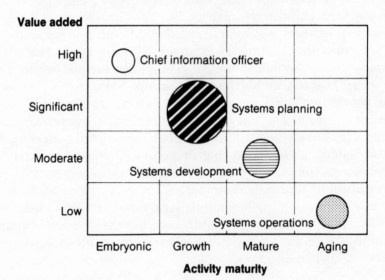

Centralize or Disperse?

The strategic perspective also suggests guidelines as to which staff functions belong where in a company. When Brunswick cut its headquarters staff in half, it decided that jobs like corporate safety director and economic analyst belonged in the plants and divisions, just as Allied Corporation decided that a similar location was where the bulk of its environmental assurance capability belonged. Companies have a number of options for placing staff activities, including:

1. Keeping them centralized at corporate headquarters.
2. Scattering them among headquarters, divisions, and plants.
3. Decentralizing them as far from headquarters as possible.
4. Keeping them centralized, but not necessarily at headquarters, while treating them as a stand-alone business by charging users for their services.
5. Purchasing them partially from outside companies.
6. Purchasing them completely from outside companies on long-term contracts.
7. Purchasing them from multiple outside providers as needed.

Depending on the expected value added and its maturity, using outside providers may be cost effective or too expensive. Generally, as an activity matures, it becomes more economical to contract it out. This can also be true, ironically, for embryonic activities in which talent is limited (and hard to hire) and the long-term impact of the issue is hard to determine. At times, the decision to go outside may have political or cultural reasons. The specialists needed for an activity may not fit the norms of the company's work force. In the following chapter we will see how People Express had to use outside people for some jobs to help maintain its homogeneous corporate culture. IBM and other nonunion companies have contracted out jobs that traditionally are filled by union workers. Much organizational planning work is done by outside consultants, because it would be difficult for an inside group to remain impartial when there are political and career implications to the alternatives being considered.

The placement of embryonic activities varies widely, frequently depending on where the issue was first noticed. At TRW in the mid-1960s, concern about equal employment opportunity and community relations first centered in an engineering unit because that was where one of its managers with a personal involvement in civil rights groups happened to be based. His outside interests made him the first in the company to be aware of changes that needed to take place in the workplace. At times, the "logical" home to consider a new issue (such as the information systems department for applications of artificial intelligence) may not be the best one, because that group is also the most threatened by the new technology or because of an implication that the unit has not been doing its job properly.

Growth staff activities are frequently concentrated at headquarters, especially when the value they add is significant and the talent to cope with them is scarce and must be shared among a variety of users. At TRW, pressure from the Department of Labor in the late 1960s helped move equal employment opportunity from an embryonic to a growth activity for the company. TRW, like many other defense contractors at that time, was facing loss of federal contracts if it did not develop and implement an acceptable affirmative action plan. TRW's main problem was that none of the staff professionals in the human resources department were knowledgeable about such plans. Employees committed to racially integrating the company, like the engineer mentioned earlier, also lacked the technical knowhow. Eventually, after a difficult search, an outsider with some experience in this area was hired. This was also the time of race riots in Cleveland, TRW's headquarters city, and the company was similarly limited in talent to manage an urban affairs program. A part-time college student with good community contacts was hired to plan such an effort, a more marginal response to a staff concern of less immediate value added.

As we've noted, by the time staff activities reach the late growth stage, more in-house talent has been trained to cope with them. At TRW, the corporate foundation staff took over the community relations efforts, and equal employment responsibilities were built into the jobs of many of the human resources staff.

During the mature phase, it is possible to turn attention of an issue from headquarters staff to divisions and plants. Instead of being considered exclusively "staff work," the activity is increasingly built into line managers' jobs. And staff people who previously performed a control staff role now become more support staff oriented as they assist the line managers. Building the company's capability to deal with mature staff issues outside of headquarters becomes a high priority. Opportunities are found to contract out parts of the work. For example, as equal employment became more a part of the management routine at TRW, the human resources staff had more time to become involved in productivity and quality-improvement projects in the late 1970s. Outside employment services handled more of the recruiting that ten years before was the key concern of TRW's newly hired affirmative action officer. And its community relations activities were broadened to include attention to international as well as domestic issues.

Managing these shifts of attention—and staff resources— has been a way of life at TRW and several other planned downsizers. But most companies have not managed staff work and size as closely. For them, the activities considered mature and aging are also those consuming most of their staff resources. These activities are the most likely downsizing targets and the ones to be most closely examined for elimination, decentralization, or contracting out.

The Ongoing
Management of Staff Size

General Electric's chief executive, John Welch, summed up this situation well when he described the evolution of strategic planning at GE. He said, "Our planning system was dynamite when we first put it in. The thinking was fresh; the form mattered little—the format got no points. It was idea oriented. We then hired a head of planning, and he hired two vice presidents, and then he hired a planner; and the books got thicker, and the printing got more sophisticated, and the covers got harder, and the drawings got better. The meetings kept getting larger. Nobody...[could] say anything with sixteen to eighteen people there." Notice that Welch did not say anything about the planning getting any *better*. Soon after he became chief executive he dispersed most of his headquarters planning group.

Managing staff strategically means paying attention to several principles:

1. Use strategic concepts such as life cycles and value added to determine staff size and location.
2. Enforce sunset laws. Close down, decentralize, or contract out mature or aging headquarters activities before starting new, embryonic, or growth ones.
3. Be wary of the myopia and tendencies of professionals to pigeonhole problems and build empires around themselves. Tie all aspects of staff work to priority business concerns, especially when making judgments about how much value an activity is adding to the company.
4. Always keep in mind alternative, competitive ways to get done what staff units are doing.

Now that we have considered some ways to evaluate staff performance and manage its size, it is appropriate to turn attention to the other major contributor to corporate bureaucracy: excess management layers.

Chapter 6

Flattening the Pyramid

"Will we revert to memos that need to be signed by *ten layers* of authority, which makes a mockery of entrepreneurship?" worried John Welch, General Electric's chairman, as GE pulled out of the early-1980s recession. He shared a concern of many business leaders as the acute need to downsize let up when the economic cycle turned upward. Some business watchers also sounded alarms about how the number of middle managers in many companies was growing three to four times faster than sales of those companies.

The concern was a very real one. While companies had let go thousands of managers, few had followed these difficult layoffs with significant redesigns of their organizations. They changed the number of managers on board without considering the corresponding changes that needed to be made in how management work was actually done. These companies that reduced their management complement without downsizing their management structure could also find easy excuses to upsize when their business situations turned more favorable.

Attacking Excess Management

Albert Casey's stay as postmaster general was brief. But this former chief executive of American Airlines moved quickly to streamline the management structure of the U.S. Postal Service. Soon after taking charge Casey eliminated one of the four layers of top management. Forty-two district offices were cut, leaving 74 divisions reporting directly to the five regional postmasters general. His goal: "To make field-management decision making more timely and responsive" by putting operating expertise closer to the people who actually sort and deliver the mail. His successor carried this decentralization further down the ranks by allowing individual postmasters more discretion in adapting to their local customer needs. As a result, several locations began to enjoy Sunday mail deliveries and evening post office hours.

Such changes in organization are certainly not limited to the public sector. Sears, Roebuck and Company made a similar move when it eliminated the territorial offices that linked their Chicago headquarters with the 24 administrative offices that are directly responsible for overseeing Sears' 800 stores. The move was for reasons similar to the Postal Service change: to speed decision making in response to a fast-changing marketplace. The four dropped territorial offices employed 1,800 people; their functions either were delegated to the administrative offices, done by a new ten-person field management office set up in Chicago, or eliminated. The change was expected to help shore up declining profit margins as well as ensure that the right merchandise got to the right stores at the right time.

Brunswick's Mercury Marine business cut out the layer of management just below its divisional level that was intended to provide sales and marketing support to each division. Instead, these functions were consolidated at Mercury Marine headquarters into a smaller unit that served all divisions. In this instance, the primary motivation was cost reduction—an estimated $6 million was saved each year—as Brunswick decided these functions were excessively decentralized.

Prudential Insurance Company of America, the nation's largest life insurer, has made several organizational shifts to better prepare it for the revolution in the financial services industry. James Melone, Prudential's president, characterized these shifts as a means of "getting the message across that we are going to move with less layers of management and more self-contained business units." These are strong words for an industry that traditionally has rivaled many government agencies in its broad range of management titles. He viewed a key purpose of downsizing management layers as getting accountability and responsibility more closely aligned with each other.

Merrill Lynch and Company, another major player in the financial services arena, has given attention to excess mid-management staffing. More than 4,000 positions have been eliminated, many in areas such as accounting, marketing, planning, and product development. Not only head counts are being reduced, either. Reporting relations are being changed so that each manager has at least six direct reports.

Executives have stopped boasting about having "management in depth." That phrase is no longer an unquestioned positive expression. Instead, attention is on minimizing the management structure between chief executive and customer. The hoped-for objectives are similar across companies: faster decision making, quicker awareness of market needs and competitor moves, and lower costs.

Many companies have found a key side benefit to cutting excess layers from the management structure: higher morale among the remaining managers. Why? The decentralization that frequently accompanies de-layering gives them bigger jobs with more real responsibility. Some feel able, for the first time, to really do their work because they are finally in control of their own operations. A middle manager is often the first to be aware that his or her boss's job does not require a full-time effort, leaving that boss too much time to meddle in subordinates' work.

In this chapter we shift attention away from headquarters staff and consider the other half of the downsizing equation: reducing the number of management layers in the corporate hierarchy. In doing so, we will examine several key issues:

1. How much does it cost to manage each employee?
2. What do managers actually do?
3. How many layers of supervision does a company need?
4. Is it possible to have too few layers?
5. How many people can one manager manage?
6. How can a manager's span of control be increased?

After reviewing these simple questions with difficult answers, we will look at several persistent problem areas. Companies seem to have chronic difficulties managing staff departments, keeping bureaucratic clutter out of their top management structures, and making matrix arrangements work. Finally, we will consider how management needs to structure itself when its primary goal is nurturing innovation.

What Does It Cost to Manage Someone?

It is very surprising that many companies with elaborate cost-accounting systems have no idea how much they spend managing each dollar of their employee payroll. Businesses with labor records that identify to the penny the labor component of each product's manufacturing costs cannot even closely estimate what it costs them to supervise their headquarters staff or first line of management. While moving an industrial engineer into an executive suite may be inappropriate on a regular basis, having at least an approximation of these costs can be useful in planning organizational streamlining.

The technique of activity cost measurement described in Chapter 4 can shed light on these issues. In addition to identifying misplaced staff work, the analysis can be used to calculate the actual cost of management in each department. This calculation permits comparison of management costs among divisions or departments in a company. It also provides a basis for comparing management productivity among companies within an industry, though as with staff ratios, these are only rough indicators. One study comparing various companies' activity costs found that, on average, insurance companies pay 55¢ in management salaries for every dollar of nonmanagement pay. Banks are just about as costly, while manufacturers, who tend to have more experience managing productivity improvement, average only 23¢ in management expense per dollar of worker cost.

The real payoff to analyzing the cost of managing payroll dollars is to see how much money can be saved if managers' spans of control are increased. One petroleum company averaged 33¢ to manage each $1 paid to its employees. It did this through an organizational structure that had, on average, 1 manager for every 5.8 workers. If this business were to improve the span of control so that each manager had seven direct reports, the potential savings would be $25 million each year. Researchers who have examined the costs of managing employees in a variety of industries have found that companies with average spans of three reports spend almost four times as much to manage each payroll dollar as do firms with average spans of eight.

Measuring the average cost of managing an employee is more difficult than simply dividing the manager's salary and benefits by the number of direct reports. That calculation assumes that 100 percent of the manager's time goes toward managing. This is an assumption that many companies make— after all, "that's what we're paying him to do, aren't we?" But, as many subordinates know, a boss does not really need or use all of his or her time to manage. An activity cost analysis of where managers' time goes can be enlightening. It quantifies the time spent managing direct reports and the people reporting to those direct reports, as well as the time that goes to individual contributor tasks. Studies have identified some managers who spend less than half their time actually managing, while others spend almost as much time "managing" their subordinates' direct reports as they spend on the subordinates themselves. This last situation should call into question either the capabilities of those subordinates or the manager's sense of what his job really involves.

Jewell Westerman, a Vice President of Temple, Barker

& Sloane, Inc., and head of its organizational planning and design consulting practice, has studied the experience of many *Fortune* 500 companies that have engaged in corporate downsizing. Despite the considerable attention the issue has received since the beginning of this decade, Westerman concludes that "from all accounts, most American workers clearly are oversupervised and undermanaged." He claims that managers in U.S. companies spend anywhere from 35 to 40 percent of their time doing the same tasks that their subordinates do. According to Westerman, they spend an equal amount of their time on administrative tasks that add little value to their companies, leaving most managers with roughly 25 percent of their time to actually manage.

Identifying opportunities for net reductions in management positions is the primary objective of these company-wide analyses. Multilayered companies frequently have such "part-time managers." As we discussed in Chapter 1, corporate compensation systems often encourage the creation of part-manager, part-individual contributor jobs like these. Regardless of their cause, these jobs frequently mean that companies are paying management salaries for nonmanagement work. They suggest that opportunities be identified to reassign the nonmanagement work and increase the number of direct reports. Frequently, these "part-time" managers are people with relatively few subordinates. Sometimes this has resulted from earlier downsizing, which eliminated several subordinate jobs without considering the impact of their elimination on their boss. The adjustments in corporate pay systems, which will be reviewed in Chapter 9, may also reduce some of the pressures companies feel when they create these "part-time" managers in the first place.

What Do Managers Do?

We have considered the organizational consequences when too much of a manager's time is spent doing things other than managing. But what are these managers actually doing when they do management work?

If you ask this question of managers, the answer probably will be along the lines, "I'm, uh ah, responsible for many things. . . ." (then they start to list the responsibilities of their subordinates). Or they may say, "Well, I make sure that everything goes all right." True responses, but not very reflective. Unfortunately, many academic observers have not done much better. Few academics have had actual experience managing, and some of the categories they use to describe what a manager does are rather general: plans, organizes, controls, coordinates, motivates, and develops subordinates. In many companies, some of these tasks, such as planning, controlling, and coordinating, are responsibilities of nonmanagers. A few observers have come a little closer to reality when they call managers gamesmen, power balancers, or people who put souls in new machines.

But some of the most useful studies of managers are those made by people who closely examine their actual daily activities. One of these, Henry Mintzberg, spotted ten characteristics of management work:

1. Most managers, because of their formal position, must represent the company as a *figurehead*.
2. They devote considerable time to serving as a *liaison* with other managers and people outside the company, from whom they need both information and assistance.
3. They must be perceived as *leaders*, setting a direction for their subordinates' work and making sure they keep to it.
4. Through the contacts they make in the first three parts of their job, they *monitor information* about their business and what is happening to it.
5. They *disseminate information* to their reports and others in the company.
6. Some managers, formally or informally, serve as *spokespersons* representing the company to the outside world.
7. To varying degrees, managers serve as *entrepreneurs* to help initiate innovation and change.

8. Many managers are responsible for *handling distur-bances* that threaten the company's normal course.
9. At least within their area of responsibility, managers serve as the primary *resource allocators*.
10. Many managers *negotiate* with employees or outsiders on behalf of the company.

Doing these tasks requires individuals who are more active than analytical, more able to shift gears quickly from subject to subject rather than spend days on one activity, and probably more attuned to talking than writing. The nature of these tasks also implies that they will be done by relatively few people. There are limits to the number of entrepreneurs, resource allocators, and negotiators that a company can contain without going off in too many directions at once. There also are constraints on the number of coordinators, disseminators, and spokespersons, if the intention is to keep communications relatively free of distortion.

How Many Management Layers Are Necessary?

Peter Drucker noted that each additional management layer in a company tends to cut in half the possibility that information is correctly transmitted, while it doubles the "noise." He observed that management levels are links in a chain. Each may add some strength, but all are additional sources of inertia, friction, and slack.

Why is information distortion such a critical issue? Cannot the problem be solved by putting computers on executives' desks which are tapped into central data bases? Not when you consider some of the types of information managers value most. Their information is not so much the spreadsheet records of past performance, but the "softer" indications of what future results will be. This information, often qualitative, gives the executive a way to calibrate the likelihood of business forecasts coming true. How confident does the sales manager seem about his forecast? What things are *just starting* to bother the customers? What novel uses are they making of a company's products that the market planners never anticipated? Is morale in an old plant high enough to justify optimism about the results of next week's union election, or should higher wage costs be budgeted?

This kind of information is usually communicated verbally and visually. It is the stuff many managers thrive on. This information has a great deal of difficulty working its way up a long chain of command, just as instructions about a shift in strategic direction have a long way to go in some companies before they reach the key employees on the front line.

Too often on visits to factories or sales offices, chief executives are amazed to see what they thought were clear statements of new company policy being totally, but not necessarily maliciously, ignored. They may find toxic chemicals still being discharged into nearby rivers, or Blacks and women kept from mainstream management jobs. Some are as surprised as John F. Kennedy was when, in the middle of the Cuban Missile Crisis, he found that outmoded rockets in Turkey he had ordered removed long ago were still there being used as an excuse by the Soviet Union for its arms buildup in Cuba. These executives often become very angry, as was Kennedy, at their subordinates, but they seldom blame the real culprit: the elongated organizational structure.

When managers pass orders on to their subordinates they usually accompany them with *their* explanation of why the changes are necessary, along with some qualifiers or amendments. What happens several layers down is that the original directive has been distorted and the accumulated qualifiers and explanations have taken on a life of their own. When a subordinate hears two messages—the official policy from "on high" and his immediate boss's interpretation of it—which message is most likely to be acted on?

Some executives try to skirt these problems by using expensive communications campaigns to carry their messages directly to each employee. Some use elaborate videotape systems; others regularly speak over the factory's public address system. A few have even taken to public radio or television commercials—not to sell products, but to convince employees listening at home that something major has changed back at the office. These efforts, sometimes of heroic proportions, are expensive. They usually require extensive headquarters staff support, and at best they only get around the real problem.

The real problem is more than just too many managers. Reducing the management head count without modifying the organizational structure may save money in the short run, but it will not necessarily improve a company's effectiveness. Improving effectiveness requires addressing the number of levels in the company. This is a lesson many *Fortune* 500 companies have learned. A Michigan State University management professor, Eugene Jennings, noted that since 1980, 89 of the 100 largest U.S. businesses have reduced their number of management layers.

But how many layers can be removed? How short can a company's hierarchy be? If the idea is to eliminate corporate bureaucracy, how can the bureaucracy be identified?

Herbert Rees, president of Eastman Kodak's internal ventures subsidiary, defines bureaucracy as the layer or layers of management between those with decision-making authority on a project and the highest level of the person working full time on it. This may be a useful working definition for those concerned with managing innovation. But for those in more steady state businesses, the example of the Roman Catholic Church suggests one outer limit for minimizing layers of authority. Church hierarchy places only one level of authority between the pope and the parish priest: the bishops. And the pope himself does double duty as the Bishop of Rome. Of course, most companies lack the church's sense of mission and impose less severe entry requirements on new recruits. And the pope has a strong headquarters staff organization and makes considerable use of committees and task forces to help with his management responsibilities.

In the secular world, People Express was able to successfully challenge—for a time—the giants of its industry by having only four levels of management. However, as we will consider in the next section, very lean structures seem capable of supporting only very lean business strategies.

Another way to get a fix on how many layers are appropriate to an organization is to examine a company's competitors. For example, at the time of the Bell System breakup, American Telephone and Telegraph faced companies like five-tiered Executone and six- to seven-leveled Rolm with an army of managers arranged in a ten- or eleven-deck hierarchy. These comparisons are a form of management benchmarking and can be a useful supplement to the similar technique described in Chapter 4 to help judge staff size. It can raise a warning flag when the difference is significant, but it still does not provide a precise norm that takes into account all the characteristics of an individual business. And it is not very helpful if a company's competitors are also bloated with management layers.

This is an area into which few management scholars have ventured. Some who espouse the contingency ("it all depends") school of management observe that tall, many-layered structures are more common among mature companies in relatively stable businesses, while short and flat structures are more prevalent among companies operating in more turbulent markets. One theoretician, though, has gone further than most in analyzing structure and layers. He is Elliott Jaques, a sociology professor based in England, with a Ph.D. from Harvard and an M.D. from Johns Hopkins. Jaques maintains that even the largest worldwide corporation can be managed with no more than *seven* managerial levels, including shop-floor supervision and chief executive. Smaller businesses require correspondingly fewer levels.

Jaques has studied organizational structures, from those of ancient China and Greece to those in modern multinationals. He noticed that almost all took on a pyramid shape, and he believes that this form reflects the distribution of human capacity in large groups of people. If everyone had similar work capacities, organizational structures would tend to be very flat. If only a small part of a population had low capacities, with the rest ranking very high, then most structures would be shaped like inverted pyramids.

His use of the word *capacity* is not intended to be confused with intelligence or what achievement tests try to measure. Instead, Jaques is referring to what he calls an individual's "time-span of discretion." This time span is the maximum period which a person is given to use his good sense, knowledge, experience, and skills to finish an assigned task. While he believes people have differing potential abilities to function at greater time spans, a person's time span at work is implied by *the kind of work his boss gives him.* Jaques feels that companies have recognized this phenomenon through their pyramidal organizations. But where he feels many companies have gone wrong is in how they have tried to break time spans into too many subdivisions by compartmentalizing assignments and degrees of authority.

What breakdowns are appropriate? To answer this, Jaques dissected hundreds and hundreds of assignments given by managers in countries throughout the world. In trying to identify target completion times—a task many bosses themselves are a little hazy about—he asked many questions about what the subordinates were expected to accomplish. Then for each of these he teased out the answer to "how long are you giving them to do it?" The results of these studies surprised him.

Jaques found that there were fairly clean breaks between the time ranges most subordinates were given to complete an assignment: up to 3 months of discretion, 3 to 12 months, 1 to 2 years, 2 to 5 years, 5 to 10 years, 10 to 20 years, and 20 years and more.

Most employees are in jobs with tasks that fit into the first of these seven categories. They have anywhere from a few minutes to up to 3 months until their projects must be completed and evaluated. First-line managers tend to have work that fits into the 3-months-to-a-year slot, while second-level managers range from 1 to 2 years. In his studies, the discretion allowed general managers with profit-loss responsibilities ranged from 2 to 5 years, with more senior executives involved in tasks that took even longer to bring to a conclusion. Jaques' data were less complete at the upper end of this spectrum, where he suggests that managers in his eighth tier are implementing 20-year strategies. Several executives, such as IBM's Thomas Watson, Sr., and Konosuke Matsushita, founder of the Japanese company that manufactures Panasonic and Quasar products, seem easily to fit this level.

Businesses may also be classified using these categories. A one-person show (a door-to-door salesman or painter) fits the up-to-3-months span. A second-level enterprise might be a small store with an owner-manager and several assistants. The 1-to-2-year span may be adequate for an organization of several dozen to several hundred employees, since it implies the existence of a middle-management tier with a 3-to-12-month span of discretion.

A fourth-rank organization might be a small stand-alone company with several functional managers reporting to the chief executive, and the managers would have two levels of management below them. This structure might also be appropriate for a division of a larger enterprise.

The next level of hierarchy (a company with its leader having responsibilities that cover a 5-to-10-year time horizon) could accommodate up to 6,000 employees, Jaques says. Next are organizations like holding companies that involve spans of over 10 years for their chief executives. This strategic horizon also characterizes the structure of some giant corporations. He feels that these can include 20,000 or more employees within a six-level management hierarchy, 10 to 20 divisions, and a group headquarters of less than 100 people.

Finally, Jaques maintains that a company with an additional management layer should be able to employ hundreds of thousands of workers, assuming that the other levels are appropriately organized and that managers are given full rein over tasks within their respective time horizons. This seven-level structure should be able to accommodate most of the world's businesses, as well as its public agencies.

While Jaques has advanced a number of psychological explanations for the existence of these categories and time spans, what he observed about the implications for managers is more interesting.

One of his findings was what happens when managers are perceived by their subordinates as "straw bosses," in other words, when those being supervised feel their immediate managers have only limited ability to make decisions about them or their work. They look to their boss's boss as their "real" manager. These situations are common in many companies, and usually indicate too many layers of supervision. In most of these cases the straw bosses occupy the same time-span level as their subordinates. There is not sufficient variation in the degrees of discretion for them to function as real managers of these people.

While Jaques has been conducting research along these lines for decades, his work has only recently started to be noticed in this country. The U.S. Army has hired Jaques to help them rethink their chain of command, perhaps to avoid repeating the mistakes described in Chapter 1. In addition to examining organizational structure, Jaques has strong views about the inappropriateness of most pay and job evaluation systems. Possibly the controversy surrounding these ideas has limited the exposure of his other, more applicable theories.

Jaques' ideas have not been given the attention they deserve by American managers. They should at least provide this challenge to organizational planners: If a company has more levels than the time-span theory implies are needed, it should be possible to specify the value added to the business by each additional layer. Determining how many levels are needed is a process of triangulation. One reference point is the current situation, another is the competitors' structures, and a third is Jaques' theory.

Is It Possible to Have Too Few Layers?

In view of the strong interest many companies have in operating with a lean management, it is important to point out that it is possible to have too few organizational layers. What is right for Merrill Lynch, Prudential, and Sears may be wrong for another business. The problems of People Express, Hewlett-Packard, and 3M illustrate the difficulties that can emerge.

People Express, a pioneer low-cost, low-price air carrier that has now folded into Texas Air Corporation, received widespread acclaim for its innovative management structure. People Express hoped to eliminate the customary split between workers and managers by making all employees managers. The conflicts that traditionally emerge between staff and line were dealt with by dividing the work so that the same group of individuals performed both tasks.

At a time when established competitors such as American, Eastern, and TWA operated with seven to eight levels of management between chief executives and pilots or passenger agents, People Express had only four. This was less management hierarchy than what the traditionally cost-conscious Northwest Airlines (six layers) or some of the other carriers spawned by deregulation, such as Air 1 (six layers) or New York Air (seven layers), employed.

The keys to People Express's lean structure were as follows:

□ *Relying on extensive employee self-management.* New recruits were selected on the basis of their potential for individual initiative, tempered by an ability to work well in team settings. Job candidates showing a need for close supervision and a desire to work in structured surroundings were screened out. Each recruit was given the title of manager, indoctrinated well in People Express's operating philosophy, and required to purchase stock in the company to feel more like an owner than an employee.

□ *Minimizing the number of job categories.* Aside from the activities of about 20 senior managers, most of the airline's work was divided into three categories: flight management, maintenance management, and customer service management. Flight managers did the work traditionally expected of pilots plus, on a rotation basis, many of the headquarters staff jobs of weather forecasting, schedule preparation, and planning for new routes. Maintenance managers kept the planes flying, and customer service managers did everything else. "Everything else" included staffing the departure gates, selling tickets and beverages during flights, and handling much of the paperwork on the ground. Work that did not fit these categories, such as baggage handling and telephone reservations, was contracted out.

    □ *Sharing the "big picture" with all employees.* This was done through an extensive communications program, aimed at the airline's employee-owners, and through cross-functional skills training. The training helped people appreciate the demands that other employees made of them so they could do their jobs properly; training also made it possible to move the work force around easily so as to quickly respond to business changes.

In the early 1980s, these practices and others were hailed as examples of how the company of the future would be managed. They were even documented in a Harvard Business School case study. Low fares and frequent schedules helped fill the planes, and People Express set off on an ambitious route expansion and acquisition campaign. The carrier soon flew across the country and then to Europe.

But, as one newspaper account of its just-before-bankruptcy purchase by Texas Air noted, "success doomed People Express." Its competitors, already experienced in managing nationwide operations, imitated its prices but not its organizational structure. They lowered costs through threats of bankruptcy, union givebacks, and low wages for new hires. In addition to these rebounded competitors, People Express's expansion helped do it in, organizationally and financially. People Express went so deeply into debt to finance the expansion that annual interest payments exceeded $60 million—far more than its yearly operating revenue. And it found that its unique, minimally layered management structure worked far better for a medium-sized airline than a large one.

Rapid expansion for People Express meant rapid influxes of new hires, more than could be thoroughly socialized into the airline's ways. The company became less homogeneous and more difficult to run by philosophy instead of direct supervision. And as the competition became more sophisticated in its responses, People Express's staff generalists were not able to do as good a job analyzing profit yields and allotting capacity to new routes as were its rivals' full-time specialists. One securities analyst commented: "They organized themselves with a very lean organization with no fat in it, but not much muscle either." He stressed that there are some important staff functions that just *must* be performed. While People Express did attempt to expand its management structure, the changes took place well after it had implemented its high-growth strategy. This upsized strategy was foiled by a severely downsized organization.

An overly lean organizational structure is a problem that has plagued *Fortune* 500 companies as well, including some most admired for their management innovativeness. Both 3M and Hewlett-Packard have faced—and addressed—problems of missing management layers.

3M is famous for its ability to turn homemade inventions into quick profits. But as many of its markets have matured and copycat versions of its products have appeared more quickly, the company's formula for making money became more dependent on concentrated marketing efforts than on rapid product development. Also, its office customers were increasingly interested in buying complex, integrated systems, not virtuoso stand-alone devices. Responding to these demands required a reorganization of 3M's operating units. Previously, 3M based its organization on the concept of small, semiautonomous, product-oriented divisions. These groups gave 3M much of its earlier entrepreneurial energy and style, but at a cost of loose coordination and communication.

Hewlett-Packard faced similar problems. Its historical decentralized management philosophy assigned the design and building of products to small divisions, but it gave responsibility for their sale to other decentralized marketing units. The result, as described by the head of one of their customer associations, was "three or four companies that don't seem to talk to each other." Products overlapped, important new markets were approached on a piecemeal basis, and technologies developed in one division were sometimes slow to migrate to other divisions. Push came to shove when HP needed to build unified computer systems to compete with IBM and other more integrated manufacturers. It then became apparent how its loose organizational design could work against developing families of products.

Both companies realized the necessity for change but were very concerned about keeping the spirit of entrepreneurship alive by simulating a small company environment. 3M first tried to use a task force on office systems to coordinate across division lines. HP initially designated an executive as "program manager" with broad authority to tap whatever divisions were necessary to provide equipment or software for a new computer line. But these half-steps met with limited success.

HP turned to regrouping its dozens of product divisions under sectors that were focused on markets rather than product types. A second management layer was created when the position of chief operating officer was established, and a centralized sales force was based in a new corporate market division. 3M made similar moves. A sector organization was set up putting their ten business groups (each with three to six small divisions) into one of four new sectors. This allowed the span of control of top executives to be cut in half, freeing them to concentrate on 3M's long-term strategies.

These moves were made very cautiously by each top management. 3M involved many managers in task forces to plan the details of the reorganization, and HP has used employee surveys and communications programs to ensure that top management and workers are not overly distanced from each other because of the new layers.

We have recalled the experiences of these three companies to emphasize how minimizing the number of management layers is not the right prescription for every situation. The popularity of operating lean and mean should not cause companies to downsize when they need to expand. The starting point of an effective streamlining effort must be the strategic plan. Both 3M and HP took theirs into account before tampering with organizational structures that had received wide acclaim. At People Express, unfortunately, an admirably lean structure could not keep pace with an expansive business strategy. Perhaps all the favorable publicity it received for its slim structure made it harder to modify the organization. In spite of the airline's problems, the People Express innovations are still worthy of consideration. They suggest ways to minimize bureaucracy when economic considerations indicate that a smaller-scale operation would be most successful. They also indicate just how sharply management hierarchy can be pruned. In Chapter 8 we will return to the issue of what recently slimmed down companies must do to operate safely with fewer layers and staff units.

How Many People Can One Manager Manage?

Flattening the pyramid means reducing the total number of managers and broadening the span of control for those remaining; that is, having each remaining manager supervise more people than before. This action raises the classic question: how many people can one individual directly oversee? As with management layers, there is no one answer that works for every company. Figure 6.1 illustrates the dilemma. Having too few direct reports wastes expensive management talent and can excessively narrow the scope of the subordinates' jobs. Having too many direct reports runs the risk of ineffectiveness by overburdening the manager and leaving the subordinates directionless and uncontrolled.

Many management theoreticians and practitioners have tried to specify an optimum point. It was also of concern to nineteenth-century militarists. Napoleon felt that 5 reports was the greatest desirable span; Karl von Clausewitz, advisor to the Prussian army, maintained that 10 was more appropriate, perhaps based on a view that German soldiers were more disciplined than their French counterparts. Henri Fayol, a French

Figure 6.1. The "optimum" span of control.

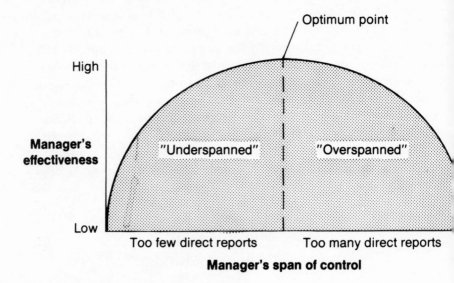

manager and early management consultant, was more flexible in his judgments. He suggested 15 direct reports for lower-level supervisors but only 4 for senior executives.

Other management observers have tried to suggest a more theoretical basis for these seat-of-the-pants judgments. Some have referred to studies which indicate that, on average, a human's span of attention is limited to six or seven things at once. For this they have reasoned that managers should not be responsible for keeping track of more than that number of direct subordinates. The most quoted of these—Englishman Lydal Urwick, who combined military and management backgrounds—stated as a principle of management that no supervisor can directly supervise more than five or, at most, six people who report to him or her and who work with each other as well.

Sears, Roebuck and Company, in either ignorance or disregard of these theoreticians, managed the post-World War II growth spurt with its headquarters merchandising vice president having 44 senior managers reporting directly to him. Their store managers each also coped, somehow, with supervising about 40 department heads.

More recently, academics have tended to favor the Sears model. As Theory Y and participative management have gained favor, the importance of organizational structure has been deemphasized. Ironically, in the 1960s and 70s, just as organization observers seemed to lose interest in classical issues like spans of control, many American companies went on the binge of adding managers and layers described in Chapter 1. Only recently have they started to shed these.

Despite these many years of pendulum swinging, the most honest answer to the question "how many people can one manager manage?" is the not so helpful: it all depends. But depends on what? This is an issue for which research and consulting experience can be more helpful. There are a series of factors which characterize a manager, his or her subordinates, the work they do, and the organizational setting in which they operate. These factors can serve as a yardstick in helping evaluate *each* managerial situation. This last point is the significant one; each manager's situation must be evaluated individually. While there are across-the-board actions a company can take to broaden its spans of control (such as investing in a computerized information network), determining the exact number of new reports each manager can cope with must be done on a one- by-one basis. The following are twelve of the more important factors involved in such judgments.

Nature of the Work Being Done

What exactly are the subordinates doing? Is the activity simple and mechanical or complex and creative? How critical are their jobs to the overall well-being of the company? How routine are the responsibilities? How many of them are being handled by the subordinates for the first time? By anyone for the first time? What is the time frame involved? Does the cycle of a typical assignment from start to finish last a day or a year? This comes back to Elliott Jaques' key concern: what is the maximum time a subordinate continues to exercise discretion without his or her results being reviewed by an overseer?

How Interdependent the Subordinates Are

The principle is simple. The more closely related the work of one subordinate is to another, the more likely their manager will be involved in coordinating work flow and in integrating the work products. The more a manager is actively doing these things, the fewer subordinates he or she can manage easily. The opposite also holds true. To the extent that a subordinate's work is relatively self-contained and can be done independently of the manager's other direct reports, the less of an integrating role the manager needs to play and the more subordinates can directly report to that manager.

Peter Drucker expressed this idea well when he commented that the real issue is not how many people report to a manager, but how many of them *who have to work with each other* report to a manager. An academic observer of organizations, James Thompson, has elaborated on this concept by characterizing three possible types of interdependence among bosses and subordinates. Each implies a different span of control, as shown in Figure 6.2.

□ *Pooled efforts.* In this arrangement, the work of each subordinate is relatively independent of that of the others. They rely on their shared manager to set a general direction for their efforts and to provide the pool of budgetary and other resources they need. This arrangement is common in staff units in which an executive may oversee the work of many specialist departments in unrelated fields (such as legal, personnel, and public relations). The executive may still be kept very busy making sure each of these departments is serving the best needs of the company as a whole, but this is a task that is more easily delegated than that of internal coordination.

□ *Sequential efforts.* In this arrangement, the output of one subordinate is the input of another. Here the situation creates greater likelihood that the manager will become involved

Figure 6.2.   Types of interdependence between manager and
direct reports.

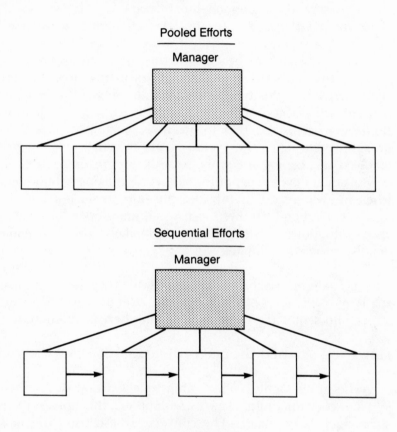

in coordinating, scheduling, and resolving conflicts among subordinates. This is typical of offices that have some of the characteristics of an assembly-line operation.

□ *Reciprocal efforts.*   In this arrangement, the work of one group becomes the input of a second, and the second's output circles back to become further input to the work of the first group. Some complex manufacturing processes are characterized by this type of interaction. So are the relations between a product design group and a marketing group when they are working together to produce an innovative product breakthrough. Then the overall manager may become deeply involved in keeping the work steadily progressing. Often in new product development this manager is the one to announce when innovating time is up and the time to start selling the product is at hand. In these reciprocal, interdependent supervisory situations the manager is most likely forced into the details of the subordinates' work.

In general, reciprocal situations tend to favor narrow spans of control. Pooled efforts can tolerate relatively wide spans, and sequential work stands somewhere in the middle.

How Well Trained the Subordinates Are

The more highly skilled subordinates are at doing their jobs and coordinating their work with others, the more of them a manager can manage. The converse is also true. In many large corporations, the work of a manager's subordinate will also be management. Spans of some upper middle-managers are narrower than the work itself seems to dictate because they are compensating for some of their direct reports' deficiencies by supervising those reports' subordinates.

How Well Trained and Capable the Manager Is

The more a manager is still learning the ropes or is basically a better individual contributor than manager, the fewer direct reports he or she can safely handle. Management expert Arch Patton has been concerned for many years that the most able managers have been attracted to staff work rather than line management. He feels that if better skilled people held line jobs, fewer staff positions would be needed and the span of control of line managers could be broadened.

Manager's Tenure

It also seems reasonable that the longer a manager stays put, the more likely he or she will develop ways to deal effectively with the current span of control. Over time, this "learning curve" effect should permit long-tenured managers to gradually increase their number of direct reports. Unfortunately, many companies move managers too frequently for this effect to take hold. In 1985, the average U.S. corporate manager stayed put for only 4.5 years.

Subordinate Turnover

The more rapidly the positions reporting to a manager turn over, the more time is needed to orient and train newcomers, and the less time is available for the manager to handle a broad span of control. The longer the tenure of a manager's subordinates, the greater the likelihood that trust and understanding of each other's needs and capabilities will make the supervisory job less difficult. As with managers, high employee turnover is a problem in many businesses. The average U.S. employee moved from one job to another at least every four years, according to a 1985 study.

Subordinate Rotation

One type of subordinate turnover facilitates broader spans of control. This involves an organized system of lateral rotation, in which subordinate A may swap jobs with subordinates B, C, D, and so on. These moves must be made carefully to avoid management by musical chairs. The switches cannot be done too frequently, and their success often depends on the investment made in cross-training and career planning. But job rotation can have a downsizing payoff by increasing each subordinate's understanding of the other's work, and thus allowing informal coordination and mutual accommodation to replace some direction and conflict resolving usually done by the manager. When the nature of the work requires sequential or reciprocal efforts, well-planned rotations can counteract the tendency of this kind of work to necessitate relatively narrow spans.

Strength of Lateral Communication Channels

The faster and more accurately that information can flow horizontally in a company or department, the less it needs to move up and down. A lot of important management time is spent "bee buzzing": learning something useful from subordinate A and telling it to subordinate B. As long as the manager maintains some way of staying informed about the critical activities of his or her people, it is usually more efficient for B to learn directly from A. Subordinate job rotation helps increase this kind of interaction; so can well-placed coffee machines and offices with partitions instead of walls. In general, one way to free managers to manage more people is to relieve them of the role of town crier.

Investment in Automated Information Systems

Unfortunately, creative architecture and coffee-pot placement cannot carry the entire burden of communication. In many situations, geography and information details require computer-based systems. To the extent these facilitate information exchange among subordinates, rather than only increase the level of detail their manager is exposed to, they can open possibilities for broader spans. Too frequently, however, the investment companies make in such systems serves to allow managers to second guess their staff better—in effect, to do their work rather than to increase management productivity. In the pre-computer era, a management theorist once advised that managers should be limited to "seven or so" subordinates because the traditional management tools of the time (yellow pads of paper and wall charts) would not allow them to cope with any more direct relationships and interrelationships. Maybe so, but computer and telecommunications networks provide tools with greater potential for control and communications.

Number of Performance Measures Needed

The fewer measures of performance a manager needs in order to know subordinates are on course, the more subordinates can be overseen. In some retail corporations it is possible for one executive to manage 20 to 25 individual store managers because a single number (profit contribution) can be calculated frequently (weekly) for each store. And in this business, this number is frequently the most critical indicator of good performance. These executives practice a form of corporate triage. They classify stores as exceeding profit targets, meeting them, or losing money. The first and last categories get most of the executive's attention, either through positive recognition or turnaround assistance. Most stores are in the middle group. In a de facto narrowing of the executive's span of control, the managerial needs of these stores are met primarily through several staff service groups.

The converse is also true: The more numbers or non-quantifiables that are needed to measure good performance, the fewer managers can be watched. This consideration often works in tandem with the investment made in information systems. The chief executive of one of Europe's largest retailers admitted he was comfortable giving his store managers a great deal of what appeared to them as operational autonomy, because the automated information system he had in place served as a safety net to allow headquarters to quickly spot weakened performance.

Use Made of Job Enrichment

Job enrichment (sometimes mislabeled "job enlargement") is the term given by industrial psychologist Frederick Herzberg to describe efforts made to consciously build self-motivating factors into the way jobs are designed. When a manager redesigns a subordinate's job with the hope of enriching it, ways are found for the subordinate to (1) assume more responsibility, (2) receive greater recognition for accomplishments, (3) feel that something concrete is being achieved, (4) develop skills and talents, and (5) feel advancement in the company will come as a result of strong performance.

While most managers intellectually agree that these factors are important, relatively few actively manage their subordinates in a way to make these abstractions concrete. Doing this usually involves more delegation on the part of the manager, which can set the stage for broader spans. Unenriched jobs (the ones most of us occupy) tend to involve fragmented work done by marginally motivated people. They seem to require relatively close supervision.

Existence of a Shared Culture

A corporation's culture is a control mechanism as much as it is anything. The existence of strong, widely shared values and beliefs, reinforced by common management practices and ways of relating to each other, can make a company more manageable: "We can get away with a lot of decentralization here; everybody thinks alike, anyway."

Everyone "thinking alike" is not something that happens by itself. Building a strong corporate culture requires a well-thought-out approach to recruitment and selection, investments in periodic employee training and retraining, consistent managers, and reinforcement by rewards and punishments. To the extent that such a shared culture exists among subordinates (and between manager and subordinates), it is more likely they will all know what to expect of each other. They will be more likely to trust each other ("because I know where he's coming from"). This allows some forms of explicit control—such as close supervision and staff police functions—to be replaced by implicit, trained-in controls. All of these factors open possibilities of operating with fewer managers and broader management spans. Mergers, restructurings, and executive turnover, unfortunately, limit a company's ability to build and maintain a stable culture. A strong culture often depends on the continuity of direction that a long-service chief executive can provide, but the average U.S. CEO in 1985 remained in place only four years.

Consider All the Factors

Taken alone, each of the factors discussed above is potentially a dangerous generalization. They have more validity when taken together. It is unwise to make span-of-control decisions based on only one, two, or three of these factors, because each proposition is true only to the extent that everything else is held constant. But in the real world nothing ever stays constant. Careful planning to broaden spans must start with a consideration of these factors together.

A potential 13th factor—the existence of an "assistant-to-the-manager" or some other form of increased staff support to help him oversee subordinates—has been deliberately omitted. While it is generally true that these supports can help a manager broaden a span of control, they also slow decision making, increase potential for confusion about who is really in charge, and add to costs. This is an issue in which tradeoffs have to be made. ITT's Harold Geneen justified his strong staff by saying it helped him eliminate layers of management and that the staff got him closer to actual facts instead of layers of managers' opinions. For an individual with his unique talents this might be true, but apparently at a cost of building a machine only one person could operate.

The previous chapters urged movement of some staff

functions to line managers. While this is a good way to down-size some headquarters units, too much migration of staff work can overburden line managers and limit their time for super-vising additional subordinates. As Figure 6.3 indicates, a bal-ance needs to be reached. The strategic approach to managing staff activities described in the previous chapter suggests dele-gating only staff work that is primarily service-providing and is relatively far along in its life cycle.

Too much staff-line interdependence can also narrow a manager's span. Having to work closely with several materials managers, staff design engineers, or accountants to get day-to-day work done adds the equivalent of one or several subordi-nates to a manager's roster. Downsizing the number and scope

Figure 6.3.   Delegating staff work to line managers.

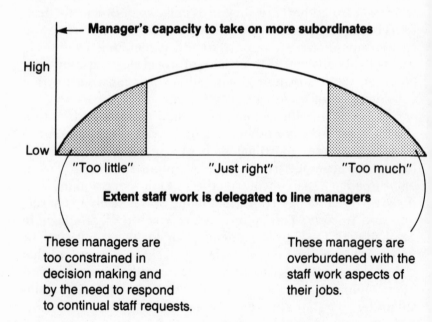

These managers are too constrained in decision making and by the need to respond to continual staff requests.

These managers are overburdened with the staff work aspects of their jobs.

of these units may allow a manager to oversee more direct reports.

How Can a Manager's Span of Control Be Increased?

The first step in flattening a company's pyramid is to closely examine the organization chart. Are there any obvious one-on-ones or one-on-twos that need immediate consideration? Examine the spans of control of all individual managers. Figure out the company's average span. Identify departments and managers that significantly exceed it. Ask whether the managers' capabilities or the nature of the work being done justify these spans. Are any managers overburdened? Identify underspanned managers. Ask why each is the way it is.

Then consider the factors just discussed. Which of them might be applied company wide to increase the overall average span? Look carefully at staff departments for examples of small spans. Consider some of the alternative ways to organize those departments, as discussed later in this chapter.

Also look carefully at the line or operating management structure. Two key reference points are a corporation's chief executive and its first tier of operating general managers with profit-and-loss responsibility (division heads in many companies). Then make sure there is a clear reason for each layer of management between the operating manager and the first-line supervisors. While many companies have reasonably broad spans in this part of their organization, it is still important to ensure these key managers do not have too much bureaucracy between them and their customers or employees. Then consider the number of layers between the division heads and the chief executive. Is value clearly added by other levels of general managers, group or sector heads, and subsidiary officers? This is where the pyramid narrows in many companies. Are there any powerful staff groups or formal committees that, in effect, add additional layers? Can their contributions be easily justified?

Then move from the organization chart to whatever data

have been collected about how managers spend their time. Consider converting part-time management positions to full-time ones by increasing the number of direct reports.

Any company-wide effort to broaden spans of control must eventually consider each manager's individual situation. This involves more than a quick redrawing of the organization chart. As these 12 factors suggest, there is no one appropriate span for every company. Many of the factors are people-specific, or they relate to the mission and nature of a department's work at a specific time. It is almost impossible to specify appropriate spans for every personnel department, auto manufacturing plant, or sales force. For one manager, 5 direct reports may be too many; for another, 12 may be too light a load. Data bases that purport to indicate the appropriate span for every quality-control department or accounts-payable unit can bury the truth in data averaging.

Too many companies have implemented span-broadening efforts without considering these factors and how they interact. The result is often solutions that either suboptimize (moving from three direct reports to five, when the manager and his or her situation could have accommodated eight or nine) or overextend the manager (who may be given what personally is an unsustainable load of seven others to supervise, when the complexity of their work and his or her inexperience as a manager suggested that five subordinates was more prudent).

To overcome these problems, use a template to evaluate each manager's situation, as shown in Figure 6.4. "Narrow span" on this chart refers to situations in which a manager has between 2 and 4 direct reports. "Wide span" refers to 9 to 12 reports and beyond. These numbers are only rough guides, especially at the wide end of the scale. The main point is to evaluate each boss-subordinate situation. The assessments first should help confirm the appropriateness of a manager's current span. Should the assessments suggest a broader span is possible, the template will indicate which factors in the company might make this possible. If the template suggests the current narrow span is most appropriate, it will identify what must be changed before a reorganization is feasible.

Figure 6.4.   Template for assessing a manager's span of control.

Favors narrow span (2-4) reports	Factor	Favors wide span (9+) reports
Complex and unique	1. Work done by subordinates	Simple and repetitive
Very interdependent (reciprocal efforts)	2. Subordinates' interdependence	Relatively independent (pooled efforts)
Minimal	3. Subordinates' training	Extensive
Minimal	4. Manager's training	Extensive
Low	5. Manager's tenure	High
High	6. Subordinates' turnover	Low
Never	7. Subordinates' rotation	Well planned
Weak	8. Lateral communication channels	Strong
Low	9. Investment in information technology	High
Many	10. Number of performance measures	Few
Minimal	11. Use of job enrichment	Common
Weak or heterogenous	12. Corporate culture	Strong and homogenous

This approach is used by some consultants in their organizational planning assignments. It can also be done in-house. An internal planning team could consist of a human resources professional along with the manager of the person whose job is being examined. Individuals can also use this list of factors to suggest ways to improve their own situations.

While this template approach is reasonably comprehensive, some managers may find it helpful to add other factors (such as geography) to their analysis. They may find that their experience with other successful reorganizations indicates that some factors should be given more weight than others. But in general most will find that reducing management layers by broadening a manager's number of direct reports involves some, if not most, of the following actions:

1. Maximizing the number of full-time managers.
2. Reducing the complexity and uniqueness of the work they supervise.
3. Having subordinates able either to function independently of each other or to easily accommodate to each other without intervention from above.
4. Providing extensive training to both managers and subordinates.
5. Minimizing turnover.
6. Encouraging well-planned job exchanges among subordinates.
7. Establishing strong communication channels to enable subordinates to coordinate with each other.
8. Investing in automated information technology.
9. Using relatively few performance measures.
10. Enriching jobs.
11. Maintaining a relatively homogeneous corporate culture.

The tactics described above are relevant for many lower- and middle-management jobs. After underspanned managers are identified, these changes can facilitate their taking on more direct reports. This, in turn, will reduce the total number of managers needed, and choices must be made among those on board based on whose skills are strongest to cope with expanded management duties. For those judged best at individual contributor work, positions need to be found, or perhaps created, to take advantage of their talents. Using this redeployment of ex-managers, combined with limiting new management promotions, some companies have been able to make major changes in their organizational structure without firing anyone.

Obviously, these tactics may not be possible for all situations. The nature of the work may be unchangeable. Rotation may be out of the question for some employees. Turnover may be difficult to control. Building a homogeneous corporate culture takes many years. Setting up a microcomputer communications network may be too costly.

Changing any of these factors requires some investment. There is no free lunch. The issue to consider when planning such a reorganization is, what level of benefit is expected to result and will it justify the cost?

How Many Is Right? The Rule of Six

After all this discussion about contingency factors and the need to judge each company's structure and management's job individually, is there not a simple guideline that can help an executive at least start to evaluate his or her company? Looking back at theory and corporate experience, it seems that Elliott Jaques, Lydal Urwick, and Merrill Lynch and Company were on to something. Let us call it The Rule of Six. We suggest that any company with more than six layers between chief executive and first-line supervisor and/or fewer than six direct reports per manager may have too much management. Determining if it does or not will take more detailed examination along the lines suggested above. The Rule of Six is intended to set an outer limit. It is a wide screen. Just because it has not been violated does not imply a company is appropriately organized. Many small companies, or large ones operating in swiftly changing markets, will rapidly approach bankruptcy or severe loss of market share with six levels of hierarchy.

Major Problem Areas

There are several chronic problem areas where this approach to span stretching needs to be supplemented with some creative organizational redesign. This especially needs to be done when top management groups, headquarters staff organizations, matrix structures, and desire for innovation are considered.

As we considered earlier, downsizing staff units involves more than reducing head count. If only this is done, the result may be staff managers with fewer direct reports and more limited management responsibilities. Their management skills may be wasted unless their department's supervisory structure is reconfigured. Often, difficult problems arise when companies try to streamline staff departments. Determining how many senior executives are necessary and how they should be configured poses some special difficulties, however. Let's consider them first.

Top Management Clutter

Effectively organizing a top management team is more of an art than a science. The relevant issues are often more related to power, influence, and mutual trust than to the optimum coordination of the work flow. Jobs are determined more by individuals' capabilities and the needs of the moment than by written position specifications. Personnel selection often depends as much on interpersonal chemistry as on track record. For some individuals, a chief operating officer reporting one-on- one to a chief executive, with a part-time chairman and a decision-making management committee working somewhere in the background, can make all the sense in the world. But a different team of executives might find this structure cumbersome and unworkable.

Apart from personality and politics, there are some structural problems that have long plagued executive suites. These include:

1. Too much bureaucracy at the top.
2. An extra executive layer between the chief executive and operating management.
3. Line and staff coming together too high in the structure.

Several companies have found that decisions are made faster when the jobs of chief executive officer and chief operating officer are consolidated. Brunswick and Celanese both eliminated the latter job. Observers have even suggested that the Celanese president and chief operating officer voluntarily resigned because a reorganization gave more power to the operating divisions, in effect working him out of a job. At Brunswick, the group vice president positions were also eliminated and all division presidents were to report directly to the chief executive.

Crown Zellerbach went even further in its downsizing decentralization. Cutbacks at the top of the company left a great deal of power in the hands of 16 managers of large plants. They were given complete accountability for plant performance, with each manager controlling credit practices and labor policies as well as marketing and sales. This reorganization reduced overhead, lowering some plant breakeven points by 30 percent.

Two giant chemical companies have also streamlined their top management structures to allow them to move quickly in spite of their size. Du Pont's executive committee members, its most powerful management group, now each have direct management responsibility for individual business lines. Previously, many of them operated in more of an advisory capacity. Britain's Imperial Chemical Industries used a top-level reorganization to help restore it to profitability. A layer of senior executives was removed and the board's size was cut.

Use of multiple management committees was curtailed, and investment decisions that used to require months of deliberation are now made in days. This quickened response time reportedly allowed the company to finalize in one day its decision to purchase Beatrice's chemical division.

Finding a solution to the problem of the overburdened chief has caused problems of its own for a number of the companies that have tried it. Offices of the president, for a time a popular way to manage, are falling into disfavor in many businesses. About half the 50 major corporations that had chairmens' or presidents' offices ten years ago have eliminated them. Some of these were formal versions of previously useful "kitchen cabinets," but Harvard Business School professor Abraham Zaleznick describes many of these offices as "deserts." Harry Levinson, the management psychologist, has also been critical of these structures, which have sometimes taken on a life of their own, leaving the rest of the company adrift. He looks at them as devices to avoid or postpone formal designation of powers. Gimmicks for often political purposes, they have never worked well as executive tools, according to Levinson.

In some corporations, the most frustrating job is that of group or sector head. Originally a way to help top management oversee diverse technologies, products, and markets, this position is becoming less relevant as companies restructure and refocus their operations. One group executive complained that he was "little more than a high-priced courier between the chief executive and the operating units." These top managers continually walk a tightrope between allowing division heads entrepreneurial elbow room and being sufficiently informed and in control so as to keep their boss comfortable.

For corporations with too many divisions for one chief executive to oversee, the group position may be the only alternative. The issue then is how to maximize its usefulness while keeping it from becoming a second-tier headquarters. Most companies tend to place similar divisions together, sometimes giving the group executive a narrow span of control. It may be possible to broaden this span, and also increase the contribution of this extra layer, by grouping divisions by common strategic mission rather than by similar products or markets. This way all start-ups are under one executive, all businesses oriented toward niche marketing and manufacturing are under another, and all focused on aggressive market-share acquisition are under a third.

Top managements are sometimes cluttered because too many types of executives report to the same person. Operations that should have been coordinated at lower levels fill agendas in the executive suite. Some of this can be dealt with by better delegation and more cross-divisional task forces, but the most difficult problems involve coordinating staff and line executives. There are often significant status and salary differences between senior line executives responsible for $500 million divisions and officers who head the human resources, public affairs, or legal activities. But in many companies these people all report to the same person.

Several companies have adopted novel top-level reporting relations that slim down layers while forcing executives to closely coordinate with each other. Exxon's top management committee long combined line and staff responsibilities, giving each committee member some of each. For example, at one point the senior vice president who was in charge of watching over Esso Middle East also had company-wide responsibility for the legal, medical, and public affairs staffs. The senior vice president dealing with employee relations was also concerned with Esso Inter-America and Exxon's mining and minerals businesses.

Alfred "Freddie" Heineken keeps his worldwide brewing businesses tightly coordinated by giving his three principal deputies charge of staff functions that are vital to the success of each other's line operations. Each deputy is responsible for results in a major geographic area of the world as well as for some worldwide staff functions. So, while one person must sell as much beer as possible in the Western Hemisphere, he must deal with someone equally concerned with sales in a different geographic territory because that person has charge of marketing and advertising. Clark Equipment Company has set up a system of four group vice presidents along these same lines as its way to prune back what even its chief executive called an overlayered company.

Figure 6.5 shows one combination of these responsibilities. Structures such as these require a close-functioning top team to work, but they can provide important payoffs in developing executive talent and unifying staff and line operations. They also help develop and test successors for the chief executive's job. When redesigning top management structures, it is impor-

Figure 6.5. Using group executives to consolidate line and staff.

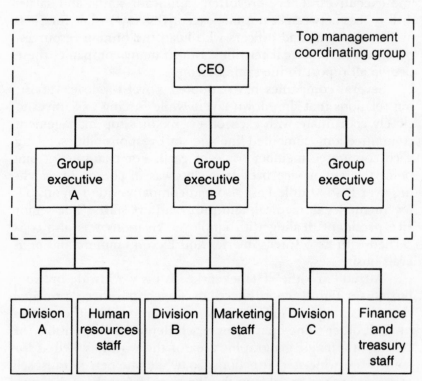

Note: In this simplified diagram, each of the three staff groups supports the work of each of the three divisions. Coordination is by mutual accommodation at the division executive level, with conflicts resolved by the top management coordinating group.

Source: Management Review, February 1984, p. 21. Used by permission.

tant to keep in mind that what is right for one company may be inappropriate for another. This is an issue that needs to be examined on a company-by-company basis.

Multiple Staff Layers

Staff functions have always been difficult for companies to organize and manage. To the extent that line managers are expected to be generalists, downsizing their number often means having those that remain do more of the same work. But staff work has tended to require specialists. Few compensation managers claim they can oversee a lawyer's work or supervise an environmental health group. Three persistent problems usually need to be addressed as companies streamline their staff hierarchies: (1) instances of layer on layer of similar staff groups, (2) part-time staff managers, and (3) excessive layers within staff departments.

The most glaring problem often creeps up on large, relatively mature companies who have gone through periods of significant growth. Their management structures frequently have four or more significant levels: headquarters, group or sector managements, divisions, and plants. In the worst case of multiple staff layers, each of these levels has fully developed staff departments that mirror those on higher and lower levels. The main work of at least one, and possibly two, of these levels is often to consolidate the work of its counterpart below. This is an expensive process with costs greater than just payroll duplication. As Peter Drucker has pointed out, layering such as this distorts communications, making it difficult to maintain consistent staff policies up and down the organization. Decision making is slowed as more experts get into the act, and overall lines of authority are confused as staff department heads must balance the demands of their line manager boss with the oversight requirements of their counterpart one layer above. Some companies try to deal with these difficulties through "dotted line" reporting or some combination of functional and administrative definitions of accountability, but these usually only add complexity to an already cluttered structure.

Other businesses, such as Harold Geneen's ITT, have tried to clear reporting channels by having all controllers report to headquarters, not to their immediate line manager. But this "solution" puts tremendous pressure on headquarters to do all the coordinating and takes away potentially useful support from the line managers.

Previously, we suggested that companies carefully question the need for sector or group management. They also need to be sure this questioning does not lead to the circular reasoning that justifies that level primarily because the staff units are there. These staff units are most likely to be redundant in companies in which it is possible to decentralize their functions.

Two approaches can be taken to deal with these layers on layers of staff. First, all operating responsibilities can be delegated to units at the plant or divisional levels. Then one level above these, either the group or corporate headquarters, *may* maintain a small policy-setting or monitoring function. In some well-managed companies this can be done by one person. There may be instances, when the group is the logical operating level, with no staff based at the divisional level. Second, a more radical delegation might involve selecting one of the four levels at which to base each staff responsibility, depending on the nature of the staff work. Staff responsibilities would then be taken away from the other three levels. Both these approaches have to be planned on company-by-company and staff-by-staff bases.

Though reducing staff layers is more troublesome than just redrawing the organization chart, a yet more difficult problem is the management of the remaining staff departments. Advancing significantly in the line or general management hierarchy usually requires demonstrated management skill. Geneen's abilities were more in the skilled use, rather than production of, staff work. However, the staff manager counterparts of many line managers tend to have less supervisory experience. They often are promoted to supervisory jobs to reward and recognize their contributions as skilled analysts and professionals. In many companies they are given management titles and salaries so they will be perceived by

their line management clients as of "equal" status. This bureaucratic practice is often ineffective and usually costly.

Many staff managers are expected to do staff work in
addition to overseeing it. Staff managers themselves are not
necessarily to blame for this situation. It is often determined by
the job evaluation methods and reinforced by the expectations
of senior executives. More than one vice president for human
resources has been expected to personally counsel a retiring
executive on how to handle his pension savings, although a
member of the compensation staff three levels down may be
just as able to handle this. Considerations of status too often
make this officer the "personnel rep" for the senior executive
group. Heads of information services units, in addition to running their expanding departments, are called upon to counsel
senior managers on personal computer purchases. The double-
pronged nature of these jobs makes it hard for their incumbents to work full time at management. And very frequently, the number of direct reports they and their subordinate
managers have is relatively low to accommodate these other
responsibilities.

This is an area in which companies can learn from the
experience of professional practices, such as large law and
architectural firms. Their partnership form of organization
allows a clear distinction between high status and management.
Frequently, they have a managing partner who is not necessarily the best lawyer or most talented architect or even the highest paid person in the firm. Decisions about the direction of the
practice are made collectively by the managing partner and the
senior practitioners. With some modification, this model could
be appropriate for some corporate staff departments. It would
allow the full-time department manager to have more direct
reports and less management hierarchy in the department.

Confusing Status with Management

Reducing the management hierarchy within staff departments is often a priority of downsizing projects. Staff groups
are frequently a company's worst offenders, with under-

spanned managers and unneeded layers of supervision. Some of this is because of their professional specialization and the corporate willingness to tolerate accountants' wanting supervision only from other accountants, and so on. But a lot of layering results from an approach to organization that confuses status with one's place in the company management hierarchy.

This is a very expensive form of confusion. Figure 6.6 illustrates the layered-organization structure of many head-

Figure 6.6. Typical narrow-span staff department.

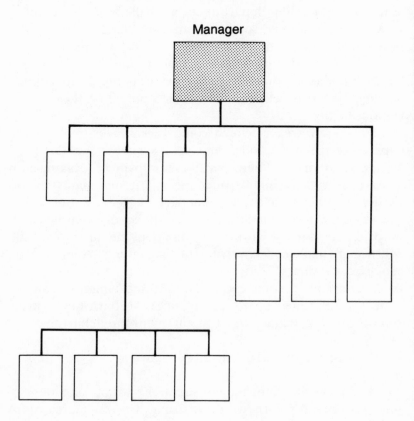

quarters staff departments. The same structural configuration applies in many computer services, engineering, finance, legal, planning, and research and development units.

In addition to multiple layers and small spans of control, a characteristic of this structure is that activities tend to become fragmented from one another. The boxes on the chart take on a meaning of their own, and over time they become barriers to easy communication and coordination. Because a hierarchy is implied, conflicts are resolved by using the chain of command. Work definitions tend to narrow. As individual work loads change, it becomes harder to balance manpower requirements across the subdepartment boundaries. Of course, vigilance on the part of the department head can keep much of this from happening, but most staff leaders have too much staff work of their own to do to also provide integration on a continuing basis.

We have already considered where these managers come from. What more streamlined alternatives are there? Figure 6.7 suggests one way out of these problems. It indicates a structure with fewer, all full-time management positions. Each has a span of control considerably wider than the part-time managers in Figure 6.6. Relative rank of staff professionals is indicated by their job titles and pay, and is shown on the chart by placing them at different levels. It is now possible to be a senior member of the department without having supervisory responsibilities.

In this streamlined alternative, work is done either by individual contributors or through teams. The team structure illustrated in Figure 6.8 interlinks the staff professionals as well as ensures that work is done by the minimum number of staff required. Some teams may be semipermanent for ongoing responsibilities; others may be set up to complete a one-time project. Some teams may have changing memberships as a task moves through different stages toward its completion. Keeping this system of project management working smoothly is a key responsibility of the department manager. The various types of teams offer a variety of leadership opportunities for department members.

In addition to its potential for cost savings by balancing

Figure 6.7.   Flatter alternative structure for a staff department.

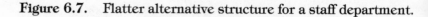
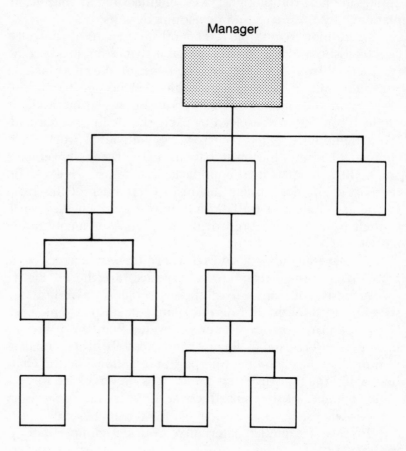

changing work loads, this structure allows department members to broaden the scope of their professional work outside of their subspecialties. This overlapping membership, if well orchestrated, can lead to better integrated staff products for the rest of the company. For example, the overlapping makes it easier to develop and maintain consistent human resource

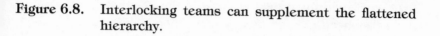

Figure 6.8. Interlocking teams can supplement the flattened hierarchy.

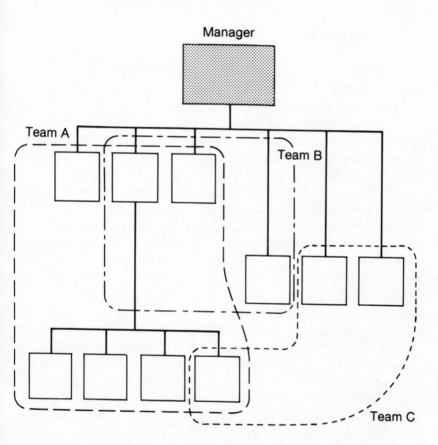

policies, since some staff people working on compensation and benefits may also contribute to the company's training policy.

Many companies have used a project-management approach to work that crosses traditional department lines, especially for technical development and introducing new products. But relatively few have tried this approach to organize work within individual staff units. Today's pressures to downsize headquarters staffs may encourage similar experiments as a way to improve productivity and effectiveness.

"Dematrixing"

Some corporations have adopted a project-oriented operation, but have kept the department and subdepartment structure in place as well. The matrix form of organization that this creates is an attempt to balance competing priorities: product-line development versus geographic expansion, keeping up to date in various technical specialties versus building a range of products. While the matrix structure received a lot of notice in the 1970s, many companies found that it created more trouble than it was worth. The layering of workers within many matrix structures added to corporate bloat. The multiple bosses this system implies created, in effect, a new layer of management that added to costs while slowing decision making.

At one point some Xerox executives felt that their efforts at new product development were strangled because of their matrix organization. Geography compounded the problems, with key design and manufacturing departments based in Rochester, New York, reporting to separate executives at Xerox's Stamford, Connecticut, headquarters. The matrix led to endless debates over design, and it did not designate any one executive the priority of getting the new products into the marketplace. At times, the only person who could resolve the conflict was the president.

While matrices can be a useful way station for a company on the path from one strategic orientation to another (most frequently when changing from a functional to a divisional organization), it is usually a poor permanent choice. By attempting to balance opposing strategic perspectives, it is not a viable way to decide how a company wants to compete and how it should organize. The conflicts inherent in two-boss systems can, over time, blunt a firm's strategic focus.

Two business-school professors who helped popularize

matrix organizations have also warned about their negative consequences. Stanley Davis of Boston University and Paul Lawrence of the Harvard Business School suggest that companies consider matrices only when nothing else works. Walter Wriston, former chairman of Citicorp—a bank that has made widespread use of global matrix structures—admits, "There are, indeed, easier ways to manage." The two Boston academics suggest using this structure only when these three conditions exist simultaneously: (1) tightly coordinated decision making is necessary in two or more of a company's most critical activities; (2) the work to be done is extremely complex and must be done amid conditions of great uncertainty; and (3) several resources vitally needed to do the work are extremely scarce. These conditions characterized the preparations for the first manned flight to the moon, but most business situations are less complex and intense.

Management consultants scan their clients' structures to identify opportunities for streamlining, and when they see a widespread use of matrices, they recognize that changes may be needed. Alternatives they frequently recommend include using the project-management approach described above, instituting policies that encourage resource sharing, and setting up small, self-contained divisions. Abolishing matrices is often recommended, too. When Xerox converted its copier business matrix to four strategic business units, it achieved a 10 percent productivity gain. Eventually, it was able to cut design time in half for some products.

Nurturing Innovation

The Janssen Pharmaceutical subsidiary of Johnson & Johnson is one of the most prolific drug discoverers in the world. Its Belgium-based president claims that one-eighth of its 2,400-person work force report directly to him—or at least think they do. While few near-billion-dollar businesses have executives with 300 direct reports, few can match Janssen's record for productive innovation. It is an example of Johnson

& Johnson's efforts to maintain an entrepreneurial atmosphere in a billion-dollar global corporation. By simulating a smaller company environment in many of its business units, it keeps on top of its rapidly changing consumer markets.

Other companies, such as Exxon in its attempt to build an office systems business, have found that trying to grow new enterprises in a hierarchy appropriate for a mature business is very difficult. Some companies have tried to get around this problem by setting up special units in which some of the standard operating procedures are suspended and hierarchy is kept at a minimum. Some, such as Lockheed with its famous skunkworks, keep these innovation-oriented ventures far from the headquarters. Others, such as Air Products and Chemicals, Allied Corporation's New Ventures Group, and the Swedish company ASEA's Innovation Unit, limit their management layers but keep activities close enough to home to allow easy transfer of the discoveries back to the parent.

Managing innovation offers special challenges to the downsizer. While many champions of innovation welcome the easier access to top management that layer reduction can bring, some also find that more visibility leads to greater expectations. They have fewer places to hide their "bootlegging" in radically streamlined operations. The successful new computer development documented in Tracy Kidder's *The Soul of a New Machine* duplicated an official project being conducted simultaneously at another Data General location. Vigorous cost cutting and elimination of all redundant activities might also have eliminated Data General's first 32-bit computer. To the extent that the downsizing is motivated by short-term cost considerations, these units may find far fewer dollars left for development projects. It is important for the innovator to consider the potential drawbacks of downsizing. While stripping away excess management can *potentially* make a company more hospitable to innovation, it will not happen just by changing the structure. And if the reductions involve major layoffs, the surviving managers may feel too insecure to deviate from the corporate norm.

The Bottom Line

This and the two previous chapters have reviewed a variety of ways to determine the optimum headquarters staff and managers to run a business. Options for restructuring and monitoring the size of an organization have been suggested. But what happens when excess staff or managers are discovered? The most frequent outcome is to remove them from the payroll. The next chapter considers how this is commonly done. And, mindful of the adverse consequences of demassing, it also considers a number of underused alternatives to layoffs.

Chapter 7

Layoffs and Alternatives to Layoffs

When some companies downsize, the cart seems to come before the horse. First they get rid of people, then they make some decisions about organizing those who remain. Only eventually, as they find their lean staff cannot do all the work that remains, do these businesses start to consider work priorities. Putting the downsizing sequence into its logical order was the subject of the last four chapters. Now it is time to face the most painful aspect of downsizing—deciding what to do with the managers and professionals whose jobs are declared "surplus."

Companies vary widely in the ways they deal with these surpluses. Consider accounts of the approaches taken by two Houston businesses, Tenneco and the Allied Bank of Texas.

At Tenneco, 1,200 employees were laid off over a six-week period. According to eyewitness accounts, many of them first found out they were no longer employed when armed guards appeared on their office floors early in the morning, along with boxes for them to use in clearing out their desks. The stunned workers were given 20 minutes to leave the building, and were watched by the guards as they packed up their belongings and emptied their lockers at the company gym. Those managers who had come to work in company cars or van pools were given coupons for taxi rides home.

Said one angry ex-employee to the *Houston Business Journal:* "This was at best an outrageous and unnecessary slaughter of human self-respect and dignity. . . .Tenneco obviously planned the day well in advance. More than 250 boxes were ordered and stockpiled for use by laid-off employees. The cab coupons also were purchased in advance. A line of cabs formed with amazing quickness around Tenneco's downtown headquarters to cart all the terminated employees away."

At the Allied Bank of Texas, department heads called divisional meetings, then read off the names of the employees to be laid off—in front of their coworkers. There was only a day's notice that there would be any layoffs at all. According to the *Journal,* the terminated employees were told to clear out their desks and leave that afternoon; they received no offers of outplacement or recommendations. Officers were given a month's salary, nonofficers two weeks' pay.

Said a laid-off manager: "Some of us had been with Allied for more than a decade. We understood the layoffs, but we didn't understand the way Allied went about implementing them. We were all stunned and disappointed."

Contrast the situations of those employees, and those of their "more fortunate" coworkers who remained employed, with those of Hewlett-Packard's work force as that company went through hard times in the 1970s:

In the early 1970s the entire electronics industry suffered a drop in orders, and most companies were laying off people in significant numbers. At Hewlett-Packard estimates indicated that it was necessary to cut back 10 percent in both output and payroll to match the decline in orders. In this company the obvious solution was to follow its competitors and lay off 10 percent of the work force. Top management, however, was committed to avoiding layoffs.

After considerable discussion, a novel solution surfaced. Management decided to require everyone from the president to the lowest paid employee to take a 10 percent cut in pay and to stay home every other Friday. By distributing the "pain" across organizational levels, Hewlett-Packard avoided both the human resources loss and the human costs associated with layoffs.

In 1974, pleased with the positive impact the layoff alternative had earlier, Hewlett-Packard used the same mechanism to cope with another business reduction. Credit for the company's committed work force, in a Silicon Valley of job hoppers, has to be attributed partly to practices such as these. A key part of Hewlett-Packard's business strategy is based on maintaining a strong corporate culture. Culture is something carried by people; high turnover makes it almost impossible to keep a consistent set of values and objectives that are followed up and down the ranks. A 10 percent layoff would have severely injured this culture; the increased voluntary turnover that most likely would have plagued the firm for years after the layoff would have impeded growth plans and added to overall personnel costs. It is unlikely the two Texas companies will, several years away from their sudden cutbacks, come out with a work force as committed to serving the company as Hewlett-Packard's.

Most companies approach downsizing implementation with tactics somewhere between these two examples. Unfortunately, few are as creative and far sighted as Hewlett-Packard. Fortunately, few employ the extreme measures that were used in Houston. Let us review the alternatives available, and consider which are appropriate when, keeping in mind that the more lead time there is, the more options are possible.

Push or Pull Strategies

Assuming an analysis indicates there are more managers or staff professionals than there is work they can usefully do, and there are no other ways they can contribute to the business, the customary reaction is to search for ways to remove these people from the payroll. There are two general means of doing this—either pushing or pulling them away.

"Push" strategies are the most direct. Whatever euphemisms are used, they involve firing employees. Even in demassing, these are often firings with cause—only the cause in this instance is an uncontrollable shift in a business situation. Sometimes the cause is employer neglect in letting the organization grow too big or allowing the market share to get too small.

Ideally, the selection of those to leave should be based on each individual's performance to date and consideration of what his or her potential can contribute to the leaner, downsized organization. In some cases, it also needs to be based on an assessment of how many good-performing, high-potential people the company can realistically support. These are always difficult judgments to make, and are made even more difficult when weak performance appraisal and career planning systems helped get the company into a sticky, overstaffed situation in the first place. These decisions also must take into account policies on the treatment of long-service, minority, female, veteran, disabled, and older employees, assuming the policies meet at least the minimum regulatory standards.

"Push" strategies can be targeted by individual, based on the above factors, or they can involve terminating relatively large numbers of employees (either across-the-board percentages of the work force or elimination of entire departments, plants, or divisions). Because it is often difficult to eliminate many full-time managers without also changing the organizational structure, these jobs are more likely cut back on a position-by-position basis. Staff professionals who function primarily as individual contributors are more susceptible to across-the-board reductions.

A "folk wisdom" about such cutbacks is that it is better to "get it all done at once as quickly as possible," so employee morale will rebound and workers will not become shell shocked from successive waves of terminations. The corollary is that "it's easier to cope with the problems that result from cutting too deeply than not cutting deeply enough." Though it is common to plan reductions with such thoughts, the wisdom on which they are based is open to question. Ideas like these have helped encourage demassing in situations where targeted downsizing would have made more sense.

It is often impossible to generalize about issues such as these; they need to be based on a careful reading of each company's situation. Improving morale usually requires that employees who are allowed to keep their jobs feel secure in them and confident in the company's leadership and direction. Single-blow cutbacks themselves will not provide this feeling. Successive waves of work-force reductions can be even more destructive, but they usually result from poor planning or unanticipated business adversity, not insensitivity to employee morale. Careful advance planning can eliminate excessive downsizing.

Limiting the human cost involved in firings is a responsibility companies must take on when they terminate employees. At a minimum, this usually involves adequate financial and benefits severance packages and outplacement assistance. Both must be provided in a way that preserves the dignity of those losing their jobs. Many companies do take this responsibility very seriously, partially out of a humanitarian concern for those laid off, partially to avoid censure from the communities in which they operate, and partially to help preserve the loyalty of those who remain. But this is an area where there is considerable room for improvement. Rod Willis, managing editor of *Management Review,* noted that "for every company that shows genuine concern, two show insensitivity in laying off employees." As was suggested in Chapter 2, consideration should also be given to the psychological needs of those charged with doing the firing and those who see themselves as the survivors.

Too few companies communicate clearly with their employees when downsizing programs are being planned. The Esmark takeover of Norton Simon was a rare exception. Donald Kelly, Esmark's chief executive, talked to the over 100 Norton Simon headquarters staff people immediately after the merger was finalized. He was direct and honest. He indicated that, as many had already anticipated, he was not going to need two holding-company staffs and that a number of them would have to leave. But he also said that he needed everyone's help for the next few months to implement the merger details. A generous severance plan was set up and some special performance bonuses were awarded to selected executives (who departed after several months) for their assistance in bringing the two companies together. The transition went much more smoothly than most megamergers, and while some employees from Norton Simon may not have been happy with the merger's impact on their careers, at least they knew where they stood. Ironically, Esmark was bought by Beatrice Companies shortly after this transition. Esmark executives initially were assured that there was room for everyone, then a short time later a number of them were fired.

"Pull" strategies produce less focused results, but are also less harsh. They generally involve offering, for a limited time, some inducement to all or to a subgroup of employees encouraging them to resign voluntarily. For older staff this includes early retirement offers, while employees further from that point in their careers may be offered a cash payment (or buyout) in exchange for leaving. Many thousands of managers and professionals have accepted these offers. For some they represent a chance to start a new career or get out of a dead-end one. For others, who felt their job security was weak, they may represent the lesser of two evils. Some employees may agree with Beebe Bourne, president of THinc., the oldest outplacement firm, who noted that "some of these packages have benefits that far outweigh staying with the company."

Among the most generous of these arrangements are the "5-5-4" early retirement plans. These plans add five years to the employee's current age and five years to the worker's service time to calculate the retirement benefits. They also add four weeks of pay for each year of service, and award this in a lump sum. Most programs are less remunerative, but few companies have had problems finding employees willing to accept them. Offering lump-sum buy-outs to those not eligible for retirement programs is also becoming common, although most companies rely on retirement efforts because these pull away the highest-paid managers, who are most likely to be in the way of others' advancement. Some companies adopted programs like the separation allowance that pays $35,000 to each Norfolk Southern locomotive engineer or fireman who voluntarily quits.

These "pull" strategies are sometimes linked with "push" approaches. The letter that invites a manager to consider early retirement or a buy-out may also warn of involuntary layoffs if the voluntary departure quotas are not met. Chevron and Exxon have taken the most evenhanded approach in this area; many employees who were terminated were given the same retirement benefits as those who accepted the voluntary offer. One chemical company took a different approach. It conducted a limited program of involuntary terminations at the same time that it offered early retirement to others. This was a stronger warning than the threats that appear in some retirement offers. One observer compared this to the practice of airline hijackers who kill a passenger or two at the outset, just to show they are serious. The chemical company, of course, intended nothing of the kind. It aimed the dismissals primarily at poor performers with limited seniority, assuming these people would not be eligible for the retirement offer. What happened, to their dismay, was that a mood of insecurity spread throughout the company, and far more employees accepted the early retirement than were budgeted for; morale was weakened for some time after.

Other companies have been surprised at the acceptance rates for their offers. Du Pont originally expected 6,500 employees to accept an early retirement option, but almost twice as many volunteered. While this heavy response rate enabled Du Pont to forego reductions it had expected to make later, it also lost employees it did not want to lose. A number of these employees had their retirements delayed or were brought back as consultants. These offers can lead to other surprising consequences, too. When a program similar to Du Pont's was offered to Manville Corporation employees, the takers included the company president.

Because this reduction strategy is such a blunt tool (companies are restricted in how finely they can target the offers), some companies have practiced subtle ways of letting staff know where they stand. According to William Morin, chairman of the largest U.S. outplacement business, "the inflection in your voice can show whether you want people to stay or leave — or the way you tilt your head." Some companies are more direct. American Motors helped avert some unwanted departures by avoiding buy-outs altogether and putting favored staff into the positions vacated by those it had previously fired. A New York company counseled a 55-year-old manager considering early retirement: "You will always have a job with us, but you'll have a position at a lower level, and you're already above that salary range now. So you can't expect you'll get any increases in salary between now and when you're 62."

These plans do produce results. Du Pont has used them to reduce its work force by 10 percent, Exxon by 15 percent of its U.S. staff. And their economics, at least in the short term, can be favorable. In the first quarter of 1985, Du Pont took a $125 million one-time charge against earnings to gain a $230 million recurring annual aftertax savings. Union Carbide, with a less generous plan, spent $70 million in up-front charges to obtain $250 million in annual savings afterward. One stock analyst and IBM watcher estimated that if 8,000 employees had accepted IBM's early retirement offer, a 40¢ per share earnings gain would result in the following year and a 50¢ per share increase in the years afterward. Another inducement encouraging businesses to consider this retirement cost strategy is the almost $100 billion surplus in overfunded U.S. corporate pension accounts.

Easing Pain: Lowering Costs

It is always easier to quantify short-term costs and benefits; numbers representing the long term are usually "softer." Often, long-term costs must be judged qualitatively and sometimes only in retrospect. This is certainly true when companies consider writing off many years of investment made in building the loyalty and skills of their human capital. Throughout this book we have been arguing for streamlined organizations, but also for doing that streamlining in ways that pinpoint problems, maximize long-term benefits, and lower costs to the individuals losing their jobs and the companies losing the employees.

In Chapter 2 we considered some of the visible costs, expected and unintended, of demassing. These costs were both human and economic, and they affected the ability of both the ex-employees and ex-employer to function effectively after cutbacks. One hidden cost, typically hard to quantify, is incurred when a business loses many of its managers and high-level staff professionals. Over the years, these people have acquired what economist Oliver Williamson calls company-specific skills. These are skills learned on the job, and they include the thousand and one things it takes to get something done well in a specific company environment (or corporate culture). The hardest of these skills to easily specify are those related to effective collaborative relationships that a manager builds up over time. These relationships allow things to get done quickly through personal trust, not bureaucratic procedure. Williamson maintains that when a manager with considerable company-specific talents leaves the firm, some productive ability is also lost. And, to make things worse, this is a loss to both company and employee, since the manager often will have no use for these talents in his or her next place of employment. When a new employee is eventually hired, he or she will have to be taught these skills, adding training costs that would not have been necessary if the old manager had stayed. This is not an argument for never losing any employee, but a reminder that turnover often brings overlooked costs with it.

The other skills that managers have are more portable. Such skills have to do with applying standard analytic techniques, running a personal computer, knowing the ins and outs of a particular industry, and the like. These talents, what Williamson calls firm-nonspecific skills, are purchasable in the labor market, though sometimes at a premium above what it costs a company to acquire these through training and executive development programs for those already hired. One danger present in the post-demassing work arena is that managers, feeling that job security is a notion of the past, may invest most of their efforts in acquiring transportable skills. To the extent that many of them ignore the need to develop company-specific talents, they will be less able to leverage their other talents. And their company's managerial effectiveness will be impaired. Considerations like these have influenced Hewlett-Packard and other cautious downsizers to give serious attention to ways of downsizing without layoffs.

Alternatives to Layoffs

The simplest way to reduce the cost and pain of downsizing is to develop options to layoffs, whether they be voluntary or forced. A number of options exist, and creative executives can certainly develop others. Some have been used extensively, but most are relatively underused. Just as layoffs are not always necessary, alternatives to them are not workable in every downsizing situation. As Figure 7.1 shows, the sensible approach depends on both the magnitude of the reduction and the amount of lead time.

Immediate Need for Action

For companies with the most acute problem—those that need to reduce payroll by 15 percent or more almost immediately—few options are available other than deep, across-the-board terminations. While businesses facing impending closure have limited options, relatively few downsizers are in need of such a drastic turnaround.

Businesses with an immediate economic threat, but one that does not require deep cuts, have more alternatives. To reduce head count (or, preferably the more useful indicator, total human resource costs) by percentages up to the low teens, the available tactics include:

1. Using "pull" offers, such as extensive voluntary buy-out or early retirement programs.

200

Figure 7.1.   Selecting an approach to downsizing.

	Less than 1 year	1-3 years	3 years+
15% +	Deep, across-the-board terminations.	Spin off business units. Series of early retirement or buy-out offers.	Close down business unit and redeploy employees. Diversification based on skills of surplus employees.
6-14%	Widespread early retirement or buy-out program. Bring subcontracted work back in-house. Pay reduction, job sharing, move to lower paying jobs.	Mobilizing the troops. Selective terminations. Retrain; redeploy. Retain; find jobs outside the company. Loan staff.	Managed attrition. Spin off staff departments.
1-5%	Selective terminations. Targeted early retirement or buy-out program.	Managed attrition. Convert staff to consultants. Market staff services outside the company.	Managed attrition (and many of the other options).
	Less than 1 year (responding to immediate economic threat)	1-3 years	3 years+

Time required for implementation

Note: Percentages indicate the approximate head-count or payroll reduction needed.

2. Bringing contracted-out work back inside the company.
3. Offering pay reductions and utilizing involuntary job-change strategies.

Pulling work done outside the company back into the house keeps otherwise surplus staff members busy, but its effectiveness depends, obviously, on how much has been contracted out and how quickly it can be brought back. It also depends a lot on the range of skills and flexibility of the work force. As companies in Japan have learned, this is a form of musical chairs that may help one company but has the net effect of making the labor surplus somebody else's problem.

Pay reduction, as a layoff alternative, has been practiced with some success by companies in the midwest Rust Bowl, Silicon Valley, and Japan. In addition to Hewlett-Packard's efforts at downsizing, their neighbor in Santa Clara, California, Intel Corporation, cut salaries by up to 10 percent to save an estimated $20 million from its 1983 payroll. Hitachi responded to a 1987 pre-tax earnings decline of 40 percent, in part, by cutting managerial and executive pay. The 6,800 Hitachi managers titled section chief and above each had 5 percent reductions; board members lost 10 percent of their salaries. As with Hewlett-Packard, this was not the first time this tactic was used. In 1975, salaries were lowered by 5 to 15 percent for a nine-month period. Reductions such as these can also be used as preludes to early retirement offers. In addition to 5 percent pay cuts for its managers and professional staff, Hewlett-Packard imposed mandatory use of vacation time and forced unpaid time off before recently offering 1,800 employees a generous early retirement window.

Other approaches can have the same net results. Motorola has used shorter work weeks as a key part of its employment security program, especially in the more cyclical parts of its business. Signetics, a Silicon Valley unit of the Dutch electronics giant, Philips N.V., has used shortened work weeks in slack periods to give managers and factory workers an alternative to layoffs. Variations on this include job sharing, in which two employees divide the work of one job between themselves; they also divide the pay and benefits. Polaroid Corporation has been able to divide jobs so that employees alternate on either half-day or every-other-month schedules. Most job sharing has been done with hourly workers, but a well-designed approach could make sense for some staff professionals. At Polaroid and Pacific Northwest Bell, employees were encouraged to take unpaid leaves of absence for a pre-specified period, with their jobs guaranteed at the period's end. For some large organizations, there are sizable cost savings from reducing paid vacation and holiday time. Others have tried lengthening the workday to avoid new hiring or to make up for employees who have left. A final approach in these circumstances is mandatory redeployment to lower paying, vacant jobs elsewhere in the company.

Most of these are temporary measures, often most useful for companies in cyclical businesses or ones with a high degree of confidence that a new product or marketing strategy will make a "hockey stick" business forecast come true. Eventually, continued salary reduction programs will cause good-performing managers to look elsewhere, and those who stay will lose confidence in the company. These programs usually only work over multiyear periods in times of national or regional depression, when employees have few other options. When used repeatedly, they can give false comfort to top management. One high-technology firm used these tactics for many years to help maintain a stable earnings record. While other layoffs were avoided, market share and product reputation declined considerably, partially because top management was kept from facing the business reasons behind the decline. Another danger of these programs lies in their execution. To be done in a way not suicidal to employee morale, they need to be applied evenhandedly. Hitachi has taken the safest approach: The higher someone is in the hierarchy, the greater percentage of pay he or she has to do without. Long-term employee commitment is easily destroyed by awarding top management large bonuses while asking others for pay givebacks.

When immediate action needs to be taken, but the magnitude of the percentage change is only in the single digits, other options are available. In addition to scaled-back versions of the tactics already considered, these include:

1. Offering narrowly targeted job buy-outs and early retirement programs.
2. Making selective terminations.
3. Reassigning people to comparable jobs elsewhere in the company.
4. Freezing actions on new positions, filling vacant jobs, salary increases, and bonuses.
5. Mobilizing the troops.

The Ohio-based manufacturer Nordson Corporation, and many other firms, have been able to prevent or postpone layoffs through a combination of hiring freezes and caps on wage increases. Shell, a planned downsizer, reduced its work force from 37,000 to 34,000 in five years through a combination of selective dismissals and attrition. Attrition coupled with hiring freezes ("watching the front door as well as the back") has helped many companies slim down. But for this formula to be helpful over the long haul, centralized planning is needed to fill vacancies by reassigning people already employed. Without this overall monitoring, downsizing will lead to payrolls in some units shrinking while others are increasing by the same amount.

Selective dismissals mobilize a downsizing mechanism most companies already have in place: their performance review system. Performance ratings can certainly be an input into decisions about forced dismissals. Their use *should* help avoid the problem of good performers losing their jobs while marginal ones stay. But for performance ratings to be useful they must also provide valid information. Many do not, usually because the systems are undermanaged or are used primarily as a way to make salary decisions, not to spot and correct performance problems.

Another form of mobilization makes use of participative management. Instead of a few senior executives or headquarters staff people trying to make detailed cutbacks and work rearrangements about individuals far away in the hierarchy, they turn the problem over to those whose jobs are at stake ("the troops"). Chapter 4 highlighted how this was done by a drug manufacturer. It also illustrated a limitation of this process: In the short run, it produces smaller cost savings. But the philosophy behind it is still useful, though unfortunately underexercised. Participative management can help build a very committed work force, a key to long-term competitive success; the process, however, depends on the possibility of a competitive future for the business that these people can share. Mobilizing the troops works best when the company's economic problem is amenable to a near-term, group solution.

This is illustrated in the way a West German food retailer managed an acquisition. When Deutscher Supermarkt Handels-GmbH bought a troubled supermarket chain, it had two options. It could restore its economic health by turnaround measures traditionally associated with the United States: closing stores, laying off employees, and drastically cutting costs and reducing assets. Or it could take the path its chief executive, Hugo Mann, chose. He conducted a careful analysis of both sides of the profit equation and found that a turnaround could also be achieved if sales were increased 5 percent company-wide. Soon after the sale was completed, he presented the managers and employees of the chain with the challenge: Find ways to increase sales by 5 percent and no one would be out of work. This encouraged teamwork, and mechanisms were put in place to implement ideas for creative ways of attracting new customers, encouraging current ones to buy more items, and differentiating the stores from those of competitors. The approach worked. Sales and profits increased, and Mann's careful analysis of the economics brought greater revenues than the asset-stripping strategy would have provided.

Mobilizing the troops, even if underused, is an attractive strategy for many executives. It can focus on cutting costs as well as increasing sales to forestall layoffs. But for it to be effective, certain internal conditions, as well as external economics, must be present:

- Strong and focused leadership must be provided from the top.
- Employees must trust the leadership enough to become very committed to improving the business for the long haul, not just in preserving their current jobs.
- Mechanisms must be put in place to short-circuit the ordinary, business-as-usual ways in which new ideas are developed, considered, and tried.

Without these in place, mobilizing the troops is a nice-sounding slogan that will only lead to misplaced expectations.

Longer-to-Implement Alternatives

The more time a company has to execute its downsizing plan, the more options are available to reduce the work force and limit the need for costly and painful layoffs. More opportunities are available to preserve and refocus past investments in training and culture building. The time available is sometimes limited by events outside the company's immediate control, but more often than not these events can be anticipated and dealt with on the company's schedule, not the outside world's. Doing so, though, requires a close link between the people who plan corporate strategy and those who plan for the company's organizational and human resource requirements. This is the point at which the process usually breaks down; too few companies build these bridges to the extent necessary. Too few take the view that organizational development is a strategic activity, at least to the extent this has been done at Hewlett-Packard, IBM, Shell, and TRW.

Taking a longer view of downsizing only works when a company is prepared to manage time well. Many rapidly implemented across-the-board layoffs happen because executives fear that prolonging the streamlining process will cause more management and human relations problems than are worth tolerating. They accept the attitude mentioned earlier, that it is best to "get it over quickly, once and for all." They are usually correct that successive layoffs over several years have a greater negative affect on morale than one big layoff that "puts the problem behind us." But this sort of reasoning ignores other, nonlayoff options which take time to execute. It also ignores the possibilities of using adversity to the company's long-term advantage through "mobilizing the troops" strategies.

Using time to the company's best advantage does not mean doing belabored analyses to keep from making hard decisions. It certainly does not mean creating an information void. This only allows employees' worst fears (about both what may happen to them and what they feel are top management's capabilities to act competently) to fester. Keeping this situation from happening requires building and maintaining employee trust through two-way communications. Just as competently managing one day's cash flow may do little to ensure there will not be problems tomorrow, top management must *continually* shape reasonable expectations by letting people know where they stand and where the company is going. The attempt here should be to drive the bad out with the good, replace rumors with authoritative information. Management needs to provide legitimate outlets for grumbling and acceptable ways for insecurities to be expressed upward. A company should manage the situation with the directness and honesty Esmark used.

Having "bought" some lead time through careful strategic planning and well-managed employee communications, what new downsizing options present themselves to a company? Refer back to Figure 7.1. Two less immediate time frames are depicted: actions requiring one to three years to complete, and those taking longer.

One- to three-year options range from spinning off entire business units to letting nature take its course through partially managed attrition. The largest potential reductions can occur when plants or entire divisions are sold off. The leveraged buy-out has become a popular form of divestiture, in which a part of the business is sold to its managers in partnership with sources of loan funds. Employee buy-outs use employee stock ownership plans to finance the sale and turn all workers into part-owners. Neither is a panacea for businesses with economic difficulties or weak managers, as was the situation when General Motors spun off its roller-bearing company in New Jersey. Business and management problems led to the unlikely situation of Hyatt-Clark's owner-employees going on strike against themselves. The third spin-off option, and the most traditional, involves selling part of the company to another firm, to whom it has more value or potential. None of these moves in themselves will solve the problem of an overstaffed organization. In fact many, as considered in Chapter 2, lead to significant layoffs. But spin-offs also may avert even deeper cutbacks than would have been required if the unit remained with its parent or was closed down.

Another mechanism that can achieve relatively large reductions in this intermediate time frame is the use of voluntary buy-outs or early retirement windows. These can be useful when a company's demographics indicate that several years must pass before the majority of employees reach minimum retirement age. A series of windows can create expectations among some employees ("well, I can always wait until the next offer") that run counter to the company's objectives; in these cases, it is more appropriate to offer the plans to different organizational units at different times. Legal constraints and differing company age distributions require that these be planned very carefully.

More moderate targets can be realized in this time period through measures such as:

1. Mobilizing the troops.
2. Making selective terminations.
3. Retraining for inside work.
4. Retraining for outside jobs.
5. Lending staff.

As we've seen, both troop mobilization and selective termination strategies are appropriate for situations requiring immediate action to produce relatively small cutbacks or cost savings. The point made by Figure 7.1 is that greater reductions or cost savings are possible using these same methods if they are managed over a longer time.

Allowing more time permits the results of training and retraining investments to pay off. Surplus people in one area of operations may still have a lot of the "company specific skills" that Williamson described, and can be retrofitted for work in areas where either: (1) new recruits would *have* to have been hired, or (2) newly created jobs "pay for themselves."

An obvious way to limit growth is to replace new hires with retrained current employees. But companies seldom think about creating new positions when they are faced with the need for cutbacks. An important economic principle about value added is often lost when companies are caught up in downsizing. That principle states that there is nothing wrong, even in a situation of overall retrenchment, with adding a new position if the value contributed by that job exceeds its costs. For companies that want to prevail—not just shrink—and have positive business possibilities, this can be a viable alternative to laying off talent already on board.

The key difficulty here is being able to wait for these new jobs to contribute the value that exceeds their cost. This takes a measure of financial strength and executive foresight. When Mazda had limited success selling its rotary-engine automobiles almost two decades ago, many workers were redeployed from offices and factories to its domestic sales force. Selling a car in Japan is a very labor-intensive, time-consuming operation. Adding more resources for sales meant selling more cars, and the action helped buy the time needed to develop better products and find a long-term financial partner.

IBM, in addition to the early retirement program already mentioned, more recently engaged in a major redeployment of talent it did not want to lose. It consolidated five headquarters marketing staffs into one, and dealt with the resulting employee surplus by moving 2,500 people to its field offices in sales and to systems engineering jobs. Almost twice this number of workers were shifted simultaneously from manufacturing facilities and laboratories to field positions. Putting these people closer to the company's customers was intended in part to help defend and rebuild relationships that had been threatened by aggressive competitors. These job reassignments were accompanied by major training investments: Many of those going into sales jobs received three-week classes as part of a ten-month program to refresh their customer-relations skills.

Retraining managers and staff professionals for work outside the company is a less tried option. Many are able to find work with the skills they have. Job search and résumé-writing skills have been provided by both downsizing employers and outplacement services, but they are, it is hoped, needed only temporarily. Some corporate training facilities and tuition-reimbursement programs allow employees to retool for career shifts. The initiative here has usually been with the individual employee, but some companies may discover retraining as a useful adjunct to planning a gradual streamlining.

Lending staff outside the company is another tactic that has received only limited use. It implies, usually, keeping surplus staff people on the payroll at least temporarily, but having them work directly for community associations, government agencies, or trade associations. Another placement that might have a more direct business benefit to the loaning company is with suppliers, subcontractors, or customers. When the downsizing objective is other than cost reduction, this option is a way to unclutter organization charts. These placements can be holding areas for talent that is needed for the long term but for whom places will not be available until more attrition occurs. More commonly, this action is a prelude to retirement. If cost reduction is still important, expense-sharing agreements may be negotiated with the recipients of the services.

When modest reduction objectives have to be met, and there are several years in which to achieve them, attrition management can come into play, too. Managing attrition, presumably with better results than the frustrated AT&T manpower planner had in Chapter 2, can be the least painful way of downsizing. As learned by Shell Oil Company and others who have used it successfully, managing attrition does not work by itself. Hiring freezes, which usually accompany attrition, tend to become hiring postponements. To get the most mileage from attrition, investments must be made in skills inventories and retraining programs, so that as openings arise, they can be filled from the internal labor pool. This pool has to be an efficient one, with mechanisms that allow for relatively easy transfer. Managers must be more willing than usual to part with their best people, if moving them will stabilize overall company size. Costs and inconveniences should be shared fairly by all units. When hiring freezes must be violated, there should be a general understanding for the reason. The cooperation and trust of the work force need to be enlisted, especially when people are expected to be geographically mobile and willing to abandon old and comfortable skills for new jobs.

In the U.S. government, where the civil service setup can

contribute to an efficient internal labor market, the Health and Human Services Department was able to eliminate 1,264 jobs without firing anyone. This 30 percent reduction was accomplished by a mix of early retirement for senior employees and a redeployment of surplus staff to other parts of the department. In Japan, an even larger reduction has been planned. As the Japanese government prepares for the privatization of its national railroad, methods are being devised to reduce employment from 307,000 to 183,000 people. A nationwide job search has been conducted to find places throughout the public and private sectors for the thousands who cannot be accommodated by traditional early retirement programs. The overall objective is to prune back the company without dismissing anyone.

It is no secret that even in companies with strong commitments to "no layoff policies," attrition results from involuntary or semivoluntary job shifts. At IBM, an observer has estimated that as many as 20 percent of those who will be requested to move to field sales and marketing jobs may decide to leave the company instead. Other companies have been less aboveboard than IBM in dealing with surplus managers. They offer them reassignments ("try the Anchorage office for a few years . . .") that have the same impact as a direct termination. Done repeatedly, this method kills the possibility of more constructive use of the redeployment tactic.

Converting headquarters staff employees into external consultants can save on office space, support staff, payroll taxes, equipment, and supplies. Here, as with benchmarking, Xerox is the industry leader. Its London-based subsidiary, Rank Xerox, set up a program for specialists in areas such as human resources, pension administration, planning, and procurement to trade their full-time jobs for two-day-a-week consulting assignments. Long-term contracts provided a measure of security and their consulting fees for the two days often came close to the size of their former paychecks. Xerox helped them become independent businessmen, and they were encouraged to find other outside clients. Low-cost furniture and office equipment were offered, and a personal computer was loaned so these new consultants could easily tap into

Xerox's data bases to do their assignments. Eventually, Rank Xerox hopes 25 percent of its headquarters professional staff positions will be converted to consultant situations. As companies lose many years of accumulated company-specific experience through early retirement programs, approaches like this are becoming more attractive.

Xerox and a number of other companies are also using the converse of this approach: They keep the staff specialists on their full-time payroll but encourage them to sell their services to customers outside the company, using the time they have left over after their in-house responsibilities. The revenues generated can help cover some or all the costs of what would otherwise be an overhead operation. The mechanics of this and its nonfinancial benefits are reviewed later in Chapter 9.

The right-hand column of Figure 7.1 lists several of the options available to businesses able to wait several years before their downsizing implementation is completed. Greater gains through attrition strategies can be achieved than possible in shorter time periods. The time is also available to spin off free-standing businesses from some staff departments, as considered in Chapter 9. But the greatest gains can come from closing down entire segments of a business. Doing this on a gradual schedule allows for redeployment of most of the staff. Some companies, such as Siemens and Sony, have also used analyses of the capabilities of staff that may be surplus in their main businesses to guide their diversification into new business areas. Diversification from such surplus talent may seem like putting the cart before the horse, but it can make sense for companies concerned with making the most of an already large investment in human resource capabilities.

Well-Orchestrated Size Control: IBM

IBM is one of the best examples of a company that manages people flow with the same high degree of attention it gives to cash flow. It joined hundreds of other companies in offering an early retirement incentive that enabled it to more than double its customary attrition rate. The recent redeployment effort outlined earlier was not a new experience for IBM. Economic troubles from 1969 to 1972 required moving over 12,000 employees from plants, offices, and laboratories short on work to others needing their talents. Five thousand of these employees required retraining and a shift in their careers as they assumed new jobs in computer programming or sales. And only a few years after this, 3,000 additional employees took new jobs as part of a continued effort to "keep the circuits balanced."

A significant amount of management attention, at all levels of the IBM hierarchy, was required to make these movements work. In addition, the company has been able—through the no-layoff practice these moves support and its other personnel policies—to maintain a high degree of employee trust in management. This trust level, in turn, allows IBM to make requests of its employees that probably would not be entertained by workers in firms lacking IBM's attention to winning its employees' commitment. Walton Burdick, in charge of IBM's human resources function, feels very strongly that full employment practices must involve a mutual commitment based on mutual trust. He notes: "People have to be willing to be retrained. And reassigned. And redeployed. And in some instances, though not all, relocated." At IBM, people protect their jobs by being flexible. The company's role is to provide resources, including spending half a billion dollars on employee education in 1985.

What this requires on a day-to-day basis is a series of interlocking practices that provide a carefully graduated way of matching company responses to increasing surpluses. The sequence is controlled from IBM's Armonk, New York, headquarters, but the practices are managed locally. Incentives are built into its system for branch locations to solve their own problems before headquarters moves in. The sequence works something like this:

1. Company size and work load are continually monitored. When staff or management surpluses occur, IBM's habitual attention to human resources

planning has already provided considerable lead time to plan responses and prepare people. Surpluses are characterized by size, expected duration (a problem for a year or two versus a permanent situation), and the types of talent affected.

2. To the greatest extent logistically and technically possible, work is moved before people are. In some manufacturing situations it is possible to shift production from one location to another to balance the overall work load; for sales and customer service work, this is obviously more difficult.

3. What IBM calls "the buffer work force" is reduced or eliminated. This includes temporary workers (hired for specific periods of time with the understanding that their contracts may not be renewed) and overtime for regular employees.

4. Pre-recruiting programs such as internships, co-op programs, and summer jobs are reduced. At this stage, employees may be encouraged to take unused vacations or to consider temporary leaves of absence.

5. The "side door" is closed by limiting transfers from other parts of the company into facilities where surpluses exist.

6. The "front door" is shut by limiting or freezing new hiring in locations with surpluses, as well as other locations. Both side- and front-door closings are intended to maximize the help that can be provided by attrition.

7. Workers in locations and job categories of surplus are asked to consider voluntary relocation to other parts of IBM. Within IBM, movement from surplus white-collar staff jobs to factory work is encouraged when necessary. In one effort called the "Voluntary Assignment in Manufacturing Program," the risk of volunteering was reduced by giving those who accepted the chance to, if they wished, return to staff jobs in their specialty after 9 or 12 months.

8. Employees finishing leaves of absence for education

and other reasons are diverted to other IBM facilities.

9. Early retirement and other "special opportunity" programs are offered.

10. Services that have been contracted out locally are brought back into the house and done by surplus workers. Having high-technology employees painting buildings and doing grounds upkeep is not the most useful way to employ their talent, but it can have a strong symbolic value in demonstrating IBM's commitment to full employment. Production that has been contracted out is also brought back in to the extent feasible.

11. An overstaffed facility can be declared "open." This allows other IBM locations to aggressively recruit its workers to join theirs; it also allows employees subject to potential displacement to select three alternative work locations. The management at these locations must either take these workers or do a considerable amount of explaining why not.

12. Employees are transferred involuntarily to comparable jobs at their current location.

13. Employees are involuntarily moved to lesser jobs in their current locations.

14. Workers are required to relocate to wherever jobs are available in other IBM facilities.

Many of these alternatives are possible because even in times of no surplus, IBM continually rotates its people and encourages multifunctional careers. Later we will consider how this kind of movement is vital for downsized companies that want to stay slim. IBM does not always go through every step or follow this exact sequence, but these items indicate the range of options it keeps available. From Option 9 onward, headquarters approval is needed before these steps may be taken. Also, IBM is concerned about the musical chairs situation so common in Japan that Option 10 can involve. More than one IBM supplier has been disappointed when told by IBM that it wants to limit the business it receives from that supplier because the supplier's work force may become too dependent on IBM for its own job security. Still, IBM suppliers such as Seagate Technology and Tandon Corporation have had to make sharp cuts in their own work forces after IBM reduced their orders.

Most companies admire IBM's management prowess, but some feel it has gone overboard to make full employment a reality. Others, including IBM, feel the benefits gained easily outweigh the costs. Obviously, companies with more limited scopes of operations, fewer locations, and fewer similar jobs will not be able to make use of all these options. But many companies can customize a sequence that fits their situations and achieves many of the same objectives. At the least, IBM's practices represent a worthwhile reference point, just as the experience of People Express has lessons about how to manage with minimal layers.

A Learning Process

Both layoffs and layoff alternatives are hard for many companies to implement effectively. This is often because they have little experience managing situations of declining size and retrenchment. Most attention since World War II has gone into managing growth, increasing production capacity, or expanding to meet new market demands. Building organizations, not taking them apart, is the task for which executives have acquired talent. The purpose of this chapter is not to single out or belittle companies that have had problems shrinking their size. Those that have handled cutbacks poorly have usually done so out of ignorance, not from some malicious desire to punish their ex-employees. Managing work-force reductions in ways that do not also cause a job security crisis is an art U.S. businesses are only just beginning to acquire.

Just as lessons about effective downsizing are now being painfully learned, few executives have been able to build experience in the new management style required to make their now-lean corporate structures operate successfully and safely. The next chapter lays out some key features of this different way of getting things done.

Chapter 8
Running Lean

"What do we do now that they're all gone?" laments a chronically overworked survivor of deep demassing. Let us look at one post-cutback worst-case scenario that this person might be facing.

Our headquarters has shrunk to a handful of people. We don't even own the building anymore. But division and plant staffing is on the increase, and what's more frustrating is that each division, now that we've given them complete hire-fire authority, is taking on the same kind of professionals and engineers that their sister groups already have. Hasn't anybody ever heard of economies of scale? Don't they realize they're going to start inventing work to keep them all busy? Have they considered what they'll do with these high-paid folks in a few years when they'll all want promotions?

Still, we are pleased, at least for the moment, because the total corporate payroll has had a big bite taken out of it. But some of the remaining staff departments are submitting pretty large capital budget requests for new computers, workstations, and telecommunications. Staff head count has gone down at the computer center, but overtime is way up and the net savings there to date seem minimal. And we are making more use of outside contractors than ever before. Two divisions have already overspent their budgets for consultants, and the year's not half over.

We haven't gone as far as Rene McPherson at Dana. He replaced 22 1/2 inches of corporate procedure manuals with a one-page philosophy statement. But we've come pretty close. The trouble is, we've had to double the size of our training program to be sure everybody understands how to apply our abbreviated standards.

Decisions do move along faster without all the layers of approval we used to have—but I'm a little concerned that our overall direction in the marketplace isn't as focused as it once was. Being quick to make decisions doesn't always mean we are making good ones. I'm starting to get concerned that our image with customers is suffering from whiplash. One day we decide to advertise our products as the cheapest available, the next month our sales campaign is focusing on how many bells and whistles each one has.

We're certainly less guilty of analysis-paralysis, but only a few of our managers know how to solo without a lot of staff backup. The result? Occasional shooting from the hip. Without the headquarters staff around to second-guess every decision, our managers' morale has sure risen, but I still wonder how many are broadly gauged enough to handle all this new responsibility.

While this example is a composite of different companies' experiences, the situations are very real. Companies that carefully plan their downsizing should be able to avoid the frustration of problems like these. But in doing so, they quickly rediscover (in case they have forgotten) the no-free-lunch rule. For every economy achieved, new costs may arise. Even when a company clearly had more managers than needed to do all the work, downsizing disrupts many long-ingrained habits. A longer-than-expected transitional period may be necessary before operations reach peak efficiency. Running lean successfully, and safely, means making trade-offs. For example, even when reducing management, a company needs to give some management attention to the problems of moving from bloated to lean.

Because most management attention during downsizing goes toward the mechanics of personnel cutbacks and the details of planning reorganization, many psychological issues are ignored or possibly delegated to a low-level staff unit. But these are the issues whose handling can make or break the entire effort. Harry Levinson has observed, from his years of consulting and company-watching, that "most organizational change flounders because the experience of loss is not taken into account. When the threats of loss are so severe as to increase people's sense of helplessness [as is often the case during downsizing], their ability to master themselves and their environments decreases. To undertake successful organizational change, an executive must anticipate and provide means of working through that loss."

One way to do this is to set up a series of task forces, each dealing with a different aspect of the organizational and system changes that must be made to support the downsizing. These teams of managers and staff professionals can focus on issues such as developing new reporting procedures, adapting the management information systems to the new structure, and finding ways to speed product development through the streamlined structure. While they are discussing these concrete issues, opportunities may arise to consider also some of the less tangible aspects of the reductions.

Having worked through this difficult period, the company will be able to face issues that will have a long-term impact on its ability to thrive with a lean structure and few staff assistants. It then needs to consider what kind of manager is going to do the best job in this new environment, what ground rules and management tools will be needed, how the corporate culture will have to adapt, and how a slimmed down headquarters staff will still be able to guide the business.

A New Breed of General Manager

A number of key players may need to change. There are managers who are comfortable in corporate bureaucracies where decision making is slow and the job scope limited, where pleasing the boss is more important than collaborating with peers to get things done, and where change is glacial at best. These people may be out of place in a streamlined corporate environment. The proverbial "bull in the china shop"—the highly aggressive and narrowly single-minded manager—may also have trouble fitting in.

What's needed may well be a new breed of manager for many recently streamlined companies: the manager who thrives in settings where expert analyses are needed, but staffs of experts are not available to deliver them; where fearsome cost competition may mandate tight expense controls, but close supervision and an army of auditors are not present. While some features of the situation are similar to those faced daily by small and medium-size companies, the lines of zeros on the financial reports will be much longer. Downsized companies still operate in upsized, often global, markets. They face threats from well-financed overseas competitors as well as new technologies started up in nearby garages.

Companies are only beginning to gain experience in running large businesses leanly. At Emerson Electric Company, a leanly managed, relentless cost-cutter, some patterns are apparent. The company's 44 divisions have been run as nearly autonomous businesses, and its cadre of division heads have been compared to princes reporting to a strong king. In addition to being strictly oriented to the bottom line, these managers are selected for their ability, when necessary, to stand up to and fight their aggressive boss, Charles Knight. Corporate staff people number less than 50, with each division head responsible for creating and implementing strategy. This situation is antithetical to the culture of mistrust that grows in many other firms. The chief executive does not lie back and let the business run itself as a loose collection of semi-independent companies. He is deeply involved in a carefully selected number of areas that are key to overall competitive performance, such as labor cost control. Knight is constantly visiting Emerson's facilities, asking challenging questions of his managers. His activist style is far different from that of the "corpocrats" U.S. Deputy Treasury Secretary Richard Darman has complained about. It is a style not without its flaws, of course. The autonomy it encourages can make it difficult for units to cooperate on projects that cross divisional lines.

At Unilever, one of the world's largest consumer products companies with over a thousand worldwide brands, a similar formula has been tried. Its 500 subsidiaries have been run by a team of executives using what one calls lion-tamer management: "Keep them well fed and never let them see that all you have is a whip and a chair." Lean headquarters may reduce some managers to this stance, but it is hoped that behavioral and computer technologies will arm them with stronger tools.

What characteristics will this new breed of manager possess? What should be looked for when new general managers must be selected? Here are some clues:

□ Because their jobs will be too big to allow time to constantly watch how well each subordinate complies with all facets of company policy, these managers will have to be better internal salespeople than police officers. They have to be good at *eliciting the commitment* of their subordinates to company plans. Their motivational skills will take precedence over their monitoring ones.

□ They will have to be well attuned to overall company strategy. Since their work load will only allow them to monitor a few performance indicators, *the indicators they select had better be the right ones.* Monitoring short-term sales at the expense of progress on product development, for example, may have been just a minor annoyance in a management-heavy company, but in a lean one it could be disastrous.

□ They will have to balance their commitment-building abilities with a keen sense of *knowing when to let go.* An executive vice president of an experienced downsizer, Wells Fargo and Company, once noted that as the bank prepared for deregulation, managers became heroes for withdrawing from a business as much as they were for making a new, big deal.

□ They will *enjoy being visible;* they will relish the roles of information spreader and spokesperson that good managers play. As masters of lavishing attention on customers, products, and high-performing subordinates, they will be comfortable both sending and receiving recognition. There may be less room for quiet introverts in these action-oriented, streamlined firms.

□ Working in what TRW's Pat Choate calls a "high-flex business environment" will require a lot of *flexibility and independence*. Aggressiveness will still be important, but must be tempered by adaptability and self-restraint. Being a self-starter will be vital, because the manager's boss may be too busy to keep providing short-term motivation. Being a self-stopper is also necessary; the lean corporate staffing will provide fewer restraints and checkpoints for overly aggressive behavior.

As at Emerson, these managers will not be desk-bound. They will not spend much of their day filling out forms and relaying information from one level of the hierarchy to another. Nor will they be nursemaids to departments of part-time managers. Tom Peters' "management-by-walking-around" will be second nature. They will trust their senses more than their computer reports for information about what is happening. Their incumbents will be expected to fuse both staff and line perspectives; more top-management appointments like Seymour Sternberg's will be made. Sternberg is now one of two executive vice presidents of Massachusetts Mutual Life Insurance Company. His duties include responsibility for one of its line business-growth areas (group life and health insurance) and several of its key staff areas (finance and information systems). His background is information systems—the industry's new key strategic technology—not sales, its traditional career path to the executive floor.

The once popular idea of the "professional" manager ("I can manage anything") will quickly become a discredited myth in streamlined companies. Fewer managers means being flexible, but also having a sound base of experience and knowledge around which to operate. Managers will have in-depth contact with key customer groups, or an understanding of critical technologies or functions, or a familiarity with the major players in their industry.

This concept was realized by TRW, a company oriented toward electronics technology. As part of a restructuring, it sold an aircraft-turbine parts foundry to a much smaller Portland, Oregon, firm that specializes in the low tech-high skill business of making precision castings. When TRW ran the foundry it lost money, partially because about a quarter of its products had to be scrapped for not meeting its customers' exacting specifications. The purchaser from Portland provided a foundry manager who knew this business inside and out. He was able to quickly spot the problems and provide hands-on instruction to correct them. The results? Scrap rates were cut in half, sales were increased, and red ink was turned into black in less than a year. Not having to bear the overhead burden of a multinational diversified manufacturer also helped. This is a story being repeated across the United States. Restructuring is turning portfolio companies managed by generalists into lean, focused stand-alone businesses run by managers able to roll up their sleeves and quickly add value.

At Pepsico, these ideas have even been built into the structure of top management. Rather than having a group of highly paid executives collectively oversee all of this food and beverage firm's businesses, each of the top three executives is allocated a specialty (the chairman and chief executive watches the restaurants, a former president oversees the Frito-Lay snack food business, and another heads the beverage units). Chief Executive D. Wayne Calloway admits that he makes no attempt to run all three, and feels this set of assignments keeps executives minding the store rather than concentrating on "numbers at headquarters." A former Pepsico president now teaching at Harvard Business School, Andrall Pearson, explained the simple logic behind the system: "If top managers don't get involved in the details of the markets they compete in, they're going to get killed by people who do."

The function of management is sometimes distinguished from that of leadership, with management concerned more about day-to-day operations of the business and leadership with visionary and strategic issues. Managers are seen as people who use rule books and procedures manuals, supplemented with frequent audits, to keep the company on track. Leaders, on the other hand, are expected to function more mystically. They seem more detached from the fray, and use their abilities to be articulate and charismatic to inspire people to action. Whatever the validity of the distinction, it is unlikely that streamlined companies are going to have room for many of both types. More people will have to assume both roles as the number of layers in the hierarchy decreases. Executives who have enjoyed the view from the top will find that their leadership is sometimes best expressed through everyday, routine contact with the troops. Companies that have been very procedure-driven will learn the virtues of using some of the softer aspects of management, such as corporate culture and training, to do the work of their recently eliminated bureaucracy. But the direction of downsized companies will not be achieved through charisma alone; the nature of the manager's tool kit will also change. So will some of the operating ground rules.

New Rules, Different Tools

"Run it like you own it" will be the instruction given to many managers of downsized businesses. And to help them feel more like owners, it is likely that good performance will be increasingly rewarded with stock (real or phantom), not just immediate cash payouts. Systems of pay-for-performance and various types of incentive pay and gain-sharing will become more widespread. Compensation systems will become instruments for line managers to use in guiding their subordinates, not just mechanisms for distributing pay equitably. General Electric and a number of other companies have already gotten several years' experience in applying executive bonus systems to their shrunken ranks of middle managers. Five thousand GE managers, each with a base pay of $50,000 or greater, were put on an incentive program that rewarded them for meeting both short- and long-term financial and nonfinancial goals.

Pay for performance also implies *no* pay for *no* performance. While it is likely that many who survive streamlining reductions will have enlarged and better-paying jobs, they may also have more risk associated with their performance. Fewer managers mean more visible ones. It will be easier to pinpoint who is behind the company's success and failure. "You run the show, or they will put someone else in to run it," explained one general manager at the leanly managed Marmon Group. At Fairchild Industries, chief executive Edward Uhl characterizes his business as "a meat-and-potatoes company....We don't have a deep palace guard. People on the corporate staff have to produce. If they don't produce, we're not interested in them." He expects that his managers "better damn well put down on paper what they're going to do and then go do it."

The bureaucratic style of many large organizations will depart along with the staff that has been laid off. Memos and reports will be short; there will be fewer staff people available to write them, and fewer managers with time to read them. At the Chevron Corporation, which has gone through a merger and a number of major reductions, departmental meetings are held monthly instead of weekly; policies and procedures have been reduced from 400 to 18, with common sense replacing detailed instructions; and the executive committee of the board is looking at capital-expenditure requests with a third fewer pages than those of previous years. The research and development group is focusing more on applications than on basic research. When a new chemical process is discovered, the key question is "What will we do with it?," not "Why is it happening?"

Downsizing also means turning many organizations on their sides. Getting things done will mean being able to work the company horizontally more than vertically, because streamlined structures will be wider than they will be tall. Being able to elicit support and cooperation from peers may be a more important skill than currying a boss's favor. Talents at negotiating will become key to obtaining resources in operations like GE's manufacturing businesses, where functional units like marketing and engineering have been centralized again. Lateral positions will be created in many slim companies. While Ford was sharply reducing its staff size, it created 20 new line product-manager positions to be sure its division heads had all the information to closely manage costs and market shifts. At Campbell Soup Company, orientation is toward customizing its products, advertising, and sales efforts to diverse regional markets. Campbell Soup followed the successful approach of another consumer goods maker, Johnson & Johnson, in dividing its factory-dominated monolithic structure into 50 small divisions, each with profit-and-loss responsibility. Sales and marketing staffs have been first combined, then regionalized. They are told to stay more attuned to their local markets and not to act as offshoots of the corporate office.

As the experiences of GE and Campbell Soup suggest, operating lean means centralizing for some companies and decentralizing for others. The trick is to focus the corporate organization on the key factors for business success, not on internally generated requirements. Many companies will reorganize to strike a new balance between staff and line, but there is no one way to organize that is appropriate for all downsized firms.

One practice that will be common in many streamlined companies, though, will be extensive use of forums that promote communication and exchange of ideas across departmental and divisional lines. For some, this may mean annual internal trade fairs where managers can show off and swap ideas for productivity improvement, new products, and new technologies. Others may accomplish the same by making extensive use of task forces, whose memberships put people together across organizational units and management levels who do not otherwise see much of each other.

Managers will also adopt some new tools to leverage their time and talents. First thought of are the now usually ubiquitous microcomputers and data terminals appearing next to every manager's desk. While these can be great time-savers and grasp-extenders, they can also become tools that promote inappropriate micromanagement and excess analysis. They can also chain managers to desks when they should be walking around, and tempt some into getting things done all by themselves instead of delegating to subordinates. Economist Lester Thurow has observed that, in many corporate accounting departments, increased automation does not lead to increased productivity. Instead, it is primarily responsible for increasing the frequency and types of accounting that are done—generating more paperwork and reports, not less!

Paul O'Neill, International Paper Company's president, has long felt that many layers of management exist only to sort and transmit information. He hopes that by the mid-1990s these will all be eliminated. Perhaps so, but past experience shows that increased spending for office automation brings with it large information bureaucracies. Too much focus has been on computerizing existing manual systems, sometimes in ways that build into the new system the jobs of those managers who do the collecting, sorting, and relaying of the information. Automation in streamlined companies starts with replanning the most critical work, then automating it. It begins with activity prioritizing, not software and hardware purchases. Obtaining the strategic results from investments in information systems that Robert Crandall of American Airlines has achieved requires continual management by line executives over the entire process. This kind of attention helped him reduce his corporate controller's organization to half the size it was five years earlier.

Making the most of personal computers will require a shift from their being used primarily as tools (to do spreadsheet analysis or to write a memo) to their becoming more of a day-to-day partner or special assistant. For this to become a reality, technological developments, such as the advances in artificial intelligence reviewed in the next chapter, will need to occur. This may also require more time for training than many overworked managers now have. For some companies, the manager-machine partnership will have to wait until a new generation of computer-literate managers takes over.

On the factory floor, computer-integrated manufacturing can be a double-edged sword. It can either promote more centralized management than is currently possible, or it can allow for significant decentralization and upgrading of factory workers' skills. The way numerically controlled machines are managed illustrates this distinction. It is common in the United States for staff programmers to be the only employ-

ees allowed to adjust their programs to production or product changes. In Europe and Japan, where no-layoff policies
and restrictive labor laws encourage companies to make the
most of their factory-floor talent, these machines tend to be
"unlocked," allowing workers to make faster and more flexible responses to changing conditions. Overseas production
workers are expected to make significant inputs into factory
equipment purchasing, rather than delegating this task to the
industrial engineering staff and the purchasing depártment.
Inventory control staff people have been eliminated in some
Japanese plants by enriching the assembly-line worker's job
with this responsibility. Procter & Gamble has been ahead of
many U.S. manufacturers in adopting these methods. Half
of their domestic-production workers are salaried technicians
charged with making and implementing most day-to-day operating decisions. This has permitted elimination of a layer of
middle management in each plant using this job category.

Running lean the Procter & Gamble way requires both
computer and behavioral technologies. Rather than just looking at what changes are possible by adding a new tool or policy, executives stand back and consider the entire picture. They
look at their overall corporate culture and ask what aspects of
it need to be changed to make lean and mean management
a workable reality. And they have learned from the cultural
anthropologists that you cannot change just one thing. Every
aspect of their company's culture is linked in some way with
every other one. New systems and management tools can help
shape the streamlined culture, but the starting point in changing a company's culture is the principal carrier of that culture:
the company's managers.

Corporate Culture Built on Trust

An important job of the new breed of managers in downsized
companies is their role in the creation of a culture that helps fill
the vacuum left by fewer staff people and supervisors. This is
a corporate culture that, at its root, is based on trust. The word

trust does not refer to openness and honesty, although these qualities are certainly important in all organizations. Instead, it is the kind of trust that Vince Lombardi worked to achieve through his coaching. He explained the effectiveness of the Green Bay Packers as: "Every man on the team trusts every other player to do what he is trained to do—win football games."

The key words here are *team, trust,* and *trained.* The kind of trust that is vital to leanly staffed organizations (whether on the football field or in the global marketplace) is that which comes from being part of a close-knit team, not being an independent player temporarily affiliated with a company. The team is formed around the leadership provided by the new breed of hands-on manager. It stays together because of its focus on common goals and through an interlocking network of relationships among team players. But the trust that keeps the team and the company together is based on more than just camaraderie; it is built on the knowledge that other players share skills and viewpoints. In short, the team has been trained together; they share a common corporate culture.

There are as many types of corporate cultures as there are corporations. Companies differ considerably in the extent to which they actively use their culture as a tool to manage their employees. Most do not. At best, their culture is something of interest to only a few managers most likely based in the personnel department. It is occasionally mentioned in a chief executive's speech, and usually forgotten soon after the speech is made. Sometimes its quirks are the subject of an interesting after-work discussion around drinks. Most managers are aware that their corporate cultures include the shared values, habits, and behaviors of the company. They know that these can have a great impact on how well the company performs. But most believe that culture does not really matter—that performance comes from good plans, skilled managers, comprehensive policies and systems, and lots of hard work. Maybe they are right, but the reality for most downsized companies is that these factors are probably in short supply. Using culture, the "softer"

side of management, may be one of the few ways to leverage
the contributions of remaining managers and staff people.

Cultures, like psychological contracts, happen whether
they are managed or not. Building a strong culture means
building compliance around at least a few key values and
practices. These can start with the basics. What do we assume
about our customers? What do we assume about the people we
work with? Lombardi's idea of a well-functioning team is one
in which everyone could count on everyone else. Is this a reasonable assumption in most U.S. companies? Not so, according to the father of statistical methods of quality management,
W. Edwards Deming. His experience and other researchers'
studies indicate that 80 percent of American managers cannot
answer with any measure of confidence these seemingly simple
questions:

1. What is my job?
2. What in it really counts?
3. How well am I doing?

Expecting a company to do well with broadened spans of
control and fewer staff monitors is rather chancy if the answers
to these questions are not easy to come by. Where close supervision may have made up for some uncertainties in the past,
a strong shared culture is going to have to do the job in the
streamlined future. This is where expanded investments in
training will be necessary. An important function of operations
such as Dana University, Disney University, McDonald's Hamburger University, and IBM's extensive employee-training programs is to build unified company cultures while teaching practical work skills. Employee-students learn not just what to do,
but how to do it *the company's* way. The objective is to replace
explicit controls (procedures manuals, rule books, and armies
of auditors) with implicit, trained-in controls. The companies
that do this well make training mandatory, not a reward or
something for when time is available.

While the mix of features that make up a corporate culture varies considerably, one factor continually leads to bloated staffing. It is what quickly teaches most managers that they will do better if they continually win, always stay in control, and keep mistakes buried. This is what, in the first chapter, we called the tendency to build corporate cultures on mistrust. A big danger many downsized companies face is that this cultural tendency may be reinforced, not eliminated, by the tough, macho atmosphere present in some lean and mean organizations. As long as this tendency predominates, sustainable streamlining and safely running lean will be very difficult to achieve.

The toughness these values encourage is brittle and only skin deep. Earlier, we reviewed the adverse consequences. These are the values that turn $50,000 mistakes into $5 million catastrophes. Keeping these catastrophes from happening requires corporate cultures that encourage learning from mistakes as well as reward quick successes.

Instead of attempting to always get it right the first time, and then putting efforts into covering up the mistakes that are bound to happen, managers in trust-based cultures are more attuned to making small commitments—low-stakes gambles— and seeing what the results are. Then they either increase the investment or pull out while the losses are minor. They are good experimenters who know how to build on each trial, not gamblers who continually start each day facing the same unfavorable odds.

Changing a company culture means changing who becomes a corporate hero, seeing that rewards and recognition are distributed to people achieving short-term success as well as to those who pave the way for long-term accomplishments.

The Lean Headquarters

While a common culture and shared values help keep an organization on course, and well-developed channels for lateral communication and coordination relieve some of the upward pressure for decisions, downsized companies still require some

central direction. While streamlining will not eliminate the
need for headquarters staff, it can have considerable impact
on what it does and how it does it.

Large companies vary widely in the size and scope of
responsibilities assigned to headquarters. Many still have hundreds, or even thousands, of employees there. For some, especially those in a single business or several closely related ones
that can be put under one roof, this may make sense. But other
companies are finding problems as their large headquarters
takes on a life of its own, almost as if it were an independent
business. One-way communications can emerge as headquarters tries to keep control of divisions and plants; the divisions
often ignore the headquarters' policies because they bear little relationship to the local situation. The usual response by
headquarters to obvious or suspected deviations from company
policy is redoubled efforts to control local units. Eventually,
these efforts dominate the communications between headquarters and field managers. Little room is left for consideration of
customer needs or competitors' moves. The way around this
morass is to delegate responsibility for operating performance
to local executives and to restrict the size of the central office.

A number of companies have managed their operations
with less than 100 people at headquarters. Dana Corporation
sells over $3 billion annually with a Toledo, Ohio, staff of 85.
And these headquarters personnel are activists, not just con-
solidators of data. When an opportunity arose to purchase the
Warner Electric Brake and Clutch Company, the staff went
into action. Chairman Gerald Mitchell approached Warner's
top management directly, telling his colleagues: "I didn't need
an investment banker to do that. We understand that company's business pretty well." His staff negotiated the deal, paid a
modest premium over the listed stock price, and saved a million dollars in investment-banker fees.

Another Midwest corporation, the Marmon Group
(owned by the family that controls the Hyatt hotels and Braniff
Airlines), has a strong aversion to top-heavy corporate staffs.
Its multibillion dollar collection of 75 companies is run by some
very busy senior executives and between 80 and 90 employees

at headquarters, including secretaries. As the Marmon Group tripled in size, it added only 35 people to its Chicago home office. The functions represented there include three operations-oriented vice presidents who help the chief executive monitor the companies, three corporate controllers, and small units for communications, human resources, public relations, and taxes. There is no planning staff, and Marmon's president, Robert Pritzker, feels they would only be counter-productive: "We don't have a staff of business analysts in our headquarters the way most companies do to analyze capital programs. Those financial people can only crunch numbers. They can't add any original thinking. They don't know anything about whether a new piece of equipment would work or whether there is a market for a product." Pritzker makes these equipment and product decisions by closely interrogating the operating people who propose them. He pays as careful attention to the thought process used by the operating managers to rationalize an expenditure as he does to the numbers themselves. He realizes that numbers are always soft until they become historical records, so as much time is spent judging people as goes into the quantitative analysis of business plans.

At CSX Corporation, even fewer workers and executives are based at its Richmond, Virginia, home office. They are supported by heavy investment in computer information systems and telecommunications links to coordinate the activities of this transportation megacarrier. A novel form of decentralized organization has been installed to put all marketing responsibilities under one roof and all operational ones under another. Both "roofs" are kept outside headquarters. This eliminates the extra corporate bureaucracy that would result from CSX functioning as a holding company with self-contained units for each of its individual rail, shipping, pipeline, and trucking operations. But it still provides a strong measure of the operational integration that railroads formerly had to achieve through monumental headquarters staffs. Another railroad-turned-megacarrier, the Seattle-based Burlington Northern Corporation, has followed this philosophy of organization, too. Less than 100 people in Seattle provide, through three departments, the direction for the entire organization. The units are finance and planning, law and corporate affairs, and human resources.

U.S. West, one of the regional telephone companies created from the Bell System splitup, maintains a 100-manager headquarters by keeping them focused on shareholder-related concerns while its operating subsidiaries concentrate on serving customers. Innovative single-business companies can find ways to keep their central staff even smaller. The steel mini-mill pioneer, Nucor Corporation, operates with 15 (including clerical workers) at its Charlotte, North Carolina, headquarters.

Running a company with staff this small requires special management practices. An important objective is to break down the traditional barriers that arise between line managers and staff professionals. Two tactics that have helped many companies lower these walls are (1) "Don't let them ever get too large," and (2) "Don't let them ever stay too long in one place." Both require the line organization doing more of what has been traditionally considered staff work and, in at least one case, giving the headquarters staff executives some line responsibilities.

At TRW, the rule has long been to limit headquarters size. Rather than concentrate power, efforts have been made over many years to delegate it to middle-level line executives. If you talk to one of them you are likely to hear: "It is my responsibility to find ways to grow this business—not . . . [the chairman's], or . . . [the president's], or . . . [my boss']." Great pains are taken not to legislate anything out of corporate headquarters. Staff vice presidents exist for company-wide issues such as productivity, quality, technical resources, manufacturing, and material and information systems—just as they do in many similar companies. The main difference lies in how these officers get things done. They have very small groups to back them up; rather than build headquarters empires, they are expected to get their work done by deputizing line managers. They are expected to serve as true catalysts, not dictators.

These headquarters executives frequently team up to

pool their talents on issues that cut across their specialties. For example, when TRW was concerned about developing productivity measurements that could be applied across its diverse business units, one of its vice presidents was given the overall mandate. He recruited a team from among other staff officers and outside experts. The group's first job was to build a communication network with the line managers throughout the company, not to study the subject in depth themselves. They appointed a steering committee of top executives to direct demonstration projects. They set up several councils made up primarily of divisional managers. They developed potential productivity measures and initiated projects in their divisions to test them. They also spread the results of their tests, and those done by the other divisional councils, throughout their groups. The staff vice presidents did most of their work behind the scenes, providing input and keeping each council aware of the other's projects. The result was a slow-to-analyze but quick-to-implement process. It was also one that built commitment to an important issue where it counted most: among the mid-level line managers.

The bulk of TRW's staff employees are distributed among the divisions. This way those line managers who are paying for the services of these staff people have more of a say in how large the units are and what they spend their time on. Staff specialists are sometimes rotated among the divisions to spread ideas developed in, say, the Cleveland human resources function to the personnel department at Redondo Beach, California. Also, it is common for line managers, before being promoted to senior general-management slots, to spend time in a staff function to broaden their development. Finally, TRW has pioneered a novel practice of technological forecasting. Rather than set up a large headquarters group to do trend analysis, or continually fund large outside research projects to predict which new technologies will be practical when, in the 1960s TRW started to pick the brains of its in-house experts. A detailed roster was prepared of all scientists, engineers, and managers on the payroll. It indicated what each's technical specialty was and who was most likely to be keeping up with developments in which fields. Then panels were selected, each with a dozen or more "experts," to cover the technologies of most interest to TRW. Each was asked, Delphic style, to predict when breakthroughs might occur or when new technologies might be commercialized. The results of these periodic surveys are analyzed by a small headquarters group, and the results are spread around the company for use in individual divisions' business planning.

While TRW has achieved good results by not letting headquarters staff size grow to the point that it is doing what line managers can do better, IBM has significantly lowered the line-staff wall by continually moving employees across it. Cross-training helps keep IBM's no-layoff practice workable. A normal career progression will have many managers doing tours in both staff and line jobs. This is a great way to be sure each perspective understands the needs of the other side. A staff manager may be more reluctant to add a new rule that will make his day go quicker, but that would lengthen the operating time of line managers, when he knows he is likely to occupy one of their slots in a year or two.

Some companies have avoided rotation because they feel it ends up with second-class staff experts, out of touch with their fields. This is more of an excuse for not carefully managing their people flow than it is a reason for avoiding well-prepared rotations. IBM, and a number of other companies that work hard to keep from developing narrow staff specialists, have found there are many other ways to keep abreast of changing fields. Consider the compensation and benefits specialty, an area in which IBM is considered among the most proficient in using it to support the company's strategic direction. Compensation is frequently considered the most technical part of the human resources field. But at one point, almost half the corporate staff people in compensation were no more than 18 months' away from holding management positions in IBM's operating divisions. And the head of the department, IBM's senior compensation expert, started his career there as a typewriter salesman.

Another reason some companies have avoided staff-line rotations is that they feel if they move a staff expert into an operating position, all the expert's specialized knowledge is lost to the company. Not completely. The person is still on the payroll and is available to advise and consult. Even more important, by spreading staff knowhow and perspective into the line organization, it just may be possible to get by with a smaller, less adversarial staff bureaucracy. Creating this kind of organization has its costs in increased training budgets and more time spent deliberately planning individuals' careers. But the real issue is, are these expenses worth the benefits a streamlined organization will bring?

Xerox has found a middle position between IBM's extensive staff-line rotation and TRW's efforts to get line managers to do staff work. Xerox works hard to see that its headquarters staff managers also have some line management duties in an area of critical competitive importance: ensuring customer satisfaction. The title of "officer of the day" is rotated among all central staff officers; each has it about a day a month. The person holding it is responsible for personally handling all customer complaints that reach headquarters that day. This executive also follows through to see that they have been resolved. On a long-term basis, each headquarters manager of director rank and above, in addition to his regular duties, has some account-management responsibilities for key Xerox customers. For example, the director of personnel administration is also charged with working closely with the Xerox team that serves the Florida state government. He visits purchasers of Xerox equipment in Tallahassee and reviews copies of sales reports and customer-satisfaction surveys.

The CEO as Roman Emperor

All of these practices, and many others, can help keep headquarters small and the company on track. But even more important are the fundamentals of running lean: managing the post-downsizing transition, selecting a new breed of manager, giving managers broad charters and new tools, and learning to use culture to manage. Maintaining a culture that works this way requires incessant training, for both managers and those managed. Running a lean and mean company puts its chief executive in a position similar to that of the Roman emperors two thousand years ago:

> One reason why the Roman empire grew so large and survived so long ... is that there was no railway, car, aeroplane, radio, paper, or telephone. Above all, no telephone. And therefore you could not maintain any illusion of direct control over a general or a provincial governor ...[nor could you] fly over and sort things out if they started to get into a mess. You appointed him, you watched his chariot and baggage train disappear over the hill in a cloud of dust ... and that was that. If there was a disaster, you would know nothing about it until months later when a messenger came panting up from the port of Ostia or galloping in down the Via Apennina to tell you that an army had been lost or a province overrun. There was, therefore, no question of appointing a man who was not fully trained, or not quite up to the job; you knew that everything depended on his being the best man for the job before he set off. And so you took great care in selecting him; but more than that, you made sure that he knew all about Rome and Roman government and the Roman army before he went out.

Chapter 9

Staying Streamlined

Even with great attention to running a lean field organization and managing it with well-selected and trained general managers, the Roman Empire crumbled. Some blame the decline on repeated onslaughts from leaner and meaner competitors from the north. Others say it was owing to a bloated, high-overhead headquarters in Rome. In spite of the suggestions made here for giving managers a piece of the business they feel they own, it is possible to become out of touch with home base. Corporate empires, as with the Roman one, will eventually crumble if attention is not paid continuously to managing a company's size. Staying downsized can be a lot harder than getting there.

The slash-and-burn approach to streamlining may produce significant short-term overhead reductions. And a combination of fear and adrenalin might even keep the survivors on course for awhile. But sustainable downsizing, in most cases, requires completely rethinking the logic behind a corporation's organization. It also requires computer networking and tools such as expert systems, as they are developed. Most important, though, are the changes needed in human resources management. Career paths need to change direction, performance appraisals have to have teeth, and pay systems must eliminate the management bias. And, paradoxically, to ensure continual productivity improvements more attention, not less, needs to be given to providing job security for those who work in downsized organizations.

Networks, Not Conglomerates

We have already stressed the importance of lowering the walls between line and staff and among the various operating divisions. To keep a streamlined organization over the long haul requires lowering another barrier, too. This is the wall between the company and its outside world. In times of rapidly growing markets, limited production capacity, and plenty of business for all comers, it made a great deal of sense to put as many parts of the business as possible under one roof. This was the era of vertical integration, when Ford Motor Company made its own steel and Greyhound built its own buses. The key to economic success, and competitive outflanking, was owning as many of the resources that went into the business as possible.

Today, this era has ended for many industries. Companies now operate in a period of vertical *dis*-integration, where competitive advantage comes to those *not* wedded to one source of supply or technology, and where attempts to build corporate size through acquisitions of dubious synergy are no longer rewarded by the stock market. Organizations will now resemble spiderwebs more than pyramids. The planning done by the large supermarket chain described in Chapter 3 was meant to bring its organization back into alignment with its competitive strengths. This is a movement happening across much of U.S. industry.

Lewis Galoob Toys Inc. does not look like a big company. To some observers, it is a very alien business creature. But it did sell over $50 million worth of toys in 1985. The ideas for the toys are purchased from independent inventors or large entertainment businesses. Engineering and design work are handled by outside contractors. The builders of the toys themselves are selected by evaluating bids from the many toy manufacturers based in Hong Kong. These businesses in turn have most of the actual work done in labor-cheap China. Common-carrier freight lines bring the finished toys to the United States, where they are sold through a network of commissioned representatives. The Galoob staff numbers just over 100, not even enough to include an accounts receivable department; revenue collecting is also contracted out. What does the Galoob company do? It manages a network of relationships, making it what the dean of the University of California at Berkeley's business school, Raymond Miles, calls "a switchboard instead of a corporation."

One of Galoob's competitors, the meteoric seller of Teddy Ruxpin talking bears and Lazer Tag, Worlds of Wonder, reached over $300 million in sales in less than two years of existence. With no time or desire to build a corporate bureaucracy, it adopted an organizational network similar to Galoob's. It hired executives like Stephen Race, who typifies the new breed of general manager cropping up in more and more streamlined corporations. Race learned flexibility and independence while he was a management consultant, where one day he would be trying to influence a Rust Bowl manufacturer to focus more on marketing than manufacturing, and the next day be flying to Brazil to help a clothing maker improve profitability. This background also taught him skills useful in influencing people who work for different bosses in companies other than his own. It is vital when one has to manage networks of contractors instead of subordinates.

These "solar system organizations," as they have been called by some observers, have outside suppliers orbiting around a small central nerve center. The solar system organization may not become *the* organization of the future, but it certainly will be among the types that add value without adding clutter. Companies like Worlds of Wonder and Galoob are in businesses in which sales can shift as rapidly as the roller coasters their young customers ride; for them, it can make strategic sense not to get overcommitted to fixed assets. This style of operating also makes sense for those who want to be driven by customer-pull, not factory-push. It has enabled consumer-product companies like the 315-person Minnetonka Corporation (Softsoap and Calvin Klein's Obsession) to challenge and occasionally out-innovate giants like Procter and Gamble. It works when a careful analysis is made of value added and comparative advantage; this sort of planning has convinced many consumer-electronics firms to leave the factories to someone else and focus their organization building on marketing, sales, and distribution. Sometimes one company's low value added is another's high: California-based Flextronics concentrates on manufacturing, procurement, and customer service for electronics firms with complementary skills.

Corporate Networking

To get enough popular Teddy Ruxpin dolls built quickly enough, Worlds of Wonder had to make some in its competitors' factories. And this new twist on corporate networking is not limited to toymakers. Before its acquisition of American Motors, Chrysler met heavy demand by having some of its full-size cars built at an idle American Motors plant in Kenosha, Wisconsin. Lee Iacocca decided it is better to rent a competitor's plant than build one he may have to shut down later. Moves like this, and greater reliance on suppliers to preassemble components, are helping build what Iacocca's lieutenant, Harold Sperlich, calls a company with enough mass to be efficient but small enough to be manageable. Ford has been following a similar strategy. Its president decided to manage size as well as market share and be willing to "live with some shortage of our ability to get our full share in a peak year."

Giving up complete self-sufficiency may be hard for some companies, but for many it will be the only way they can stay downsized. To preserve some of its cutbacks, Du Pont is starting to buy rather than to develop all its own technologies. A number of established companies have found it useful to develop close relationships with embryonic, "Silicon Valley-like" firms already with the state-of-the-art technologies they are interested in, and contract with them to do R&D and product development. This strategic partnering (the small outfits receive money not otherwise as easily available to fund

their growth) is more effective than duplicating their innovative environments in a larger company. It also often has better
results than directly purchasing these start-ups, a move that
too often drives the creative talent elsewhere.

Vertical Dis-Integration and Decentralization

The corporate raider's traditional call to action is "this
company is worth more dead than alive." It may make more
sense to say: "Many individual businesses under a broad corporate umbrella will not be alive and kicking until their super-
structures are killed off." Some companies have had a history
of not letting this superstructure form: Hewlett-Packard, Johnson & Johnson, and 3M. Others, such as Campbell Soup, have
used reorganization to limit their influence. Bankers Trust
New York Corporation, long a typical banking miniconglom-
erate, has become one of the leading corporate investment
banks by narrowing its scope, selling off its consumer branch-
es, and focusing its organization on what it does best. Eastman
Kodak has capitalized on its 10 percent work-force reduction,
which included 25 percent cuts in its top management, by making a major overhaul in its basic organizational design. This
historically integrated company was broken into 17 smaller,
autonomous business units as a response to its chief executive's
objective to find a way to encourage a major corporation to
behave like a small company.

"How big is too big?" is a question many executives are
starting to ask. Like the issue we examined earlier of how
many people can one manager manage, the best answer is still,
"It all depends." But some guidelines are starting to emerge.
According to Alonzo McDonald, former president of Bendix:
"When it comes to motivating people, you hit diseconomies of
scale early." For some companies, this has meant limiting divisions to 10,000 people; factories to 1,000; and offices to 100.
While these numbers are arbitrary and need to be determined
on a company-by-company basis, the principle behind them is
not arbitrary. Ralph Cordiner, reorganizer of General Electric
in the 1950s, felt it was important to keep a decentralized unit

small enough so a good manager could get his arms around it. Peter Drucker has taken this advice and expanded it a little, saying that the rule is that a small group of executives "four or five maybe—can still tell without having to consult charts, records, or organization manuals, who the key people are in the unit, where they are, what their assignments are and how they perform, where they came from, and where they are likely to go."

In Europe, the intellectual home of corporate bureaucracy, companies are also starting to search for ways to prune back overgrown structures. To help arrest declines in profit and market share, West Germany's global air carrier, Lufthansa, is planning early retirement and redeployment strategies to eliminate management layers. The objective is to build a company of profit centers around groups of interrelated air routes, instead of running Lufthansa as one worldwide, tightly integrated system. Another German firm, Siemens, has already moved further along these same lines. For many years it has been known as "Ma Siemens," Germany's largest privately owned bureaucracy. Now, under the leadership of a new activist chief executive, large—but, in the European style, lay-off-less—staff reductions have been made over several years. To make use of the possibilities these reductions have offered, considerable management attention has gone into setting up meetings and other forums to bring together the managers and staff people who develop Siemens' products with those who sell and market them.

But some companies have always managed to stay lean. The innovative French resort operator, Club Mediterranee, follows IBM's rotation scheme as it continually moves generalist staff (but of the carefully specified "Club Med mold") between headquarters and field, as well as among its vacation villages. Another French business also illustrates how a company can become big without becoming bureaucratic. Carrefour S.A., the $6 billion pioneer of the hypermarket concept (gargantuan stores selling food and other goods), keeps its company expanding but its organization lean by decentralizing as many functions as possible. A headquarters staff of less than

20 (including secretaries) guides the business. Almost half these people are involved in human resource management, one of the key ways Carrefour keeps control and ensures consistency in its operations. Only one layer of management is between the central office and the stores, a tier of regional managers. Each of these has, at most, five assistants.

Continued attention to employee training at all levels is what makes the lean structure work. In a typical year, two out of every three workers receive some form of training; Carrefour spends over 2 percent of its payroll costs on these programs. Providing the training is a responsibility of line managers at all levels, not of a separate staff-development bureaucracy. Individual departments within Carrefour's hypermarkets are run as profit centers. The best-performing department in a given specialty throughout the Carrefour system—say, casual clothing or frozen foods—is expected to play a key role in managing that specialty on a company-wide basis. In addition to being responsible to a store manager for its own profit plan, this clothing or food unit also helps other clothing or food department managers to select merchandise, train staff, and develop business plans. The lateral networks created by this cross-company interchange help tie what can easily become a very fragmented business together, and help maintain the small headquarters staffing over the long run.

While it may seem that companies like Club Med and Carrefour are very decentralized, in fact the opposite is true. They stay lean by actually having more central control over their far-flung stores and resorts than do some companies that keep tens of thousands of employees all at one location. But they substitute "soft" controls (focused cultures, carefully selected employees, mandatory training) for "hard" ones (staff, supervisors, systems). These companies all seem to "manage by mission." Their company philosophies include, as Carrefour's does, nice-sounding phrases about people being important and the need to be responsible to all of a company's constituencies. But they also make it clear what is expected of each person.

W. Edwards Deming would be very pleased with them. At Carrefour, employees are told of their responsibilities in four areas: people, merchandise, money, and assets. Job descriptions are built around these areas; training programs are keyed to teach the skills needed to perform in each; performance reviews provide regular reports on how well each is handled.

Across the Atlantic, Frederick Smith, founder of Federal Express, achieves a similar result by making videos so he can be seen by his package carriers across the United States as he continually emphasizes the importance of the boxes and envelopes they handle. By stressing how critical the contents of these packages are to their recipients, he has turned what could be an ordinary, routine delivery job into an important mission. And this, along with investment in a state-of-the-art information network, has allowed him to run Federal Express with far fewer managers than would otherwise be needed to provide the same consistently high level of service.

Selling Staff Services

In addition to maintaining their lean management structures, companies that stay streamlined well into the 1990s will have found ways to keep the size and scope of their headquarters staffs in check. The experiences of Carrefour, TRW, Xerox, and others indicate that this is possible, but it does require some creative reorganization. As we considered in Chapter 5, a key to effectively managing staff resources is to treat them less like overhead and more like actual businesses. Some companies have carried this philosophy further and found ways to turn overhead into profit.

In the last several years an increasing number of companies, including Control Data, Morgan Stanley & Company, Parsons Brinckerhoff, Polaroid, Security Pacific National Bank, Union Carbide, and Xerox, have turned carefully selected headquarters staff functions into businesses that sell their wares outside the home company. Control Data provides personnel services to other businesses for a fee; Parsons' public relations department has become an accredited advertising agency; and Xerox sells logistics and distribution services to customers of its reprographic equipment.

Some of the better managed efforts to sell staff businesses follow the three-step model outlined in Figure 9.1; not all of

Figure 9.1. Converting staff overhead into stand-alone businesses.

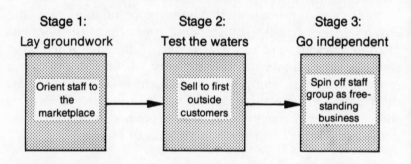

Stage 1: Lay groundwork	Stage 2: Test the waters	Stage 3: Go independent
Orient staff to the marketplace	Sell to first outside customers	Spin off staff group as free-standing business

Stage 1: Lay groundwork	Stage 2: Test the waters	Stage 3: Go independent
1. Select objectives.	1. Package or repackage products or services for outside customers.	1. Depending on external market demand, plan partial or complete spin off of staff unit.
2. Identify staff functions that are candidates for becoming independent businesses with external customers.	2. Develop marketing program; sell to external market as well as serving internal customers.	2. Determine extent of independence that unit will have.
3. Identify the specific products or services they could sell.	3. Manage the ongoing conflicts that emerge between internal and external customers.	3. Consider adding more management or marketing talent to unit before it becomes independent.
4. Assess feasibility based on market needs and internal capabilities.	4. Monitor sales performance and customer satisfaction.	
5. Set up procedures for pricing and cost accounting.	5. Be sure that the leader of the staff unit has appropriate management skills to operate a potential stand-alone business.	
6. Remove functions from general overhead budget; charge back their services to internal users.		
7. Start training to emphasize business-building skills.		

these companies have progressed to the third stage, but most are at least bringing extra revenues into their company. They have several objectives in mind when doing this—one of the more exciting and entrepreneurial approaches to staying lean:

1. Lower overhead costs.
2. Make profits.
3. Build a broader staff service than their own company can afford alone.
4. Bring more customer-orientation to their headquarters staff.
5. Retain high performers by adding new challenges to their jobs.

As more companies realize that managing staff functions is easier to discuss than implement, selling staff services will be viewed as an increasingly valuable tool in keeping headquarters slim. Companies will also find a growing variety of ways to get staff work done without putting people on the payroll. Conference Board economists estimate that a quarter of the U.S. work force is now made of contingent employees (part-timers and contract employees). Some temporary agencies are starting to provide as-needed managers and staff professionals, especially in financial and engineering functions. "Business services" is now the Bureau of Labor Statistics' fastest growing industrial category, as more companies are buying rather than owning the talent for their operations. Some consulting firms are also reformating their services to take on more day-to-day responsibility for areas in which they formerly only provided advice or input.

The objective of these reconfigurations in the shape of a corporation is to increase management's value added while decreasing management's costs. Paul Strassmann, former strategy planner at Xerox, calculates that American management productivity is fairly weak. His measures of return on management indicate that managements of most U.S. companies are barely paying their own way. The purpose of steps such as corporate networking, vertical dis-integration, selling staff services, and buying instead of making is to significantly increase this kind of return.

Expert Systems Instead of Experts?

For many years, the promises of artificial intelligence (AI) have been slow to deliver. By the early 1990s, however, this situation may be very different. A combination of heavy investment by many corporations in the development of "expert systems" and the spread of new hardware technologies such as neural-net computers and parallel processors will move AI from the laboratory to the office desk and factory floor.

The field of artificial intelligence includes work in robotics, machine vision, natural-language processing (getting computers to understand everyday English, not just computerese), and expert-system building. Putting aside the interesting philosophical question of to what extent machines can actually think or mimic human thought processes, it is worth considering how work in this field is being applied. The first two areas are already having considerable impact on manufacturing technology and strategy. They are creating factories without factory workers, allowing for quick-changeover manufacturing, and helping make economical short production runs of highly customized products.

While it is unlikely that, in the foreseeable future, robots will occupy the desks of corporate planners or compensation analysts, it is more likely that staff will receive some help from computer-based expert systems. These are computer programs that mimic the thought processes used by acknowledged experts in solving problems in a particular field. The programs usually include a large data base of up-to-date facts. They also include rules that experts use to make inferences about a problem and determine what needs to be done. These rules form the heart of the expert system. Eliciting these rules from the guru in a field is usually not very straightforward. Most of us are unaware of all the steps we actually take to solve a problem; and after we become good at something, we develop many shortcuts to a useful answer. The builder of an expert system learns what the shortcuts are, then reduces them to a computer code. Eliciting this knowhow is the most difficult part of the process; in fact, how well it is done often determines how useful the final system is and how far beyond the obvious it goes.

When the "finished" system is ready for a novice, it usually displays a series of questions on a computer screen to describe the particular problem at hand. Then the program uses its rules and knowledge bases to figure out other questions to ask. When this phase of consultation is over, the expert system matches the patterns in the information provided with those its rules suggest are typical situations. From this it can characterize, or diagnose, a problem and suggest some courses of action. The programming is usually done in such a way as to also give an indication of how confident the system is in its recommendations, sometimes based on asking the user how confident he or she feels in the accuracy of the background observations provided. Many expert systems also are able to explain the chain of reasoning used to reach a particular conclusion, something that can help give users more confidence in what is being suggested. The word *finished* was put in quotes earlier because some of these systems are open ended: They get smarter with use. They remember the features of each problem they are used to solve (and the solutions they came up with) and use these to add more shortcuts to their lists of rules.

These expert systems have great potential to make scarce and costly expertise available to a wider audience. Many are still in demonstration or prototype stages, but they have often been useful enough to convince companies to continue funding their development. Their use in leveraging expensive staff talent is illustrated by ExperTAX, an expert system used by the accounting firm Coopers & Lybrand. It draws on the knowledge and experience of 40 senior tax partners to provide an easy-to-use, question-and-answer format for their 96 offices around the United States. The system is intended to be used by junior auditors to provide advice to smaller clients who would not usually be able to afford the attention of top tax professionals. It cost over $1 million to build and can be run from a desktop personal computer. Its internal logic includes 2,000 rules elicited from these senior partners by observing them at work on a variety of client problems. The system was not built to replace accountants; its focus is to enhance the level of advice its staff can provide, not just to automate a manual process.

Some companies have built expert systems around the knowhow of skilled, one-of-a-kind professionals nearing retirement. General Electric captured the knowledge of their foremost expert on maintenance of diesel-electric locomotives. Now they are able to have the system available around the country at customer maintenance locations, rather than fly the expert to the scene of a malfunctioning engine (or hauling the locomotive to him, as often was the case before the expert system was built). A number of these systems have been developed to assist with financial planning, to determine credit worthiness for bank loans, and to help insurance underwriters calculate premiums for complex risks. While many of these corporate-oriented applications are still in their infancy, enough have been used to mark expert systems as something organizational designers should watch closely. As their development progresses, these systems should facilitate more leanly staffed headquarters and fewer management layers.

The real payoff of artificial intelligence is in what managers can do because of it. Research in natural-language processing should eventually allow managers to have an intelligent "front end" on their desktop computer. Managers will be able to easily access corporate data bases, strategic planning models, or financial and operational analysis packages by typing their requests into the terminal in day-to-day English. They will state what they want to know and let the "intelligent" program select which data bases have the information or what models need to be run to determine the solution. This will help end the computer literacy problems managers face today.

A second general application of artificial intelligence is the possibility that managers may have a dozen or more automated assistants in the form of individual expert systems. The "assistants" will help them identify and solve problems in areas they used to bring to their bosses or staff assistants for help. These may include everything from doing annual budget planning to customizing advice on how to best develop subordinates for promotion.

Will expert systems completely replace staff experts? No, not completely. But they will leverage their skills and knowledge. They will allow managers to factor more considerations into decision making than they otherwise might. They will allow companies to track the implications of more embryonic staff issues than they usually do, and to do it in a way that does not add to staff size. And as staff issues become more mature, expert systems will allow more of these issues to be handled by line management, not the central office.

Human Resources Planning, Not Personnel Administration

Reorganization and computers alone will not be enough to keep businesses slim. Without an effective watchdog function, downsized companies will be a transient phenomenon. In the first chapter we considered a dozen forces driving corporate bloat, from decentralized management philosophies to government regulation. We also looked at how some common human resource practices, such as upward-only career development and compensation systems biased toward managers, can lead to excess middle management. Some of these forces have been temporarily checked by restructuring, but all are still very much alive and waiting for an easing of economic pressures to exert their ballooning influences again.

Maryann Keller, an automobile industry analyst, has had many opportunities to compare the Japanese and American ways of managing. She notes "The Japanese regard cost control as something you wake up every morning and do. Americans have always thought of it as a project. You cut costs 20 percent and say: 'Whew! That's over.' We can't afford to think that way anymore." This warning certainly applies to downsizing as well. Without changing the way corporations are managed, it will be business as usual, and mid-level bloat will return. These are partially people issues, but the job is far bigger than the scope of the traditional personnel function. The issues of organizational planning involve power and strategy more than building relationships and administrative procedures.

Staying streamlined requires, in most companies, a strengthened human resources function. This does not necessarily imply a bigger staff department, but more attention must be paid to human resources management by senior executives and line managers. Planning and monitoring the size and shape of a company is a general-management responsibility, not something to be delegated to a staff unit. It needs to be closely related to the business planning process.

In recent years, there has been considerable talk, and minimal action, on the importance of closely integrating human resources and strategy planning. In most companies, it is unrealistic to expect the initiative for this to come from personnel experts, though they certainly have a valuable role to play. Leadership on this, if it is going to be kept from being just another staff-talking-to-other-staff activity, has to start at the top. Much of the detailed planning is also best left to senior line managers, some of whom—it is hoped—will have had experience working in the human resources function at some point in their careers.

As they prepare to stay downsized, it can make sense for some firms to move the training function out of the personnel area and group it with other culture-building and control units such as finance, information systems, and communications. But, even with redeployments such as these, there is still plenty the human resources group can do to keep the company downsized. Here are a few of the key action areas:

□ *Make it hard to get hired.* They can develop detailed selection criteria for new recruits that take into account their fit with overall company culture as well as the requirements of the job. They can deliberately understaff, using contractors and part-time employees as buffers to absorb the swings of a cyclical business. They can continually look for ways—short of hiring people—to get work done which adds only low value to the company.

□ *Make it hard for poor performers to stay.* They can put real teeth into the performance review process. They can adopt a simple single system that can be applied from top to bottom, and see that it evaluates a small number of performance targets that are linked to each job's mission. They can also ensure that *how* a person accomplishes a job is rated as well as *what* is accomplished. They can obtain relevant input to the review process by having managers rated by their subordinates and staff by their internal customers, as well as by their bosses. They can use the results of the reviews primarily to improve performance, not to distribute salary increases. This implies taking a no-nonsense approach to performance assessment. Rodney Plimpton, Vice President of Temple, Barker & Sloane, Inc. and a specialist in organizational issues, describes this notion as being "individually compassionate but collectively ruthless."

□ *Slow down the upward-only fast track.* They can design career paths that cover more horizontal territory than vertical, that include more functional specialties than hierarchial levels. They can try to keep people out of mid-level and senior staff jobs until they have had some experience in the line organization. They can limit appointments to key line executive positions to managers who have spent some of their careers in the human resource function. They should not assume that all good performers will stay for their entire careers, or even that such a situation is the most desirable.

□ *Keep the pay system from building excess management back into the company.* They can adjust aspects of the compensation and job evaluation systems that lead to bloated management. They can look hard at two-track pay scales, but be sure the nonmanagement side applies to all staff professionals, not just R&D types. They can consider applying skill-based pay to staff workers, and examine the possibility of customizing their job evaluation criteria to match the skills essential to their company.

Providing Job Security:
The Downsizing Paradox

In many companies, downsizing is clearly a shock to most of the employees. They may have built up expectations over many years of service in the belief that they have proved themselves, passed some sort of tenure point, and now have jobs for life. Breaking the bonds, spoken or implicit, that have been formed is one of the most wrenching aspects of downsizing. And one of the most disruptive. James Olson, AT&T's chairman, asks: "Do you know how tough it is asking people to support your strategy when you know you can't promise all of them jobs when this is over?" Olson certainly fights an uphill battle, as do other companies trying to build commitment to a new strategy at the same time as they impose continuing staff reductions. At General Electric, John Welch has had to eliminate a quarter of GE's jobs. For the 350,000 remaining, he has redefined what it means to work at GE: "The job of the enterprise is to provide an exciting atmosphere that's open and fair, where people have the resources to go out and win. The job of the people is to take advantage of this playing field and put out 110 percent. . . . The people who get in trouble in our company are those who carry around the anchor of the past."

Welch's view is a good statement of the way the employer-employee relationship is being redefined. Planned downsizers like GE, as well as companies that have been less focused in their reductions, have a sometimes elongated period of transition and consolidation while reshaping their organizations, systems, and strategies. Strong leadership from the top, like that Welch provides, is essential to moving effectively through this period. But at the close of this period, many companies may find it to their advantage to rethink something paradoxical to the idea of downsizing: managing the company to provide as high a degree of job security as possible for those remaining.

At post-downsized Apple Computer, temporary help is used to staff up to 10 percent of its jobs. Michael Ahearn, Apple's staffing manager, says: "If we bring someone on board full time, there is an implied obligation that the job won't disappear."

The vice president of Sony of America, Samadi Wada, provides a Japanese-eye view of what happens when workers and managers are continually concerned about how long their jobs will last: "I understand why some American companies fail to gain the loyalty and dedication of their employees. Employees cannot care for an employer who is prepared to take their livelihood away at the first sign of trouble." As we have considered in Chapter 7, IBM is an American company that has taken this point of view to heart. It defends its costs and inconveniences by citing concrete benefits to its business, such as its ability to cut out two-thirds of the cost of product manufacturing through the skill and smarts of its work force. IBM maintains that these achievements would have been impossible without the productive and committed work force that its full employment practices have helped produce. Other employers committed to providing employment security, like the Lincoln Electric Company, cite the same benefits occurring for the same reasons.

Many U.S. manufacturers have found the secret to continued productivity improvement in making sure that the people a company expects to deliver it know that they are not paving their way to an unemployment line. This applies in the office as well as the factory, to staff professionals and middle managers as well as assembly workers. It is a view that companies concerned about staying streamlined, not just temporarily lean, should consider.

Balanced Attention to
All the Corporation's Constituencies

Many private-sector executives have become as skilled at balancing the interests of competing groups as have seasoned members of Congress. Most know that the myth of the company as a short-term profit maximizer is just that, and that they must constantly respond to multiple constituencies. Coping with the sometimes conflicting demands of government regulators, unions, employees, supplier cartels, local communities, Wall Street, shareholders, retirees, and customers requires statesmanship coupled with a strong sense of direction. This sense of direction—the view of a company's overall mission—is something that cannot be learned in business school. Executives develop, personalize, and pull together teams to support that mission throughout their careers. It is a critical management tool for companies trying to ensure a future for themselves in the twenty-first century. Just getting by through balancing competing interests may make for an exciting career, but it will not necessarily build a business that will prevail. This kind of corporate gamesmanship is doomed, because what may be in the immediate best interests of one constituency will not always serve this group, let alone the others, in the long haul.

Through most of the 1960s and '70s, the stock market rewarded companies that maintained strong growth rates, often through unrelated acquisitions, and that achieved ever-increasing earnings, even if those earnings were generated by underinvesting in their base businesses. Sticking to the knitting was dull, usually unrewarding—something considered suitable for old women. By the mid-1980s, the piper had to be paid. Many companies lost their competitive advantage to more focused overseas rivals, and bloated corporate structures were strangling both profits and good ideas for the future. And the stockmarket, which has always favored the short-term, switched loyalty to value generated by lean companies with equity returns better than any nearby safer alternative. The restructuring that resulted has caused more turmoil than many industries have seen since the Depression. Some companies with clear missions and purposes are taking advantage of the turmoil to reposition themselves to provide sustainable value for their customers. Reactions of others are keyed more to immediate fears of corporate raiders and the current price of capital. They are still leaving themselves open to being tossed around by the concerns of the moment.

Mission-driven businesses, like Apple Computer, Chrysler, TRW, and Xerox, are no strangers to restructurings or the downsizing that frequently accompanies them. But through careful planning and follow-through, they have built organizations that are stronger, not just smaller. While not losing sight of the stock market, they also have not ignored their employees' needs. Corporate missions are built on the interrelated needs of all a company's constituencies. To the extent that one of these groups must be emphasized for a time, a "correction" in corporate attention will eventually follow and provide attention to the requirements of the others as well. These companies work hard to avoid the bitter criticism of one long-service oil company manager: "We used to be a community. . . .Now it's clear there is only one important group—the shareholders." Planned downsizers, while reacting to immediate pressures, are preparing for future challenges by not forgetting the employees they will have to count on to meet those challenges.

A Demographic Kicker

The demographics of the 1980s have been a challenge for many companies and managers. The postwar baby boom reached mid-management age just at a time when restructuring and downsizing eliminated many of the positions they hoped to move into. Companies that have responded to this by working hard to provide job security for those who remain are one step ahead of others, with loyal and committed people to deal with the demographics of the 1990s. But while the U.S. work force grew by 2.6 percent in the 1970s, this growth will slow to 1.1 percent by 1995. The coming of age by the "baby bust" generation will lead to labor shortages, not continued surpluses. Companies will be running lean because they have to, not because they want to reduce overhead.

These labor shortages have already reached industries

dependent on entry-level workers. In many regions of the United States, the minimum wage is something to laugh at. While redeployment of the by-then-aging baby boomers will absorb some of the slack, and making better use of women, minorities, and retirement age managers will also help, the going will not be easy for many companies in the 1990s. Labor shortages and high salaries will drive many companies to try the tactics we have been considering in the last two chapters. And the greatest advantage will go to the mission-driven, planned downsizers who have prepared for this situation all along.

Appendix:
How Job Evaluation Favors Managers

Because job evaluations often lead to management bloat, it is worth considering their causes in more detail than is appropriate in the main text. Without addressing this problem, it is likely that many of the management layers shed during downsizing will reappear on the organization chart of several years hence.

The experience of a rapidly growing biotechnology company illustrates this problem and its consequences rather clearly. Like many entrepreneurial start-ups, it grew rapidly and without a lot of initial concern for consistency in personnel practices. Management attention was focused more on engineering new molecules and finding investors to support the long product-development cycle these required. As the company added new scientists and executives, each was paid what the market seemed to require at the moment of hiring. The consequences of this ad hoc salary setting caught up with the company after several years. There were complaints of similarly qualified individuals doing similar work but receiving very different paychecks. Some people quit, and the chief executive soon realized that this was the time to formalize a consistent salary structure.

Many of the common job-evaluation techniques were considered by a team of the company's scientist-managers. They selected one method that appeared comprehensive and allowed for easy quantification of judgments about individual jobs. The opportunities it provided for peer decision making also appealed to the scientists. But the factors used and how points were weighted quickly indicated that the method had a sharp bias. Managers were rewarded with job evaluation points at the expense of stellar-performing individual contributors.

By looking inside the "black box" of job evaluation, the team soon found why. This scheme rated jobs on 12 factors, with the maximum points available for each factor, as shown in Table A.1.

Upon first consideration, the system seemed appropriate for this high-technology company. Only the last two factors seemed directly related to management work, and they only covered 110 points (20 percent) of those available. But the scientists on the task force insisted upon applying the experimental method before they would accept it for company-wide use.

Table A.1. Job evaluation factors and points.

Factor	Total Points
1. Knowledge	70
2. Work experience	70
3. Freedom from supervision	50
4. Independent judgment	60
5. Accountability and responsibility	60
6. Work relationships	50
7. Work environment	25
8. Manual skill	15
9. Hazards and risks in the work environment	25
10. Physical labor	15
11. Number of people supervised	70
12. Nature of managerial responsibilities	40
Total	550

After a series of trial ratings of management and nonmanagement jobs, it was quickly apparent that the senior management positions scored close to the 550 total points, while few of the senior scientist jobs received as many as half the total points. Because the company's business strategy was more dependent on scientific achievement than managerial prowess, the team agreed something was wrong.

A close examination of the ten other factors revealed that, to receive the upper range of points in four of them, it was necessary to have managerial responsibilities. The biased factors were: freedom from supervision, independent judgment, accountability and responsibility, and work relationships. These four factors accounted for an additional 220 points in this system. Allowing that it was hard for nonmanagement jobs to get more than 100 of these additional points, the system kept almost half of its total points from nonmanagers! Since these points were to be used to determine salary levels, the potential problems could have been very significant. Ad hoc salary discrimination was easier to explain in this company of well-trained number watchers than was the systematic variety. When they reviewed several other common approaches to job evaluation, similar problems emerged.

This genetic engineering company eventually solved its problem by adopting a custom-designed job evaluation scale that provided alternative ways to rate jobs on these bias-prone factors. While their situation was rather specialized, it does offer a warning for companies in a wide range of businesses. The scientific curiosity of their staff led them to challenge some implicit features of many job evaluation systems that other executives take for granted or assume are being taken care of by their compensation specialists. These systems are used because of the other benefits they provide or the expense of changing them. What is too often ignored is the cost of maintaining the systems: excess managers and slow decision making from the extra layers that eventually must be created to accommodate them.

Another example illustrates the difficulties that can plague companies with management-oriented compensation systems.

In this second case, the difficulties were faced by a large chemical company planning a reorganization. The head of one of its major headquarters units, a 150-person staff department, needed a small policy-planning unit reporting directly to him to give more focus and cohesion to the work of the diverse group of professionals in the department. He agreed that the best person to head the new 2- to 3-person unit would be the manager of a 54-person group within the department. But he was reluctant to make the appointment because he was certain that the new job, with fewer people to supervise, would not be rated high enough by the company's job evaluation committee to allow the favored manager to hold it and keep his current salary.

He thought this was ridiculous. The new job would have a much greater impact on the overall usefulness of the department to the company than did the entire 54-person unit. Unfortunately, he had too many scars from previous battles with the job evaluation system to take on this fight. So he compromised. He appointed the manager to the new post, but also let him keep responsibility for most of his old operation as well. An acceptable alternative? Not really. The manager ended up chronically overloaded and never was able to give sufficient time to the policy-planning tasks.

Notes

INTRODUCTION

Page

1   Richard Darman said: Hobart Rowen, "U.S. Official Raps Business Executives," *Washington Post,* Nov. 8, 1986, p. G1.
1   Just after World War II: Amanda Bennett, "Chevron Corp. Has Big Challenge Coping with Worker Cutback," *Wall Street Journal,* Nov. 4, 1986, p. 1.
1   "It was almost": Arch Patton, "Industry's Misguided Shift to Staff Jobs," *Business Week,* Apr. 5, 1982, p. 12.
1   In 1980: Mark Green and John Berry, "The Forces Behind White-Collar Layoffs," *New York Times,* Oct. 13, 1985, p. F3.
2   "Where we were hiring": Ibid.
2   But almost all: Lester Thurow, "White-Collar Overhead," *Across the Board,* Nov. 1986, p. 26.

CHAPTER 1: THE BULGE IN THE CORPORATE PYRAMID

Page

6   "A salesman hears": Robert Reich, *The Next American Frontier* (New York: Times Books, a Division of Random House, Inc., 1983), pp. 143–144.

Page

8   GM's costs: Maralyn Edid and William Hampton, "Detroit vs. Japan: Now What's the Problem?," *Business Week,* Sept. 1, 1986, p. 74.

8   Chairman Roger Smith: Anne Fisher, "GM Is Tougher than You Think," *Fortune,* Nov. 10, 1986, p. 56.

8   An observer of GM: Ibid., p. 60.

8   25 percent fewer: William Hampton, "GM's Shuffle: The Calm Before the Slaughter?," *Business Week,* Feb. 17, 1986, p. 35.

8   Figure 1.1: John Neuman, "OVA: Avoid Slash and Burn Overhead Reduction," *Management Review,* Jan. 1987, p. 38.

8   In electrical machinery: Reich, p. 142.

8   By 1976: Ibid.

8   Some estimates indicate: "A Telephone Stock to Reach Out and Touch?," *Fortune,* Nov. 10, 1986, p. 172.

8   One large and wealthy: Betsy Morris, "RJR Nabisco Is Jolted by Chief Who Arrived Through a Takeover," *Wall Street Journal,* Jan. 20, 1987, p. 31.

9   Half its work force: Reich, p. 142.

10   This "chain of command": Edward Luttwak, *The Pentagon and the Art of War* (New York: Simon and Schuster, Inc., 1985), p. 51.

11   300,000 British troops: Henry Mintzberg, *The Structuring of Organizations* (Englewood Cliffs, N.J.: Prentice-Hall, Inc., 1979), p. 345.

11   He attributes: Luttwak, pp. 18–19.

11   Become managers instead: Ibid., p. 192.

12   Iran-hostage rescue: Ibid., pp. 44–45.

12   Israeli commando experts: Ibid., p. 44.

13   Tiny 315-employee: Steven Greenhouse, "Minnetonka's Struggle to Stay One Step Ahead," *New York Times,* Dec. 28, 1986, p. F8.

17   Sustainer of management layering: Edward Lawler III, "What's Wrong with Point-Factor Job Evaluation," *Compensation and Benefits Review,* Mar.-Apr. 1986, pp. 20–28.

21   Build disappointment: Harry Levinson, *Psychological Man* (Cambridge, Mass.: The Levinson Institute, 1976), p. 56.

22   Chris Argyris has: Chris Argyris and Donald Schön, *Organizational Learning: A Theory of Action Perspective* (Reading, Mass.: Addison-Wesley Publishing Company, 1978).

Page

24   Korean Airlines: Richard Witkin, "Korean Pilot Offers New
       Theory on Downed Plane," *New York Times,* Dec. 28, 1986,
       p. 8.
26   Ford Motor Company needed: "A New Target: Reducing Staff
       and Levels," *Business Week,* Dec. 21, 1981, p. 69.
26   "Managing Our Way": Robert Hayes and William Abernathy,
       "Managing Our Way to Economic Decline," *Harvard Business
       Review,* July–Aug. 1980, pp. 67–77.
26   *Theory Z:* William Ouchi, *Theory Z: How American Business Can
       Meet the Japanese Challenge* (Reading, Mass.: Addison-Wesley,
       1981).
26   *The Art of Japanese Management:* Richard Pascale and Anthony
       Athos, *The Art of Japanese Management* (New York: Simon and
       Schuster, Inc., 1981).
26   *In Search of Excellence:* Thomas J. Peters and Robert H.
       Waterman, Jr., *In Search of Excellence: Lessons from America's Best-
       Run Companies* (New York: Harper & Row, 1982).
26   "There is, then": Thomas Peters and Nancy Austin, *A Passion
       for Excellence: The Leadership Difference* (New York: Random
       House, 1985).
27   Peters' examination: Peters and Waterman.

CHAPTER 2: DEMASSING: A BLUNT RESPONSE

Page

28   Conference Board estimate: Susan Sanderson and Lawrence
       Schein, "Sizing Up the Downsizing Era," *Across The Board,* Nov.
       1986, pp. 15–16.
28   Bureau of Labor Statistics: "A New Era for Management,"
       Business Week, Apr. 25, 1983, p. 50.
28   Search firm estimates: Earl Gottschalk, Jr., "More Ex-Managers
       Seek to Turn Hobbies Into Full-Time Businesses," *Wall Street
       Journal,* Dec. 23, 1986, p. 23.
28   Other reports suggest: Sanderson and Schein.
30   International Telephone and Telegraph: "Cost-Saving Efforts
       Spread," *Washington Post,* Sept. 19, 1986, p. G2.

Page

30 General Electric's purchase: Howard Banks [ed.] "The New Wave of Firings at the Top," *Forbes*, Aug. 25, 1986, p. 25.

30 Cutbacks at Eastman Kodak: David Armon, "Kodak Plans Major Layoffs, Cost-Cutting," *Washington Post*, Feb. 12, 1986, p. F1.

30 Brunswick Corporation's: "A Slimmed-Down Brunswick Is Proving Wall Street Wrong," *Business Week*, May 28, 1984, pp. 90–98.

31 Tektronix planned: Mike Tharp, "Tektronix Sets Layoff of 2,000," *Wall Street Journal*, May 22, 1986, p. 4.

31 Hewlett-Packard offered: Brenton Schlender, "Hewlett to Offer 1,800 a Program to Retire Early," *Wall Street Journal*, June 13, 1986.

31 Victor Technologies, found: Erik Larson, "Victor Expected to Cut 500 More from Its Staff," *Wall Street Journal*, Sept. 20, 1983, p. 4

31 Xerox's disk drive: John Eckhouse, "Xerox Dumping Shugart—1,650 Jobs in Peril," *San Francisco Chronicle*, Jan. 17, 1985, p. 29.

31 CBS' in-house medical: Peter Boyer, "Trauma Time on Network TV," *New York Times*, Nov. 2, 1986, p. F28.

31 Time Inc., spent: Mark Vamos, "Trouble in Paradise: A Jolt of Reality at Time Inc.," *Business Week*, Feb. 17, 1986, p. 40.

33 For 29 consecutive quarters: Dale Buss, "Ford Is Riding High with Smart Execution and Slashed Capacity," *Wall Street Journal*, Oct. 7, 1986, p. 14.

33 Satellite-linked computer networks: Kenneth Noble, "America's Service Economy Begins to Blossom—Overseas," *New York Times*, Dec. 14, 1986.

34 Industry watchers predict: "Minding the Store," *New York Times*, Oct. 12, 1986.

35 An Exxon employee relations: Richard Schmidt, "Major Oil Firms Are Slashing Jobs as Takeovers Rise, Demand Sags," *Wall Street Journal*, Apr. 19, 1984.

35 At Phillips Petroleum: "Labor Letter," *Wall Street Journal*, May 6, 1986, p. 1.

35 Texas-based Mostek: Cynthia Green, "Middle Managers Are Still Sitting Ducks," *Business Week*, Sept. 16, 1985, p. 34.

35 MCI: Elizabeth Tucker and Michael Schrage, "MCI Cuts Its

Page

Workforce by 2,400," *Washington Post,* Dec. 4, 1986, p. D9.

36 Thousands of management: John Keller, "A Leaner AT&T Could Cost Thousands of Jobs," *Business Week,* Sept. 25, 1986, p. 50.

36 Texas Air Corporation's: "Lorenzo Moves into Top Slot at Eastern Air," *Asian Wall Street Journal,* Oct. 20, 1986, p. 2.

36 Northwest Airlines: "Cost-Saving Efforts Spread," *Washington Post,* Sept. 19, 1986, p. G2.

37 Spicemaker McCormick: "McCormick & Co. to Cut 400 Employees Across the Board," *Washington Business Journal,* Aug. 25, 1986, p. 2.

37 Control Data Corporation's restructuring: "Commercial Credit Sets Headquarters Layoffs, Appoints Six Officials," *Wall Street Journal,* Dec. 9, 1986, p. 8.

38 An attempt by GAF: John Nielson, "Management Layoffs Won't Quit," *Fortune,* Oct. 28, 1985, p. 48.

38 Ted Turner's attempted acquisition: Green.

38 Crocker National Corporation: Richard Schmidt, "Wells Fargo Takeover of Crocker is Yielding Profit but Some Pain," *Wall Street Journal,* Aug. 5, 1986, p. 1.

39 The U.S. government: "LBOing the Federal Payroll," *Forbes,* Dec. 15, 1986, p. 130.

39 British Air cut: "The New Pizazz at British Airways," *Business Week,* Mar. 14, 1983, pp. 50–52.

40 D. Quinn Mills calls: Michael Schrage, "'Outplacement' Thrives as U.S. Firms Regroup," *Washington Post,* Dec. 28, 1986, p. K2.

41 Outplacement has increased: Craig Mellow, "Out-Placement Passages," *Across the Board,* Nov. 1986, p. 39.

43 "Our last layoff": Patricia Paris, "Chesebrough-Pond's Malaise," *Business Week,* June 3, 1985, p. 6A.

43 One management observer: Thomas Horton, "Wasting the Work Force," [unpublished speech], 1986.

43 As Thomas Horton: Ibid.

44 "Unfortunately, a lot of": Schrage.

44 "Management broke the": Rod Willis, "What's Happening to America's Middle Managers?," *Management Review,* Jan. 1987, p. 27.

44 Study by the American Society: Felix Kessler, "Managers Without a Company," *Fortune,* Oct. 28, 1985, p. 54.

Page

45 A middle manager: Janet Guyon, "As Profits Lag, AT&T Eases Computer Push, Plans Further Job Cuts," *Wall Street Journal*, Nov. 11, 1986, p. 32.

47 One of the several thousand: Daniel Karatzas, "Jack Welch's General Electric," *Fortune*, Aug. 4, 1986, p. 17.

47 Studies of companies: Richard Norman, *Management and Statesmanship* (Stockholm: Scandinavian Institutes for Administrative Research, 1976).

48 At least one has warned: Clare Ansberry, "Kodak, Aided by Cost-Cutting Program, Posts 6.9% Rise in Fiscal 3rd-Period Net," *Wall Street Journal*, Nov. 4, 1986, p. 5.

48 Celanese Corporation had gone: Patricia Gray and Terence Roth, "Celanese Gets $2.72 Billion Bid from Hoechst," *Wall Street Journal*, Nov. 4, 1986, p. 22.

49 Surveys by Opinion Research: Peter Behr and David Vise, "Big U.S. Corporations Launch New Wave of Cutbacks," *Washington Post*, Sept. 14, 1986, p. K4.

50 The chief economist: Kessler, p. 52.

51 A 1986 survey, conducted: "BW/Harris Executive Poll: No Job Is Forever," *Business Week*, Aug. 4, 1986, p. 49.

52 Rex Adams: Sanderson and Schein, p. 22.

53 They lack the job: Green.

CHAPTER 3: PLANNED DOWNSIZING:
A SUSTAINABLE ALTERNATIVE

Page

56 "Indiscriminate, impermanent": "Firms Can Improve Overall Health by Restructuring," *TBS NewsView*, Fall 1986, p. 6.

56 Some companies have been: "For Middle Managers the Squeeze Is Still On," *Business Week*, Aug. 8, 1983, p. 23.

56 Shell has followed: Toni Mack, "'It's Time to Take Risks'," *Forbes*, Oct. 6, 1986, p. 125.

56 "We didn't let": Ibid., p. 126.

62 Paul Strassmann: "A Conversation with Paul A. Strassmann," *Organizational Dynamics*, Autumn 1985, p. 27.

62 The Strategic Planning Institute: *Management Productivity and Information Technology* (Cambridge, Mass.: The Strategic Plan-

Page

ning Institute, 1983), p. 30.

62 The ROM for all of: "A Conversation with Paul A. Strassmann," p. 31.

62 "They buy more": Ibid., p. 27.

64 "Value chain.": Michael Porter, *Competitive Advantage: Creating
and Sustaining Superior Performance* (New York: The Free Press,
A Division of Macmillan, Inc., 1985), pp. 36–52.

65 Donald Kane: Interview with Donald Kane, Manager of Corporate Organization Planning, General Electric Company, Jan.
25, 1984.

66 Problems of a large steel company: Thomas O'Boyle and Carol
Hymowitz, "Graham's U.S. Steel Streamlining Takes Toll on
His Relations with Employees," *Wall Street Journal,* Aug. 17,
1984, p. 23.

66 Another manager: "Graham Is Trying to Forge a Tougher
U.S. Steel," *Business Week,* Oct. 10, 1983, p. 106.

66 Eastman Kodak has also: Leslie Helm, "Kicking the Single-
Product Habit at Kodak," *Business Week,* Dec. 1, 1986, pp. 36–
37.

66 A multi-industry study: *Seeking and Destroying the Wealth Dissipators* (Chicago: A.T. Kearney, Inc., 1984).

66 Average annual percent increases: Ibid., p. 3.

67 Measures of management efficiency: Ibid., p. 5.

68 Performers averaged: Ibid., p. 3.

CHAPTER 4: PINPOINTING EXCESS STAFF

Page

69 "There are two ways": "A New Era for Management," *Business
Week,* Apr. 25, 1983, p. 52.

70 When "Hubie" Clark: "The Shrinking of Middle Management," *Business Week,* Apr. 25, 1983, p. 55.

71 Legions protecting: Edward Luttwak, *The Grand Strategy of
the Roman Empire* (Baltimore: Johns Hopkins University Press,
1976), p. 14.

71 General Motors, Du Pont, and Sears: Alfred Chandler, Jr.,
Strategy and Structure, (Cambridge, Mass.: M.I.T. Press, 1962).

Page

73 Lester Thurow: Lester Thurow, "White-Collar Overhead," *Across the Board,* Nov. 1986, p. 27.

74 "We've been rewarding": "A New Era for Management," *Business Week,* Apr. 25, 1983, p. 52.

75 Arch Patton: Arch Patton, "Industry's Misguided Shift to Staff Jobs," *Business Week,* Apr. 5, 1982, p. 12.

75 "The United States puts": Ibid.

76 "What has always frustrated": "The Shrinking of Middle Management," *Business Week,* Apr. 25, 1983, p. 56.

77 Geneen's numbers-driven: Richard Pascale and Anthony Athos, *The Art of Japanese Management* (New York: Simon and Schuster, 1981), pp. 58–78.

78 The French purchaser: Thane Peterson, "CGE Plans to Savage ITT in Order to Save It," *Business Week,* Dec. 29, 1986, p. 49.

78 Henry Mintzberg: Henry Mintzberg, *The Structuring of Organizations,* (Englewood Cliffs, N.J.: Prentice-Hall, Inc., 1979), p. 29–34.

80 William Johnson: *Positioning Corporate Staff for the 1990s* (Houston: American Productivity Center and Cresap, McCormick and Paget, 1986), p. 15.

82 Judge, jury, and executioner: Ibid., p. 16.

87 General Electric acquired NBC: Peter Boyer, "Trauma Time on Network TV," *New York Times,* Nov. 2, 1986, p. 1F.

98 Denver's IntraWest Bank: "The Shrinking of Middle Management," *Business Week,* Apr. 25, 1983, p. 56.

99 Xerox, probably more: "How Xerox Speeds Up the Birth of New Products," *Business Week,* Mar. 19, 1984, p. 58.

99 L. L. Bean's warehouse: Frances Gaither Tucker, Seymour Zivan and Robert Camp, "How to Measure Yourself Against the Best," *Harvard Business Review,* Jan.–Feb. 1987, p. 9.

100 Common Staffing Study: "IBM Plan Measures Efficiency of Non-Manufacturing Employees," *Commerce America,* Mar. 29, 1976.

101 Division heads at Emerson Electric: "The Shrinking of Middle Management," *Business Week,* Apr. 25, 1983, p. 56.

102 Weyerhaeuser Company: Ibid.

102 Acme-Cleveland: Ibid.

102 Let's first consider the steps: John Neuman, "OVA: Avoid

Slash and Burn Overhead Reduction," *Management Review,* Jan. 1987, pp. 34–39.

107   Many modern organization observers: John Kotter, *Organizational Dynamics* (Reading, Mass.: Addison-Wesley Publishing Company, 1978).

107   [Xerox] also charges each staff function: Interview with Richard Randazzo, director of personnel administration, Xerox Corporation, on Aug. 19, 1985.

108   Domino's Pizza: Interview with Donald Vlcek, President, Domino's Pizza Distribution Company, on Aug. 22, 1985.

109   Activity cost measurement: Gregory Hendrick, "Organizational Structure: The Source of Low Productivity," *Advanced Management Journal,* Winter, 1982.

111   When GE examined: *Employee Effectiveness: Introspect* (Bridgeport, Conn.: General Electric Company, no date), p. 3.

CHAPTER 5: MANAGING STAFF STRATEGICALLY

116   Michael Porter feels: Michael Porter, *Competitive Strategy: Techniques for Analyzing Industries and Competitors* (New York: The Free Press, A Division of Macmillan Publishing Co., Inc., 1980), p. 4.

122   Four distinct maturity phases: Arnoldo Hax and Nicolas Majluf, *Strategic Management: An Integrative Perspective* (Englewood Cliffs, N.J.: Prentice-Hall, Inc., 1984), p. 182–208.

128   One manufacturer: "The Shrinking of Middle Management," *Business Week,* Apr. 25, 1983, p. 55.

129   Chrysler to cut: "A New Era for Management," *Business Week,* Apr. 25, 1983, p. 53.

130   Chief scientist: "General Electric Co. Names Schmidt, 63, Firm's Chief Scientist," *Wall Street Journal,* July 29, 1986, p. 14.

131   Chief information officers: Gordon Bock, "Management's Newest Star," *Business Week,* Oct. 13, 1986, pp. 160–172.

137   "Our planning system": Richard Hamermesh, "Making Planning Strategic," *Harvard Business Review,* July–Aug. 1986, p. 117.

CHAPTER 6: FLATTENING THE PYRAMID

Page

139   "Will we revert": Nat Snyderman, "GE Is Doing the Things the
       U.S. Must Do to Be Competitive," *Electronic News*, Oct. 3, 1983,
       p. B.

139   Albert Casey's: "Management Cut by Postal Service," *Washington Post*, Mar. 25, 1986, p. A15.

140   "To make field-management": Ibid.

140   Sears, Roebuck and Company: Caroline Mayer, "Sears to Close
       4 Offices, Cut Management Layer," *Washington Post*, Apr. 15,
       1986, p. D3.

140   Brunswick's Mercury Marine: Maggie McComas, "Cutting
       Costs Without Killing the Business," *Fortune*, Oct. 13, 1986, p.
       76.

140   Prudential Insurance Company: "Prudential Shifting Top
       Management," *New York Times*, Aug. 16, 1984, p. D2.

141   "Getting the message": Ibid.

141   Merrill Lynch: Steve Swartz, "Merrill Lynch, Racing Growing
       Competition, Reaches a Crossroads," *Asian Wall Street Journal*,
       Aug. 13, 1986, p. 16.

142   One study: Ellis Cose, "Do We Pay Too Much for Management?" *USA Today*, Mar. 25, 1983, p. 3B.

143   One petroleum company: "Span-of-Control Analysis: Improving the Lot of the Part-time Manager," *Productivity*, Sept. 1985.

144   "From all accounts": "Corporate Bureaucracy Clogs Output,
       Cripples Productivity," *TBS NewsViews*, Fall 1985, p. 3.

145   Ten characteristics: Henry Mintzberg, *The Nature of Managerial
       Work* (New York: Harper & Row, 1973), pp. 54–99.

146   Peter Drucker noted: Peter Drucker, *Management: Tasks,
       Responsibilities, Practices* (New York: Harper & Row, 1973),
       p. 546.

147   As John F. Kennedy was: Graham Allison, *Essence of Decision:
       Explaining the Cuban Missile Crisis* (Boston: Little, Brown and
       Company, 1971), pp. 141–142.

148   Since 1980: John Nielsen, "Management Layoffs Won't Quit,"
       Fortune, Oct. 28, 1985, p. 46.

148   Herbert Rees: Herbert Rees, "The Definition of Bureaucracy,"
       INC., Aug. 1986, p. 84.

Page

149 Jaques maintains: Susan Rasky, "Corporate Psychologist: Elliott Jaques," *New York Times*, Feb. 17, 1985, p. 8F. Also "Conversation with Elliott Jaques," *Organizational Dynamics*, Spring 1977, pp. 24–43. Also Jerry Gray [ed.], *The Glacier Project: Concepts and Critiques* (New York: Crane, Russak & Company, Inc., 1976).

154 "Success doomed": Frances Burns, "Success Doomed People Express," *Washington Post*, Dec. 20, 1986, p. E2.

155 "They organized themselves": Ibid. Reprinted with permission of United Press International, ©1986.

155 Reorganization of 3M's: "3M's Problems in the Office of the Future," *Business Week*, Oct. 13, 1980, p. 123. Also "3M Looks Beyond Luck and Fast Profits," *Business Week*, Feb. 23, 1981, p. 44. Also "3M's Aggressive New Consumer Drive," *Business Week*, July 18, 1984, pp. 114–122.

155 Hewlett-Packard: "Why Hewlett-Packard Overhauled Its Management," *Business Week*, July 30, 1984, pp. 111–112. Also Bro Uttal, "Mettle-Test Time for John Young," *Fortune*, Apr. 29, 1985, pp. 242–248.

155 "Three or four": "Can John Young Redesign Hewlett-Packard?," *Business Week*, Dec. 6, 1982, p. 72.

157 Figure 6.1 illustrates: For another perspective on Figure 6.1, consult David Van Fleet and Arthur Bedeian, "A History of the Span of Management," *Academy of Management Review*, July 1977, p. 360.

157 Many management theoreticians: Ibid., p. 358.

158 No supervisor can: Ibid.

158 Sears, Roebuck and Company: Henry Mintzberg, *The Structuring of Organizations* (Englewood Cliffs, N.J.: Prentice-Hall, Inc., 1979), p. 134.

160 Peter Drucker: Drucker, p. 412.

160 James Thompson: James Thompson, *Organizations in Action* (New York: McGraw-Hill, 1967).

163 Arch Patton: Arch Patton, "Industry's Misguided Shift to Staff Jobs," *Business Week*, Apr. 5, 1982, p. 12.

163 Average U.S. corporate manager: Robert Reich, *Tales of a New America* (New York: Times Books, a Division of Random House, Inc., 1987), p. 142.

Page

163   Average U.S. employee: Ibid.
165   The chief executive: Interview with Sir John Sainsbury, Managing Director, Sainsbury's PLC, Nov. 23, 1983.
166   Frederick Herzberg: Frederick Herzberg, *Work and the Nature of Man* (Cleveland: The World Publishing Company, 1966).
167   Average U.S. CEO: Reich.
167   ITT's Harold Geneen justified: Richard Pascale and Anthony Athos, *The Art of Japanese Management* (New York: Simon and Schuster, 1981), pp. 58–78.
175   The Celanese president: "Celanese: Weaving a New Pattern to Survive a Cyclical Economy," *Business Week*, Aug. 15, 1983, p. 116.
175   At Brunswick: "The Shrinking of Middle Management," *Business Week*, Apr. 25, 1983, p. 54.
175   Crown Zellerbach: Ibid., p. 56.
175   Du Pont's executive committee: "What's Causing the Scratches in Du Pont's Teflon?," *Business Week*, Dec. 8, 1986, p. 61.
175   Imperial Chemical Industries: Stephanie Cooke and John Tarpey, "Behind the Stunning Comeback at Britain's ICI," *Business Week*, June 3, 1985, pp. 62–63.
176   Abraham Zaleznick: N. Kleinfield, "When Many Chiefs Think as One," *New York Times*, Oct. 28, 1984, p. F1.
176   Harry Levinson: Ibid.
176   "Little more than": "The Frustrations of the Group Executive," *Business Week*, Sept. 25, 1978, p. 102.
177   "Freddie" Heineken keeps: David Tinnin, "The Heady Success of Holland's Heineken," *Fortune*, Nov. 16, 1981, p. 169–173.
177   Clark Equipment Company: "Clark Equipment: A Survival Effort that Depends on Streamlining," *Business Week*, Dec. 6, 1982, p. 93.
186   Some Xerox executives felt: "How Xerox Speeds Up the Birth of New Products," *Business Week*, Mar. 19, 1984, p. 58.
186   Two business-school professors: Stanley Davis and Paul Lawrence, *Matrix* (Reading, Mass.: Addison-Wesley Publishing Company, 1977).
187   "There are, indeed": Ibid., p. vi.
187   When Xerox converted: "How Xerox Speeds Up the Birth of New Products," *Business Week*, Mar. 19, 1984, p. 58.
187   Janssen Pharmaceutical: Joan Hamilton and Joyce Heard,

Page

"Why There's No Stopping Drugmaker Paul Janssen," *Business Week,* Nov. 10, 1986, p. 88F.

188 New computer development: Tracy Kidder, *The Soul of a New Machine* (New York: Avon Books, A Division of the Hearst Corporation, 1981).

CHAPTER 7: LAYOFFS AND ALTERNATIVES TO LAYOFFS

Page

190 "At Tenneco, 1,200": Rod Willis, "What's Happening to America's Middle Managers?," *Management Review,* Jan. 1987, p. 28.

191 "In the early 1970s": Lee Perry, "Least-Cost Alternatives to Layoffs in Declining Industries," *Organizational Dynamics,* Spring 1986, p. 48.

194 "For every company": Willis.

194 The Esmark takeover: Myron Magnet, "Help! My Company Has Just Been Taken Over," *Fortune,* July 9, 1984, p. 48.

195 "Some of these packages": Michael Schrage, "Outplacement Thrives as U.S. Firms Regroup," *Washington Post,* Dec. 28, 1986, p. K2.

195 Among the most generous: Bruce Nussbaum, "The End of Corporate Loyalty?," *Business Week,* Aug. 4, 1986, p. 45.

196 Norfolk Southern: Johnnie Roberts, "Norfolk Southern Offers Incentives to Cut Work Force," *Wall Street Journal,* Oct. 14, 1986, p. 24.

196 Du Pont originally: Nussbaum.

196 Manville Corporation: Perry, p. 56.

197 "The inflection in": Nussbaum, p. 48.

197 American Motors: Amanda Bennett and Douglas Sease, "To Reduce Their Costs Big Companies Lay Off White Collar Workers," *Wall Street Journal,* May 22, 1986, p. 1.

197 "You will always": Janet Bamford, "Hang Tough, or Take the Gold Watch Early?," *Forbes,* May 5, 1986, p. 159.

197 Du Pont took: Nussbaum, p. 43.

197 Union Carbide: John Nielson, "Management Layoffs Won't Quit," *Fortune,* Oct. 28, 1985, p. 49.

197 One stock analyst: Michael Schrage, "IBM Offers Incentives to Cut Staff," *Washington Post,* Sept. 13, 1986, p. C1.

Page

198   Oliver Williamson: Perry, pp. 49–51.
201   Intel Corporation: "A Flood of Pink Slips for Middle Manage-
      ment," *Business Week,* Dec. 20, 1982, p. 21.
201   Hitachi: "Hitachi Will Cut Salaries Because of Yen's Strength,"
      Wall Street Journal, Sept. 30, 1986.
201   Hewlett-Packard: Brenton Schlender, "Hewlett to Offer 1,800
      a Program to Retire Early," *Wall Street Journal,* June 13, 1986.
201   Motorola: Perry, p. 55.
201   Signetics: Selwyn Feinstein, "'Short-Time' Pay Fails to Catch
      on as a Way to Hold Down Layoffs," *Wall Street Journal,* Feb.
      3, 1987.
201   Polaroid: Perry, p. 52.
201   Pacific Northwest Bell: Ibid.
203   Nordson Corporation: "A Flood of Pink Slips for Middle Man-
      agement," *Business Week,* Dec. 20, 1982, p. 21.
203   Shell: Toni Mack, "'It's Time to Take Risks'," *Forbes,* Oct. 6,
      1986, p. 125.
204   West German food retailer: John Whitney, "Effective Turn-
      arounds Do Not Require Employee Turnovers," *Wall Street
      Journal,* Jan. 12, 1987.
208   Major redeployment: Carol Loomis, "IBM's Big Blues: A Leg-
      end Tries to Remake Itself," *Fortune,* Jan. 19, 1987, p. 52.
210   Health and Human Services: Mike Causey, "How to Run a
      RIF," *Washington Post,* Aug. 19, 1984, p. C2.
210   As the Japanese government prepares: "Japan to Cut Size of
      Railway Work Force—Without Lay-offs," *The Nation: Thailand's
      English-Language Newspaper,* May 30, 1986, p. 30.
210   An observer has estimated: Loomis, p. 52.
210   Rank Xerox: "Casting Executives as Consultants," *Business
      Week,* Aug. 30, 1982, p. 46–51.
211   Sony: "Sony: A Diversification Plan Tuned to the People Fac-
      tor," *Business Week,* Feb. 9, 1981, pp. 88–89.
212   Economic troubles: Buck Rogers, *The IBM Way* (New York:
      Harper & Row, 1986), p. 12.
212   "People have to be": Loomis. ©1987 Time Inc. All rights
      reserved.
212   The sequence: Leonard Greenhalgh, Robert McKersie and
      Roderick Gilkey, "Rebalancing the Workforce at IBM: A
      Case Study of Redeployment and Revitalization," *Organiza-
      tional Dynamics,* Spring 1986, pp. 30–47. Also Aaron Bernstein,

Page

"IBM's Fancy Footwork to Sidestep Layoffs," *Business Week,* July 7, 1986, pp. 54–55.
215   Seagate Technology and Tandon: Ibid., p. 55.
215   Cause a job security crisis: Perry, p. 48–61.

CHAPTER 8: RUNNING LEAN

Page

218   "Most organizational change flounders": Harry Levinson, *Psychological Man* (Cambridge, Mass.: The Levinson Institute Inc., 1976), p. 83.
219   At Emerson Electric: "Emerson Electric: High Profits from Low Tech," *Business Week,* Apr. 4, 1983, pp. 58–62.
220   At Unilever: "Unilever: Back to Minding the Store in Europe with the Lines It Knows Best," *Business Week,* Mar. 14, 1983, pp. 138–139.
220   "Keep them well fed": Ibid., p. 138.
220   Wells Fargo: "Wells Fargo Takeover of Crocker Is Yielding Profit But Some Pain," *Wall Street Journal,* Aug. 5, 1986, p. 12.
221   "High-flex": Norman Jonas and Joan Berger, "Do All These Deals Help or Hurt the U.S. Economy?," *Business Week,* Nov. 24, 1986, p. 86.
221   [TRW] sold an: Myron Magnet, "Restructuring Really Works," *Fortune,* Mar. 2, 1987, p. 43.
222   At Pepsico: Steven Prokesch, "Remaking the American CEO," *New York Times,* Jan. 25, 1987, p. 8F.
222   "If top managers": Ibid.
223   General Electric: "The Shrinking of Middle Management," *Business Week,* Apr. 25, 1983, p. 56.
223   "You run the show": "How Bob Pritzker Runs a $3 Billion Empire," *Business Week,* Mar. 7, 1983, p. 65.
224   "A meat-and-potatoes company": Joel Dreyfus, "Handing Down the Old Hands' Wisdom," *Fortune,* June 13, 1983, pp. 98–100. ©1983 Time Inc. All rights reserved.
224   "Better damn well": Ibid., p. 100.
224   At the Chevron Corporation: Amanda Bennett, "Chevron Corp. Has Big Challenge Coping with Worker Cutback," *Wall Street Journal,* Nov. 4, 1986, p. 1.
224   GE's manufacturing: Peter Nulty, "How Managers Will Man

Page

age," *Fortune,* Feb. 2, 1987, p. 50.

224　Campbell Soup: Christine Dugas, "Marketing's New Look," *Business Week,* Jan. 26, 1987, p. 64–69.

225　Lester Thurow has observed: Lester Thurow, "White-Collar Overhead," *Across the Board,* Nov. 1986, p. 27.

226　Paul O'Neill: *Positioning Corporate Staff for the 1990s* (Houston: American Productivity Center and Cresap, McCormick and Paget, 1986), p. 14.

226　Reduce his corporate controller's: Ibid.

226　Numerically controlled machines: Thurow, p. 30.

227　Procter & Gamble: Jolie Solomon and John Bussey, "Pressed by Its Rivals, Procter & Gamble Co. Is Altering Its Ways," *Wall Street Journal,* May 20, 1985, p. 22.

228　"Every man on": Arch Patton, "When Executives Bail Out to Move Up," *Business Week,* Sept. 13, 1982, p. 13.

229　80 percent of American managers: *Seeking and Destroying the Wealth Dissipators* (Chicago: A.T. Kearney, Inc., 1984), p. 4.

230　Learning from mistakes: Chris Argyris and Donald Schön, *Organizational Learning: A Theory of Action Perspective* (Reading, Mass.: Addison-Wesley Publishing Company, 1978).

231　One-way communications: Ibid., p. 227.

231　Dana Corporation: "Homegrown Wisdom," *Forbes,* Feb. 11, 1985, p. 168.

231　"I didn't need": Ibid.

231　Marmon Group: "How Bob Pritzker Runs a $3 Billion Empire," *Business Week,* Mar. 7, 1983, pp. 64–69.

232　"We don't have": Ibid., p. 65.

233　Nucor: "Steel from the Workshop," *Forbes,* Apr. 30, 1984, p. 74.

233　"It is my responsibility": "TRW Leads a Revolution in Managing Technology," *Business Week,* Nov. 15, 1982, p. 126.

233　Get things done: Ibid., pp. 124–130.

234　A novel practice of technological forecasting: Harper North and Donald Pyke, "'Probes' of the Technological Future," *Harvard Business Review,* May–June 1969, pp. 68–76.

236　Xerox has found: Interview with Richard Randazzo, director of personnel administration, Xerox Corporation, on Aug. 19, 1985.

237　"One reason why": Anthony Jay, *Management and Machiavelli*

Page

(London: Penguin, 1970) as quoted in: Henry Mintzberg, *The Structuring of Organizations* (Englewood Cliffs, N.J.: Prentice-Hall, Inc., 1979), p. 420.

CHAPTER 9: STAYING STREAMLINED

Page

239 Lewis Galoob Toys: John Wilson, "And Now, the Post-Industrial Corporation," *Business Week*, Mar. 3, 1986, p. 64.

240 "A switchboard": Ibid.

241 Flextronics concentrates: Ibid., p. 66.

241 Chrysler met: William Hampton, "The Next Act At Chrysler," *Business Week*, Nov. 3, 1986, pp. 66–72.

241 "Live with some shortage": Jerry Flint, "Ford's Defensive Posture," *Forbes*, Dec. 15, 1986, p. 52.

241 Its [Du Pont's] cutbacks: "What's Causing the Scratches in Du Pont's Teflon?" *Business Week*, Dec. 8, 1986, p. 60.

242 Bankers Trust: Gary Hector, "Bankers Trust Takes on Wall Street," *Fortune*, Jan. 9, 1984, pp. 104–107.

242 "When it comes": Alonzo McDonald, "Of Floating Factories and Mating Dinosaurs," *Harvard Business Review*, Nov.–Dec. 1986, p. 83.

242 Ralph Cordiner: Peter Drucker, *Management Tasks, Responsibilities, Practices* (New York: Harper & Row, 1973), p. 581.

243 "Four or five": Ibid.

243 Lufthansa, is: Susan Carey, "Lufthansa Jettisons Bureaucratic Baggage," *Wall Street Journal*, Sept. 30, 1986, p. 36.

243 Siemens: John Tagliabue, "Taking The 'Ma' Out of 'Ma Siemens'," *New York Times*, Nov. 2, 1986, p. 6F.

243 Carrefour: Maxwell Stern, "Why Training Receives Top Priority in French Retailing," *International Trends in Retailing*, Fall 1985, pp. 57–68. Also Roger Ricklefs, "French Hypermarkets Check Out the U.S.," *Wall Street Journal*, May 20, 1986, p. 32.

245 Frederick Smith: Interview with Frederick Smith, Chairman, Federal Express Company, on Dec. 9, 1983.

245 Control Data provides: "Sending the Staff Out to Solve Other Companies' Problems," *Business Week*, Jan. 16, 1984, p. 54.

Page

245 Parsons' public relations: Charlotte Forbes, "Making a Position Inexpendable," *Management Review,* Jan. 1987, p. 31.

247 Conference Board economists: Michael Pollock and Aaron Bernstein, "The Disposable Employee Is Becoming a Fact of Corporate Life," *Business Week,* Dec. 15, 1986, p. 52.

247 Bureau of Labor Statistics': Sharon Rubinstein, "These 'Temps' Don't Just Answer the Phone," *Business Week,* June 2, 1986, p. 74.

248 Expert systems: Paul Harmon and David King, *Expert Systems: Artificial Intelligence in Business* (New York: John Wiley & Sons, Inc., 1985).

249 ExperTAX: Dennis Kneale, "How Coopers & Lybrand Put Expertise into Its Computers," *Wall Street Journal,* Nov. 14, 1986, p. 33.

250 General Electric: Harmon and King, pp. 160–163.

251 "The Japanese regard": John Nielsen, "Management Layoffs Won't Quit," *Fortune,* Oct. 28, 1985, p. 47. ©1985 Time Inc. All rights reserved.

253 Rodney Plimpton: "Firms Having to Cut Employees Should Take Decisive Action," *TBS NewsViews,* Winter 1985, p. 6.

253 Two-track pay scales: Claudia Deutsch, "Holding on to Technical Talent," *New York Times,* Nov. 16, 1986, p. 9.

253 Skill-based pay: Jim Talley, "Wanted: Do-It-All Employees," *Washington Post,* Aug. 31, 1986, p. H4.

254 "Do you know": John Keller, "Can Jim Olson's Grand Design Get AT&T Going?," *Business Week,* Dec. 22, 1986, p. 48.

254 "The job of the enterprise": "The Man Who Brought GE to Life," *Fortune,* Jan. 5, 1987, pp. 76–77. ©1987 Time Inc. All rights reserved.

255 "If we bring someone": Pollock and Bernstein.

255 "I understand why": James Bolt, "Job Security: Its Time Has Come," *Harvard Business Review,* Nov.–Dec. 1983, p. 118.

255 These achievements: Ibid., p. 116.

257 "We used to be": Bruce Nussbaum, "The End of Corporate Loyalty?," *Business Week,* Aug. 4, 1986, p. 44.

257 The U.S. work force: Susan Sanderson and Lawrence Schein, "Sizing Up the Downsizing Era," *Across the Board,* Nov. 1986, p. 23.

Index